Bulgarian
PHRASEBOOK & DICTIONARY

Acknowledgments
Associate Publisher Mina Patria
Associate Product Director Angela Tinson
Product Editor Elizabeth Jones
Series Designer James Hardy
Language Writer Ronelle Alexander
Cover Image Researcher Naomi Parker

Thanks
Samantha Forge, Larissa Frost, Carol Jackson, Chris Love, Kirsty Moore,
Wayne Murphy, Stefan Nikolov, Branislava Vladisavljevic

Published by Lonely Planet Publications Pty Ltd
ABN 36 005 607 983

2nd Edition – April 2014
ISBN 978 1 74179 331 4
Text © Lonely Planet 2014
Cover Image Rila Monastery, Sofia Province, Bulgaria, Matteo
Carassale / 4CORNERS ©
Printed in China 10 9 8 7 6 5 4 3 2 1

Contact lonelyplanet.com/contact

MIX
Paper from
responsible sources

FSC™ C021741

acknowledgments

Editor Branislava Vladisavljevic would like to acknowledge the following people for their contributions to this phrasebook:

Ronelle Alexander for the comprehensive translations, cultural information and extensive notes on Bulgarian grammar and pronunciation. Ronelle teaches at the University of California in Berkeley, California. She travels frequently to Bulgaria, both its cities and villages, and has grown to love the country and its culture over the years.

Among Ronelle's many Bulgarian-connected friends, those who have given input on this book, and whom she wishes to acknowledge, include Lauren Brody, Olga Mladenova, Malvina Rousseva, Milena Savova, Roumen Starkovski, Vladimir and Kiril Zhobov, and Aglaia and Kremena Zhobova.

make the most of this phrasebook ...

Anyone can speak another language! It's all about confidence. Don't worry if you can't remember your school language lessons or if you've never learnt a language before. Even if you learn the very basics (on the inside covers of this book), your travel experience will be the better for it. You have nothing to lose and everything to gain when the locals hear you making an effort.

finding things in this book

For easy navigation, this book is in sections. The Tools chapters are the ones you'll thumb through time and again. The Practical section covers basic travel situations like catching transport and finding a bed. The Social section gives you conversational phrases, pick-up lines, the ability to express opinions – so you can get to know people. Food has a section all of its own: gourmets and vegetarians are covered and local dishes feature. Safe Travel equips you with health and police phrases, just in case. Remember the colours of each section and you'll find everything easily; or use the comprehensive Index. Otherwise, check the two-way traveller's Dictionary for the word you need.

being understood

Throughout this book you'll see coloured phrases on each page. They're phonetic guides to help you pronounce the language. Start with them to get a feel for how the language sounds. The pronunciation chapter in Tools will explain more, but you can be confident that if you read the coloured phrase, you'll be understood.

communication tips

Body language, ways of doing things, sense of humour – all have a role to play in every culture. 'Local talk' boxes show you common ways of saying things, or everyday language to drop into conversation. 'Listen for ...' boxes supply the phrases you may hear. They start with the foreign language and then lead in to the phonetic guide and the English translation.

about bulgarian 8

basics 11

practical 49

social 111

CONTENTS

bulgarian

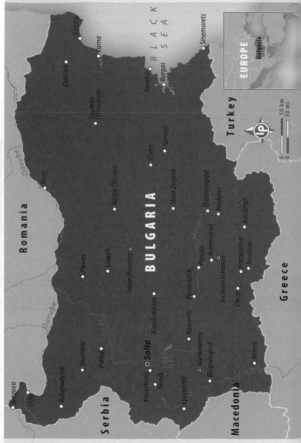

■ official language

For more details, see the **introduction**

Surprisingly, the name of the oldest South Slavic literary language, Bulgarian, isn't of Slavic origin at all. It's one of a handful of words remaining in Bulgarian from the language of the Bulgars, a Turkic people who invaded the eastern Balkans in the late 7th century. Along with their language, they assimilated with the local Slavs who had crossed the Danube and settled in the Balkan peninsula at the dawn of the 6th century.

As a member of the South Slavic group of languages, Bulgarian has Macedonian and Serbian as its closest relatives. However, it also shares similarities with the non-Slavic languages in the so-called Balkan linguistic union (Romanian, Albanian and Greek), as a result of multilingualism and prolonged contact between the Balkan peoples. These foreign influences explain many of its grammatical features – for example, its simplified noun system, which sets Bulgarian (and Macedonian) apart from other Slavic languages. In addition, numerous Turkish words entered Bulgarian over five centuries of Ottoman rule. In the 19th century, many of these Turkish loanwords were eliminated from the language. Their place was partially filled by Russian words, as Russian has influenced Bulgarian through both Bulgaria's ties with the Orthodox Church and long-standing cultural links with Russia.

Old Bulgarian (which is very similar to Old Church Slavonic) was the first Slavic language recorded in

---

at a glance ...

language name:
Bulgarian

name in language:
български
buhl·gar·skee

language family:
South Slavic

approximate number of speakers: 9 million

key country: Bulgaria

close relatives:
Macedonian, Serbian, Russian

---

about bulgarian

9

written form in religious literature from the 9th century. The central figures in the development of the Slavic literary language were Saints Cyril and Methodius, missionaries of the Byzantine emperor who invented the Glagolitic alphabet around AD 863 and used it to translate Greek liturgical texts into Old Church Slavonic. Their disciples devised the Cyrillic alphabet (based on Greek and Glagolitic) in which Bulgarian has been written ever since.

In its modern version, standardised after the last spelling reform in 1945, the Bulgarian alphabet is very similar to the Russian Cyrillic alphabet. Today, Bulgarians celebrate St Cyril and Methodius Day as a national holiday on the 24th of May (also known as the Day of Bulgarian Culture or the Cyrillic Alphabet Day). On joining the European Union in January 2007, Bulgaria also had the honour of introducing the Cyrillic alphabet to the EU as its third official writing system, alongside the Roman and Greek alphabets.

Modern Bulgarian has about 9 million speakers and is the official language of Bulgaria, with Bulgarian-speaking minorities in Ukraine, Moldova, Romania, Serbia, Hungary, Greece and Turkey. The literary standard is based on the northeastern dialects. The transitional dialects spoken around the borders between Bulgaria, Serbia and Macedonia are very similar to one another and this has provoked sensitive political issues over the centuries.

This book gives you the practical phrases you need to get by as well as all the fun, spontaneous phrases that lead to a more successful interaction with Bulgarian people and a deeper understanding of their culture. Local knowledge, new relationships and a sense of satisfaction are on the tip of your tongue. So don't just stand there, say something!

abbreviations used in this book

a	adjective	n	(after English) noun
adv	adverb	n	(after Bulgarian) neuter
f	feminine	pl	plural
inf	informal	pol	polite
lit	literally	sg	singular
m	masculine	v	verb

Even if you're not familiar with the Cyrillic alphabet, you'll soon realise that Bulgarian is easy to read. There's generally a one-to-one correspondence between the written form and pronunciation, and the sounds found in Bulgarian are familiar to English speakers. Read the coloured pronunciation guides as if you were reading English, and then move on to the Cyrillic script as you gain confidence.

vowel sounds

Bulgarian vowel sounds all have equivalents in English. To make yourself sound more like a native, just remember that in Bulgarian vowels in unstressed syllables are generally pronounced shorter and weaker than in stressed syllables.

symbol	english equivalent	bulgarian example	transliteration
a	father	дата	*da*·ta
ai	aisle	май	mai
e	ten	лек	lek
ee	feet	бира	*bee*·ra
o	lot	вода	vo·*da*
oo	boot	тук	took
uh	ago	къде, часа	kuh·*de*, cha·*suh*

consonant sounds

Bulgarian consonant sounds are pretty straightforward, as they all have equivalents in English. The only sound you might trip over is ts, which can occur at the start of words. Try saying 'cats', then 'ats', then 'ts' to get the idea.

pronunciation

symbol	english equivalent	bulgarian example	transliteration
b	bit	брат	brat
ch	chop	чист	cheest
d	day	душ	doosh
f	fun	фенерче	fe·ner·che
g	goat	гума	goo·ma
h	hard	хотел	ho·tel
k	king	карта	kar·ta
l	lump	билет	bee·let
m	my	масло	mas·lo
n	not	нула	noo·la
p	put	грип	greep
r	rib	утро	oot·ro
s	sit	син	seen
sh	ship	шест	shest
t	ton	сто	sto
ts	cats	крадец	kra·dets
v	vet	вчера	vche·ra
y	yes	брой	broy
z	zoo	зад	zad
zh	pleasure	плаж	plazh

word stress & intonation

There's no general rule regarding word stress in Bulgarian – stress can fall on any syllable and sometimes changes in different grammatical forms of the same word. Just follow our coloured pronunciation guides, in which the stressed syllable is in italics.

An important aspect of Bulgarian pronunciation is stress on certain single-syllable words following negation. Several commonly used single-syllable words (given in the list on the opposite page) are not stressed, but lean upon the following word and are pronounced together with it. However, when one of these words comes in between *не* ne (not) and a verb, it carries a very strong stress, as shown in the example phrases.

ви	vee	са	suh
ги	gee	се	se
го	go	си	see
е	e	сме	sme
им	eem	сте	ste
й	ee	съм	suhm
ме	me	те	te
ми	mee	ти	tee
ни	nee	я	ya

I feel well.	Добре ми е.	do·*bre* mee e
I don't feel well.	Не ми е добре.	ne *mee* e do·*bre*
My name is …	Аз се казвам …	*az* se *kaz*·vam …
My name isn't …	Аз не се казвам …	*az* ne *se kaz*·vam …

For reasons of consistency, in our coloured pronunciation guides word stress is only marked (with italics) in words with more than one syllable, but if you keep this general rule in mind you can easily apply it to relevant phrases in this book.

reading & writing

Bulgarian spelling is almost entirely phonetic, meaning that there's generally a one to one correspondence between the letters and the sounds they represent. There are some exceptions, however. For example, there are a few instances when the letter 'a' is pronounced uh (not a), even (and in fact most noticeably) when accented. You don't have to worry about these rules, though, as our coloured pronunciation guides show the correct pronunciation of sounds in the context of any given phrase.

Bulgarian uses the Cyrillic alphabet, which was developed in the 9th century on the basis of the Greek alphabet. In its modern version, it's very similar to the Russian Cyrillic alphabet. Note that the letter 'ь' (er *ma*·luhk) has no sound of its own – it appears only before the vowel 'o' to indicate that the preceding consonant is pronounced 'soft' (ie followed by a slight 'y' sound), eg *шофьор* sho·*fyor* (driver). There's no upper-case

13

form of this letter as it never occurs at the beginning of a word. Be careful not to confuse it with the letter 'ь' (er gol·*yam*), pronounced uh (as in 'ago'), which has both upper- and lower-case forms and is a fully fledged vowel in Bulgarian.

For spelling purposes (eg when you spell your name to book into a hotel), the pronunciation of each letter is provided in the first box below. The letters are presented in alphabetical order (reading down the page) and words in the **menu decoder** and **bulgarian–english dictionary** are also listed in this order.

alphabet					
А а	a	К к	kuh	Ф ф	fuh
Б б	buh	Л л	luh	Х х	huh
В в	vuh	М м	muh	Ц ц	tsuh
Г г	guh	Н н	nuh	Ч ч	chuh
Д д	duh	О о	o	Ш ш	shuh
Е е	e	П п	puh	Щ щ	shtuh
Ж ж	zhuh	Р р	ruh	Ъ ъ	er gol·*yam*
З з	zuh	С с	suh	ь	er *ma*·luhk
И и	ee	Т т	tuh	Ю ю	yoo
Й й	ee *krat*·ko	У у	oo	Я я	ya

Just as letters in the Latin alphabet look different when they're in roman font (like 'a') as opposed to italics (like '*a*'), so do some Cyrillic letters. To eyes accustomed to the English alphabet, understanding that 'дата' and '*дата*' are both forms of *da*·ta (date) can be a challenge. Here's the Bulgarian Cyrillic alphabet in both roman and italic font to help you with menus, schedules and signs.

italic cyrillic									
Аа	Бб	Вв	Гг	Дд	Ее	Жж	Зз	Ии	Йй
Аа	*Бб*	*Вв*	*Гг*	*Дд*	*Ее*	*Жж*	*Зз*	*Ии*	*Йй*
Кк	Лл	Мм	Нн	Оо	Пп	Рр	Сс	Тт	Уу
Кк	*Лл*	*Мм*	*Нн*	*Оо*	*Пп*	*Рр*	*Сс*	*Тт*	*Уу*
Фф	Хх	Цц	Чч	Шш	Щщ	Ъъ	ь	Юю	Яя
Фф	*Хх*	*Цц*	*Чч*	*Шш*	*Щщ*	*Ъъ*	*ь*	*Юю*	*Яя*

a–z phrasebuilder
граматичен речник

contents

The list below shows which grammatical structures you can use to say what you want. Look under each function – in alphabetical order – for information on how to build your own phrases. For example, to tell the taxi driver where your hotel is, look for **giving instructions** and you'll be directed to information on **demonstratives** and **prepositions**. A **glossary** of grammatical terms is included at the end of this chapter to help you.

adjectives & adverbs

Adjectives in Bulgarian come before the noun they modify. They change form to agree with the noun in gender and number, and can have the definite article ('the' in English) attached to them (see **articles**, **gender** and **plurals**). In the singular, masculine adjectives usually end in a consonant or in -и -i, feminine adjectives in -a -a and neuter ones in -o -o. Plural adjectives of all genders end in -и -i. In the **dictionaries** and word lists in this book, adjectives are given in the masculine form only.

singular		
nice city	хубав град m	*hoo·*bav grad
nice picture	хубава картина f	*hoo·*ba·va kar·*tee·*na
nice village	хубаво село n	*hoo·*ba·vo *se·*lo
plural		
nice cities	хубави градове m	*hoo·*ba·vee gra·do·*ve*
nice pictures	хубави картини f	*hoo·*ba·vee kar·*tee·*ne
nice villages	хубави села n	*hoo·*ba·vee se·*la*

Adverbs don't change their form and can be placed before or after the verb they refer to (see also **verbs**). Adverbs often have the neuter singular form of adjectives (ending in -o -o). Less frequently they end in -e -e or -и -i.

fast train	бърз влак	buhrz vlak
	(lit: fast train)	
Drive fast.	Карай бързо.	*ka·*rai *buhr·*zo
	(lit: drive-you fast)	

articles

Bulgarian has only a definite article (like 'the' in English) – so 'a room' is стая *sta·*ya (lit: room) and 'the room' is стаята *sta·*ya·ta (lit: room-the). As shown by this example, the definite article in Bulgarian is an ending attached to the noun. The table below shows different forms of the definite article in the singular depending on the noun's gender. In the plural, nouns which end in -a -a (in their plural form) add the article -та -ta, and all other nouns add the article -те -te (see **gender** and **plurals**).

a city	град m	grad
a picture	картина f	kar·*tee*·na
a village	село n	*se*·lo

singular		
the city	градът m	gra·*duht*
the picture	картината f	kar·*tee*·na·ta
the village	селото n	*se*·lo·to
plural		
the cities	градовете m	gra·do·*ve*·te
the pictures	картините f	kar·*tee*·nee·te
the villages	селата n	se·*la*·ta

When the definite article is added to masculine nouns, they have a subject form (ending in -ът -uht) and an object form (ending in -a, but pronounced as if it were spelled -ъ -uh).

The city is big.	Градът е голям.	gra·*duht* e go·*lyam*
	(lit: city-the is big)	
We live in the city.	Живеем в града.	zhee·*ve*·em v gra·*duh*
	(lit: live-we in city-the)	

If the noun is accompanied by an adjective, the definite article is attached to the adjective instead of the noun. For masculine nouns the article on the adjective takes the form -ият -ee·yuht.

the big suitcase	големият куфар m	go·*le*·mee·yuht *koo*·far
	(lit: big-the suitcase)	
the small bag	малката чанта f	*mal*·ka·ta *chan*·ta
	(lit: small-the bag)	
the nice village	хубавото село n	*hoo*·ba·vo·to *se*·lo
	(lit: nice-the village)	

be

describing people/things • making statements

In Bulgarian, the verb съм suhm (be) changes in person and number to match the subject of the sentence. The present tense forms of the verb 'be' are given in the table below. See also **negatives** and **verbs**.

be – present tense			
I	am	съм	suhm
you sg inf	are	си	see
you sg pol		сте	ste
he/she/it	is	е	e
we		сме	sme
you pl	are	сте	ste
they		са	suh

demonstratives

giving instructions • indicating location • pointing things out

Words for 'this' and 'that' in Bulgarian change form for number, and in the singular for gender as well, to agree with the noun they refer to. They're placed before the noun. See also **gender** and **plurals**.

demonstratives					
	m sg	**f sg**	**n sg**	**pl**	
this	този *to*·zee	тази *ta*·zee	това to·*va*	**these**	тези *te*·zee
that	онзи *on*·zee	онази o·*na*·zee	онова o·no·*va*	**those**	онези o·*ne*·zee

gender

naming people/things

Bulgarian nouns have grammatical gender – masculine (m), feminine (f) or neuter (n). It's important to know a noun's gender, as it dictates the form of the adjective, definite article or demonstrative accompanying the noun, as well as the form of the pronoun used to refer to the noun.

The rules for determining the gender of nouns are fairly regular: most masculine nouns end in a consonant, feminine nouns generally end in -a -a or -я -ya (although there are a number of feminine nouns which end in a consonant), and neuter nouns usually end in -e -e or -o -o. All the nouns in this book's word lists, **dictionaries** and **menu decoder** have gender marked. See also **plurals**.

град m	grad	**city**
картина f	kar·*tee*·na	**picture**
село n	*se*·lo	**village**

have

possessing

An easy way of expressing possession in Bulgarian is by using the verb имам *ee*·mam (have). The present tense forms of this verb, both affirmative and negative, are shown in the tables below. See also **possessives**.

have – present tense (affirmative)			
I		имам	*ee*·mam
you sg inf	have	имаш	*ee*·mash
you sg pol		имате	*ee*·ma·te
he/she/it	has	има	*ee*·ma
we		имаме	*ee*·ma·me
you pl	have	имате	*ee*·ma·te
they		имат	*ee*·mat

have – present tense (negative)			
I		нямам	*nya*·mam
you sg inf	don't have	нямаш	*nya*·mash
you sg pol		нямате	*nya*·ma·te
he/she/it	doesn't have	няма	*nya*·ma
we		нямаме	*nya*·ma·me
you pl	don't have	нямате	*nya*·ma·te
they		нямат	*nya*·mat

negatives

negating

To form negatives in Bulgarian, simply put the word не ne (not) before the verb. Bulgarian also uses double negatives, as shown below. For the negative forms of 'have', see above.

I eat fish.	Ям риба. (lit: eat-I fish)	yam *ree*·ba
I don't eat eggs.	Не ям яйца. (lit: not eat-I eggs)	ne yam yai·*tsa*
I don't eat any meat.	Не ям никакво месо. (lit: not eat-I no-sort meat)	ne yam *nee*·kak·vo me·*so*

nouns

naming people/things

Bulgarian nouns take different endings in plural and when they are used with a definite article. For more information, see **articles**, **gender** and **plurals**.

personal pronouns

doing things • making statements • possessing

Personal pronouns ('I', 'you' etc) are frequently omitted in Bulgarian as the subject of a sentence, if the verb endings make it clear who is referred to (see **verbs**). Their main use in the subject role is for emphasis.

Do you eat meat?
Ядеш ли месо?   ya·*desh* lee me·*so*
(lit: eat-you *question particle* meat)
I don't eat meat.
Не ям месо.   ne yam me·*so*
(lit: no eat-I meat)
I'm from Australia, and he's from America.
Аз съм от Австралия,   az suhm ot av·*stra*·lee·ya
а той е от Америка.   a toy e ot a·*me*·ree·ka
(lit: I am from Australia
and he is from America)

subject pronouns					
I	аз	az	**we**	ние	*nee*·e
you sg inf	ти	tee	**you** pl	вие	*vee*·e
you sg pol	вие	*vee*·e			
he	той	toy	**they**	те	te
she	тя	tya			
it	то	to			

Bulgarian has both an informal and a polite word for 'you' – basically, unless you know the person well, use the polite form, вие *vee*·e, and the matching second-person plural form of the verb. See the box **all about you** on page 138 for more information. Note also that 'it' is expressed by pronouns meaning 'he/him' or 'she/her' if the noun it refers to is of masculine or feminine gender.

The direct and indirect object pronouns ('me', 'us' etc) have both a short and a long version (separated in the tables below with a slash). Note that the long forms of the indirect object pronouns correspond to those of the direct object pronouns preceded by the preposition на na (to) (eg like 'me' and 'to me' in English).

direct object pronouns (short/long)

me	ме/мене	me/ *me*·ne	us	ни/нас	nee/nas
you sg inf	те/тебе	te/*te*·be	you pl	ви/вас	vee/vas
you sg pol	ви/вас	vee/vas			
him	го/него	go/*ne*·go	them	ги/тях	gee/tyah
her	я/нея	ya/*ne*·ya			
it	го/него	go/*ne*·go			

indirect object pronouns (short/long)

me	ми/ на мене	mee/ na *me*·ne	us	ни/ на нас	nee/ na nas
you sg inf	ти/ на тебе	tee/ na *te*·be	you pl	ви/ на вас	vee/ na vas
you sg pol	ви/ на вас	vee/ na vas			
him	му/ на него	moo/ na *ne*·go	them	им/ на тях	eem/ na tyah
her	й/ на нея	ee/ na *ne*·ya			
it	го/ на него	go/ na *ne*·go			

The long forms are used for contrast or after prepositions, while the short forms are used elsewhere. With verbs, the short forms of direct object pronouns are more frequently used than the long ones, but with prepositions, only the long forms are used.

I gave it to him.
Дадох му га. *da·*doh moo ga
(lit: gave-I to-him it)

I gave it to her, but not to him.
Дадох га на нея, *da·*doh ga na *ne·*ya
а не на него. a ne na *ne·*go
(lit: gave-I it to her but not to him)

The short forms of the direct object pronouns are normally placed before the verb (unless the verb is first in the sentence, in which case they come after the verb), while the long forms are placed after the verb.

He knows me.
Той ме познава. toy me poz·*na·*va
(lit: he me knows-he)

He knows me, but not you.
Той познава мене, toy poz·*na·*va *me·*ne
а не тебе. a ne *te·*be
(lit: he knows-he me but not you)

Sometimes the short form is used together with the long form in the sentence to refer to the same object.

I'm cold.
На мене ми е студено. na *me·*ne mee e stoo·*de·*no
(lit: to me to-me is cold)

The short form can also be used to refer to a noun object in the same sentence when it's necessary to make clear that the noun is acting as an object rather than a subject.

Mara doesn't know that person.
Мара този човек *ma·*ra to·zee cho·*vek*
не го познава. ne go poz·*na·*va
(lit: Mara that person not him knows-she)

See also **gender** and **plurals**.

plurals

Plurals of nouns are formed by using a variety of endings – the most common endings are shown in the table below. Note that masculine nouns which denote objects have separate forms when they're used with cardinal numbers and words expressing quantity, eg 'several'. For more on these forms, see the **numbers & amounts** chapter. See also **gender**.

singular & plural nouns				
pencil	молив m	*mo*·leev	моливи m pl	*mo*·lee·vee
city	град m	grad	градове m pl	gra·do·*ve*
picture	картина f	kar·*tee*·na	картини f pl	kar·*tee*·nee
candle	свещ f	svesht	свещи f pl	*svesh*·tee
village	село n	*se*·lo	села n pl	se·*la*
piece	парче n	par·*che*	парчета n pl	par·*che*·ta

possessives

As in English, possession can be expressed in Bulgarian by using the verb 'have' (see **have**) or by using possessive adjectives (eg 'my' and 'your') before the noun. Just like other adjectives, Bulgarian possessive adjectives can have the definite article attached to them, and they change to match the number and gender of the noun they go with (see **articles**, **gender** and **plurals**).

possessive adjectives

	m sg	f sg	n sg	pl
my	мой *moy*	моя *mo·ya*	мое *mo·ye*	мои *mo·yee*
your sg inf	твой *tvoy*	твоя *tvo·ya*	твое *tvo·ye*	твои *tvo·yee*
your sg pol	ваш *vash*	ваша *va·sha*	ваше *va·she*	ваши *va·shee*
his	негов *ne·gov*	негова *ne·go·va*	негово *ne·go·vo*	негови *ne·go·vee*
her	неин *ne·een*	нейна *ney·na*	нейно *ney·no*	нейни *ney·nee*
our	наш *nash*	наша *na·sha*	наше *na·she*	наши *na·shee*
your pl	ваш *vash*	ваша *va·sha*	ваше *va·she*	ваши *va·shee*
their	техен *te·hen*	тяхна *tyah·na*	тяхно *tyah·no*	техни *teh·nee*

Another way of expressing possession is by placing the short form of the indirect pronoun after the thing possessed.

my handbag
чантата ми   *chan·ta·ta mee*
(lit: handbag-the to-me)

If the possessor is indicated with a noun, it must be expressed using the construction 'на na (of) + noun' after the object possessed:

the girl's handbag
чантата на момичето   *chan·ta·ta na mo·mee·che·to*
(lit: handbag-the of girl-the)

prepositions

giving instructions • indicating location • pointing things out

In Bulgarian, prepositions are used to show relationships between words in a sentence, just like in English.

prepositions					
about	за	za	on	на	na
at	на	na	to (place)	в	v
from (place)	от	ot	to (time)	до	do
from (time)	от	ot	with	с	s
in	в	v	without	без	bez

For the use of the preposition 'to' with indirect objects, see **personal pronouns**. For the use of the preposition 'of' with direct objects to indicate possession, see **possessives**.

questions

asking questions

To form a yes/no question in Bulgarian, place the verb at the start of the sentence and insert the particle ли lee (indicating a question) immediately after the main verb.

I speak English.
> Говоря английски.   go·*vor*·yuh ang·*leey*·skee
> (lit: speak-I English)

Do you speak English?
> Говорите ли английски?   go·*vo*·ree·te lee ang·*leey*·skee
> (lit: speak-you *question particle* English)

To ask for specific information, just add one of the question words (shown on the next page) to the start of a sentence:

question words		
How?	Как?	kak
How many/much?	Колко?	*kol·ko*
What?	Какво?	kak·*vo*
When?	Кога?	ko·*ga*
Where?	Къде?	kuh·*de*
Who?	Кой? m sg Коя? f sg Кое? n sg Кои? pl	koy ko·*ya* ko·*e* ko·*ee*
Why?	Защо?	zash·*to*

verbs

doing things • making statements

There's no infinitive in Bulgarian. In dictionaries, Bulgarian verbs are given in the first person singular present tense form. The present tense form is used after the conjunction да da (that) in a meaning similar to the English infinitive.

I want to learn Bulgarian.

Искам да уча	*ees·*kam da *oo·*chuh
български.	*buhl·*gar·skee
(lit: want-I that learn-I Bulgarian)	

Verbs in Bulgarian change form to match the person and number of the subject in a sentence. There are three different classes of verbs, depending on the verb stem. The verb stem is the basic form of the verb left after taking off the ending -ш -sh from the present tense second person singular form of the verb. The three classes are: the -e -e stem (eg пишеш *pee·*shesh 'write'), the -и -i stem (eg говориш go·*vo·*reesh 'speak') and the -a -a stem (eg искаш *ees·*kash 'want').

verbal aspect

Most Bulgarian verbs have two 'aspects' – meaning that an English verb can usually be translated into Bulgarian in two different ways (eg 'answer' can be either отговоря ot·go·*vor*·yuh or отговарям ot·go·*var*·yam). The first form is called the 'perfective aspect' and refers to completed single actions in the present, past or future. The second form is called the 'imperfective aspect' and is used for habitual or continuing actions in the present, past or future. Note, however, that there are a number of very common verbs referring to basic actions which are not marked for aspect – their form simply designates the action (eg 'drink', 'eat', 'read', 'speak'). Where applicable, Bulgarian verbs in this book's **dictionaries** are given in both perfective and imperfective aspects.

I saw him yesterday.

Вчера го видях.   *vche*·ra go vee·*dyah*

(lit: yesterday him saw-I – *ie perfective aspect*)

I used to see him often.

Виждал съм го често.   *veezh*·dal suhm go *ches*·to

(lit: seen am-I him often – *ie imperfective aspect*)

present tense

The present tense is formed from the verb stem (the -e -e, -и -i or -a -a stem) and a set of endings. See also **negatives**.

'read' – present tense (-e stem)			
I		чета	che·*tuh*
you sg inf	read	четеш	che·*tesh*
you sg pol		четете	che·*te*·te
he/she	reads	чете	che·te
we		четем	che·*tem*
you pl	read	четете	che·*te*·te
they		четат	che·*tuht*

'speak' – present tense (-i stem)			
I		говоря	go·*vor*·yuh
you sg inf	speak	говориш	go·*vor*·eesh
you sg pol		говорите	go·*vor*·ee·te
he/she	speaks	говори	go·*vor*·ee
we		говорим	go·*vor*·eem
you pl	speak	говорите	go·*vor*·ee·te
they		говорят	go·*vor*·yuht

'want' – present tense (-a stem)			
I		искам	*ees*·kam
you sg inf	want	искаш	*ees*·kash
you sg pol		искате	*ees*·ka·te
he/she	wants	иска	*ees*·ka
we		искаме	*ees*·ka·me
you pl	want	искате	*ees*·ka·te
they		искат	*ees*·kat

past tense

There are two simple past tenses in Bulgarian (plus several compound ones). The two simple past tenses are the imperfect tense (used to describe an action in progress over a period of time), and the aorist tense (used to describe the fact of an action – usually completed, but not necessarily). The examples of these tenses are shown in the tables on the page opposite. Both tenses can be used in both the perfective and imperfective aspects. See also **negatives**.

'read' – imperfect tense			
I	was reading	четях	che·*tyah*
you sg inf	were reading	четеше	che·*te*·she
you sg pol		четяхте	che·*tyah*·te
he/she	was reading	четеше	che·*te*·she
we		четяхме	che·*tyah*·me
you pl	were reading	четяхте	che·*tyah*·te
they		четяха	che·*tya*·ha
'read' – aorist tense			
I		четох	*che*·toh
you sg inf		чете	*che*·te
you sg pol		четохте	*che*·toh·te
he/she	read	чете	*che*·te
we		четохме	*che*·toh·me
you pl		четохте	*che*·toh·te
they		четоха	*che*·to·ha

future tense

The future tense is formed from the present tense forms and the word ще shte. For the negative forms, the construction няма да *nya*·ma da is used instead of ще.

'read' – future tense (affirmative)			
I		ще чета	shte che·*tuh*
you sg inf		ще четеш	shte che·*tesh*
you sg pol		ще четете	shte che·*te*
he/she	will read	ще чете	shte che·*te*·te
we		ще четем	shte che·*tem*
you pl		ще четете	shte che·*te*·te
they		ще четат	shte che·*tuht*

'read' – future tense (negative)			
I		няма да чета	*nya·ma da che·tuh*
you sg inf		няма да четеш	*nya·ma da che·tesh*
you sg pol		няма да четете	*nya·ma da che·te·te*
he/she	will not read	няма да чете	*nya·ma da che·te*
we		няма да четем	*nya·ma da che·tem*
you pl		няма да четете	*nya·ma da che·te·te*
they		няма да четат	*nya·ma da che·tuht*

word order

making statements

In Bulgarian, there are strict rules regarding the position of single-syllable words relative to one another and to the verb when used in a sentence with negation. Generally, however, you can stick to the subject–verb–object order, just like in English.

Ivan doesn't eat meat.
 Иван не яде месо.　　　　　　　*ee·van* ne ya·de me·so
 (lit: Ivan not eats-he meat)

See also **negatives** and **questions**.

glossary

adjective	a word that describes something – 'The invention of the **Cyrillic** alphabet …'
adverb	a word that explains how an action is done – '… is **traditionally** linked with the Byzantine missionaries St Cyril and Methodius …'
article	the words 'a', 'an' and 'the'
aspect	most Bulgarian *verbs* express one of two aspects – *perfective* or *imperfective*
demonstrative	a word that means 'this' or 'that'
direct object	the thing or person in the sentence that's the direct recipient of the action – '… who invented **the Glagolitic alphabet** in the 9th century …'
gender	classification of *nouns* into classes (masculine, feminine and neuter), requiring other words (eg *adjectives*) to belong to the same class
imperfective	verbal *aspect* denoting a repeated action or an action in progress – '… while they **were translating** Greek texts into Old Church Slavonic.'
indirect object	the person or thing in the sentence that is the indirect recipient of the action – 'They contributed **to the development** of the Cyrillic alphabet …'
infinitive	the dictionary form of a verb – '… which has been used **to write** Bulgarian since the 10th century.'
noun	a thing, person or idea – 'The **author** of the Cyrillic **alphabet** is probably **St Clement** …'
number	whether a word is singular or plural – '… who was the **disciple** of the two **brothers**.'
object	see *direct object* and *indirect object*
perfective	verbal *aspect* denoting a completed action – 'He most likely **based** the Cyrillic alphabet on the Glagolitic script.'

a–z phrasebuilder

personal pronoun	a word that means 'I', 'you' etc
possessive adjective	a word that means 'my', 'your' etc
preposition	a word like 'for' or 'before' in English
subject	the thing or person in the sentence that does the action – '**The alphabet** spread across Eastern Europe with the Orthodox Christianity …'
tense	form of a *verb* that shows the time of the action – 'eat' (present), 'ate' (past), 'will eat' (future)
verb	the word that shows what action happens – '… and it **developed** regional variations.'
verb stem	the part of a verb which does not change – '**writ**e' in '**writ**ing' and '**writ**ten'

language difficulties

Do you speak (English)?
Говорите/Говориш ли
(английски)? pol/inf

go·vo·ree·te/go·vo·reesh lee
(an·gleey·skee)

Does anyone speak (English)?
Говори ли някой тук
(английски)?

go·vo·ree lee nya·koy took
(an·gleey·skee)

Do you understand (me)?
Разбирате/Разбираш
ли (ме)? pol/inf

raz·bee·ra·te/raz·bee·rash
lee (me)

I (don't) understand.
(Не) Разбирам.

(ne) raz·bee·ram

I speak (English).
Говоря (английски).

go·vor·yuh (an·gleey·skee)

I don't speak Bulgarian.
Не говоря български.

ne go·vor·yuh buhl·gar·skee

I speak a little.
Говоря малко.

go·vor·yuh mal·ko

---

false friends

магазин m   ma·ga·zeen   store/shop
not 'magazine', which is *списание* n spee·sa·nee·e

митинг m   mee·teeng   political rally
not 'appointment', which is *среща* f sresh·ta

паста f   pas·ta   pastry/paste
not 'spaghetti', which is *макарони* m ma·ka·ro·nee

презерватив m   pre·zer·va·teev   condom
not 'stabiliser', which is *стабилизатор* m sta·bee·lee·za·tor

хол m   hol   living room
not 'hall' or 'entry area', which is *антре* n an·tre

I'd like to learn some Bulgarian.

Искам да науча малко   *ees*·kam da na·*oo*·chuh *mal*·ko
български.   *buhl*·gar·skee

Let's speak Bulgarian.

Хайде да говорим   *hai*·de da go·*vo*·reem
български.   *buhl*·gar·skee

What's this called in Bulgarian?

Как се казва това   kak se *kaz*·va to·*va*
на български?   na *buhl*·gar·skee

What does (влак) **mean?**

Какво значи (влак)?   *kak*·vo *zna*·chee (vlak)

Pardon?

Моля?   *mol*·yuh

How do you …?	Как се …?	kak se …
pronounce this	произнася това	pro·eez·*nas*·ya to·*va*
write (*shtuhr*·kel)	пише (щъркел)	*pee*·she (*shtuhr*·kel)

Could you please …?	Моля да …	*mol*·yuh da …
repeat that	повторите/ повториш това **pol/inf**	pov·*to*·ree·te/ pov·*to*·reesh to·*va*
speak more slowly	говорите/ говориш по-бавно **pol/inf**	go·*vo*·ree·te/ go·*vo*·reesh *po*·bav·no
write it down	напишете/ напишеш това **pol/inf**	na·*pee*·she·te/ na·*pee*·shesh to·*va*

---

yes or no?

In Bulgaria, shaking your head from side to side means 'yes', while moving it up and down means 'no'. Although these gestures are the opposite of those used by English speakers, there are enough other cues (eg smiles or frowns) to ensure that there's less confusion than you might expect. Of course, it's always a good bet to verify the meaning by using the words *да* da (yes) or *не* ne (no).

cardinal numbers

After numbers or the words *колко* kol·ko (how much/many) and *няколко* nya·kol·ko (several), add the ending *-а* -a to masculine nouns – eg *молив* mo·leev (pencil), *два/няколко молива* dva/nya·kol·ko mo·lee·va (two/several pencils).

The numbers 'one' and 'two' (and higher numbers adding 'one' or 'two') change form depending on the gender of the noun following them. When counting in general, the neuter gender is used – *едно, две, …* ed·no, dve … (one, two, …).

0	нула	noo·la
1	един m	e·deen
	една f	ed·na
	едно n	ed·no
2	два/две m/f&n	dva/dve
3	три	tree
4	четири	che·tee·ree
5	пет	pet
6	шест	shest
7	седем	se·dem
8	осем	o·sem
9	девет	de·vet
10	десет	de·set
11	единайсет	e·dee·nai·set
12	дванайсет	dva·nai·set
13	тринайсет	tree·nai·set
14	четиринайсет	che·tee·ree·nai·set
15	петнайсет	pet·nai·set
16	шестнайсет	shest·nai·set
17	седемнайсет	se·dem·nai·set
18	осемнайсет	o·sem·nai·set
19	деветнайсет	de·vet·nai·set
20	двайсет	dvai·set

21	двайсет и един/	*dvai*·set ee e·*deen*/
	една/едно **m/f/n**	ed·*na*/ed·*no*
22	двайсет и	*dvai*·set ee
	два/две **m/f&n**	dva/dve
30	трийсет	*tree*·set
40	четирийсет	che·*tee*·ree·set
50	петдесет	pet·de·*set*
60	шестдесет	shest·de·*set*
70	седемдесет	se·dem·de·*set*
80	осемдесет	o·sem·de·*set*
90	деветдесет	de·vet·de·*set*
100	сто	sto
200	двеста	*dve*·sta
1000	хиляда	heel·*ya*·da
1,000,000	един милион	e·*deen* mee·lee·*yon*

ordinal numbers

Ordinal numbers are formed by adding -*u* -ee to the cardinal number. In some cases, though, the form of the cardinal number changes (most notably in 'first' and 'second', as shown below). Ordinal numbers are abbreviated in writing by adding the last two letters of the written form to the numeral, eg *18-mu* for *осемнайсети* o·sem·*nai*·stee (18th/eighteenth). Dates are written with the number first and read as the ordinal number, eg *18 октомври* o·sem·*nai*·stee ok·*tom*·vree (18 October).

1st	първи	*puhr*·vee
2nd	втори	*vto*·ree
3rd	трети	*tre*·tee
4th	четвърти	chet·*vuhr*·tee
5th	пети	*pe*·tee

Петър пет плета плете преплита;
преплети, Петре, петте плета.
*pe·*tuhr pet *ple·te* ple·*te* pre·*plee·*ta
pre·ple·*tee pet·*re pet·*te ple·*ta
(Peter is weaving and interweaving five hedges;
weave, Peter, the five hedges.)

Шейсет и шест шишета от швепс се сушат
на шейсет и шест шосета.
shey·*set* ee shest shee·*she·*ta ot shveps se *soo·*shat
na shey·*set* ee shest sho·*se·*ta
(Sixty-six bottles of Schweppes are drying out
on sixty-six roads.)

fractions & decimals

Fractions are formed from a cardinal number followed by the
plural form of the ordinal number, eg *три четвърти* tree
*chet·*vuhr·tee (three-quarters).

a quarter	една четвърт	ed·*na chet·*vuhrt
a third	една трета	ed·*na tre·*ta
a half	половин	po·lo·*veen*
all	всичко	*vseech·*ko
none	нищо	*neesh·*to

Decimals are written as in English, except that a comma is used
instead of a dot. In speech, the phrase *цяло и tsya·*lo ee is used
for the English 'point'.

3.14	три цяло и четиринайсет	tree *tsya·*lo ee che·tee·ree·*nai·*set
4.2	четири цяло и две	che·tee·ree *tsya·*lo ee dve
5.1	пет цяло и едно	pet *tsya·*lo ee ed·*no*

useful amounts

How much/many?	Колко?	kol·ko
Please give me …	Дайте ми,	dai·te mee
	моля …	mol·yuh …
(100) grams	(сто) грама	(sto) gra·ma
half a dozen	половин	po·lo·veen
	дузина	doo·zee·na
a dozen	дузина	doo·zee·na
half a kilo	половин	po·lo·veen
	килограм	kee·lo·gram
a kilo	един килограм	e·deen kee·lo·gram
a bottle	шише	shee·she
a jar	буркан	bur·kan
a packet	опаковка	o·pa·kov·ka
a slice	филия	fee·lee·ya
a tin	кутия	koo·tee·ya
a few	няколко	nya·kol·ko
less	по-малко	po·mal·ko
(just) a little	(само) малко	(sa·mo) mal·ko
a lot	много	mno·go
many	много	mno·go
more	повече	po·ve·che
some	няколко	nya·kol·ko

For more amounts, see **self-catering**, page 176.

handy hints

- Bulgarians finger-count by holding the palm face up and flat, and starting with the little finger.
- The entire hand is used for beckoning, and tilting the head in the intended direction equates to 'pointing'.
- Indicating height and length with the use of hands is done as in English; otherwise hand gestures are avoided.
- Using a single finger for any purpose (counting, pointing etc) is considered rude.

telling the time

The 24-hour clock is the norm in formal contexts, but in most informal situations the 12-hour clock is used. Minutes up to half-past the hour are added, eg 10.20 is *десет и двайсет* de·set ee *dvai*·set (lit: ten and twenty). Minutes after half-past are subtracted from the next hour, so that 10.50 is *единайсет без десет* e·dee·*nai*·set bez de·set (lit: eleven without ten). Note also that the form *час* chas (o'clock) is used with 'one' and numbers adding 'one', but *часа* cha·*suh* is used with other numbers.

What time is it?	Колко е часът?	*kol*·ko e cha·*suht*
It's one o'clock.	Часът е един.	cha·*suht* e e·*deen*
It's (two) o'clock.	(Два) часа е.	(dva) cha·*suh* e
Five past (two).	(Два) и пет.	(dva) ee pet
Quarter past (two).	(Два) и петнайсет.	(dva) ee pet·*nai*·set
Half past (two).	(Два) и половина.	(dva) ee po·lo·*vee*·na
Quarter to (three).	(Три) без петнайсет.	(tree) bez pet·*nai*·set
Twenty to (three).	(Три) без двайсет.	(tree) bez *dvai*·set
am	сутрин	*soo*·treen
pm	следобед	sle·*do*·bed
At what time ...?	В колко часа ...?	v *kol*·ko cha·*suh* ...
At (five).	В (пет).	v (pet)
At (7.57pm).	В (деветнайсет и петдесет и седем).	v (de·vet·*nai*·set ee pet·de·*set* ee *se*·dem)

Times during the day are expressed in the following way:

сутринта	soo·treen·*ta*	**in the morning (4–10am)**
през деня	prez den·*yuh*	**during the day (10am–5pm)**
следобед	sle·*do*·bed	**in the afternoon (2–6pm)**
вечерта	ve·cher·*ta*	**in the evening (6–11pm)**
през нощта	prez nosht·*ta*	**during the night (11pm–4am)**

the calendar

календарът

days of the week

Monday	понеделник m	po·ne·*del*·neek
Tuesday	вторник m	*vtor*·neek
Wednesday	сряда f	*srya*·da
Thursday	четвъртък m	chet·*vuhr*·tuhk
Friday	петък m	*pe*·tuhk
Saturday	събота f	*suh*·bo·ta
Sunday	неделя f	ne·*del*·ya

months

January	януари m	ya·noo·*a*·ree
February	февруари m	fev·roo·*a*·ree
March	март m	mart
April	април m	ap·*reel*
May	май m	mai
June	юни m	*yoo*·nee
July	юли m	*yoo*·lee
August	август m	*av*·goost
September	септември m	sep·*tem*·vree
October	октомври m	ok·*tom*·vree
November	ноември m	no·*em*·vree
December	декември m	de·*kem*·vree

dates

What date is it today?
Коя дата е днес?   ko·*ya da*·ta e dnes

It's (18 October).
(Осемнайсети октомври). (o·sem·*nai*·stee ok·*tom*·vree)

seasons

spring	пролет f	*pro*·let
summer	лято n	*lya*·to
autumn/fall	есен f	*e*·sen
winter	зима f	*zee*·ma

> ### spring symbols
>
> During the first week of March, small decorations of red and white yarn are worn pinned to the lapel. They're called *мартеници mar*·te·nee·tsee and symbolise spring. The month of March is personified as an old woman or grandmother – *баба Марта ba*·ba *mar*·ta.

present

настоящето

now	сега	se·*ga*
today	днес	dnes
tonight	довечера	do·*ve*·che·ra
this ...	днес ...	dnes ...
morning	сутринта	soo·treen·*ta*
afternoon	следобед	sle·*do*·bed

this ...	този ... m	*to*-zee ...
	тази ... f	*ta*-zee ...
week	седмица f	*sed*-mee-tsa
month	месец m	*me*-sets
year	година f	go-*dee*-na

past

day before yesterday	онзи ден	*on*-zee den
(three days) ago	преди (три дена)	pre-*dee* (tree *de*-na)
since (May)	от (май)	ot (mai)
last ...	миналият ... m	*mee*-na-lee-yuht ...
	миналата ... f	*mee*-na-la-ta ...
night	нощ f	nosht
week	седмица f	*sed*-mee-tsa
month	месец m	*me*-sets
year	година f	go-*dee*-na
yesterday ...	вчера ...	*vche*-ra ...
morning	сутринта	soo-treen-*ta*
afternoon	следобед	sle-*do*-bed
evening	снощи	*snosh*-tee

reading through the ages

Bulgarian equivalents of the abbreviations BC and AD are *преди н.е.* for *преди нашата ера* pre-*dee* na-sha-ta *e*-ra (before our era), and *от н.е.* for *от нашата ера* ot na-sha-ta *e*-ra (from our era). Since the fall of communism the older forms – *пр. Хр.* for *преди Христос* pre-*dee* hrees-*tos* (before Christ) and *след Хр.* for *след Христос* sled hrees-*tos* (after Christ) – are returning into use.

In Bulgarian, Roman numerals are used for centuries, and the abbreviation *в.* stands for *век* vek (century) – for example *IV в. пр. Хр.* (4th century BC).

future

day after tomorrow	в други ден	v *droo*·gee den
in (six days)	след (шест дена)	sled (shest *de*·na)
until (June)	до (юни)	do (*yoo*·nee)
next ...	следващият ... m	*sled*·vash·tee·yuht ...
	следващата ... f	*sled*·vash·ta·ta ...
week	седмица f	*sed*·mee·tsa
month	месец m	*me*·sets
year	година f	go·*dee*·na
tomorrow ...	утре ...	*oo*·tre ...
morning	сутринта	soo·treen·*ta*
afternoon	следобед	sle·*do*·bed
evening	вечер	*ve*·cher

during the day

afternoon	следобед m	sle·*do*·bed
dawn	зора f	*zo*·ra
day	ден m	den
evening	вечер f	*ve*·cher
midday/noon	обяд m	ob·*yad*
midnight	полунощ f	po·loo·*nosht*
morning	утро n	*oot*·ro
night	нощ f	nosht
sunrise	изгрев слънце m	*eez*·grev *sluhn*·tse
sunset	залез слънце m	*za*·lez *sluhn*·tse

Christmas	Коледа f	*ko·le·*da
New Year	Нова година f	*no·*va go·*dee·*na

The traditional greetings are *Честита Коледа!* ches·*tee·*ta *ko·le·*da (Merry Christmas!) and *Честита Нова година!* ches·*tee·*ta *no·*va go·*dee·*na (Happy New Year!). The abbreviation *ЧНГ* is seen everywhere and biscuits are even baked in the shape of the letters. A popular custom on New Year's morning is *сурвакане* soor·*va·*ka·ne. Using decorated branches of cornelwood, young children strike their elders lightly on the back, chanting *Сурва сурва година, весела година, живо здраво догодина, догодина до амина* soor·va soor·va go·*dee·*na *ve·*se·la go·*dee·*na *zhee·*vo *zdra·*vo do·go·*dee·*na do a·*mee·*na (lit: happy happy year, joyous year, live healthily next year, next year to amen). The adults give them shiny new coins in return.

Easter	Великден m	ve·*leek·*den

The traditional Easter greeting is *Христос возкресе!* hris·*tos* voz·*kre·*se (Christ has risen!). The proper reply is *Во истина возкресе!* vo ees·*tee·*na voz·*kre·*se (Truly he has risen!).

St Cyril and	Ден на Св.	den na *sve·*tee
Methodius	Кирил и	*kee·*reel ee
Day	Методи m	me·*to·*dee

A holiday dear to Bulgarians, the 24th of May honours the founders of *кирилица* kee·ree·*lee·*tsa (the Cyrillic alphabet). Everything closes, and the whole country partakes in festivals and parades celebrating the alphabet named after St Cyril (for more information, see **introduction**, page 10).

3 March	3 март m	*tre·*tee mart

During the communist era the national holiday was *9 септември* de·*ve·*tee sep·*tem·*vree (9 September), the date of Bulgaria's liberation from fascism in WWII. Since the collapse of communism in 1989, the national holiday has reverted to the 3rd of March, the date of the 1878 San Stefano treaty and the creation of what Bulgarians consider to be the true Bulgarian state (whose borders were considerably reduced by the Congress of Berlin in July of the same year).

The Bulgarian currency is the *лев* lev (almost always used in the counting form *лева* le·va), which comprises 100 *стотинки* sto·teen·kee. A common slang word for the lev is *кинт* keent. With Bulgaria's entry into the EU in 2007, it has committed to replace the lev with the *евро* ev·ro (euro). The changeover in currency is likely to be effective by 2016, with a period of two years during which both the lev and the euro will be accepted.

How much is it?
Колко струва? *kol*·ko *stroo*·va

Can you write down the price?
Моля, напишете цената. *mol*·yuh na·pee·*she*·te tse·*na*·ta

Do I have to pay?
Трябва ли да платя? *tryab*·va lee da plat·*yuh*

There's a mistake in the bill.
Има грешка в сметката. *ee*·ma *gresh*·ka v *smet*·ka·ta

Do you accept ...?	Приемате ли ...?	pree·*e*·ma·te lee ...
credit cards	кредитни	kre·*deet*·nee
	карти	*kar*·tee
debit cards	дебитни	de·*beet*·nee
	карти	*kar*·tee
travellers	пътнически	puht·*nee*·ches·kee
cheques	чекове	*che*·ko·ve
I'd like ...,	Дайте ми	*dai*·te mee
please.	моля ...	*mol*·yuh ...
my change	ресто	*res*·to
a receipt	квитанция	kvee·*tan*·tsee·ya
I'd like ...	Искам ...	*ees*·kam ...
a refund	да ми се	da mee se
	върнат	*vuhr*·nuht
	парите	pa·*ree*·te
to return this	да върна това	da *vuhr*·nuh to·*va*

I'd like to …	Искам да …	*ees·*kam da …
cash a cheque	осребря чек	o·sreb·*ryuh* chek
change a	обменя	ob·men·*yuh*
travellers	пътнически	puht·*nee·*ches·kee
cheque	чек	chek
change money	сменя пари	smen·*yuh* pa·*ree*
get a cash	изтегля пари	eez·*teg·*lyuh pa·*ree*
advance	от кредитната	ot kre·*deet·*na·ta
	си карта	see *kar·*ta
get change for	разваля тази	raz·*val·*yuh *ta·*zee
this note	банкнота	bank·*no·*ta
withdraw	тегля пари	*teg·*lyuh pa·*ree*
money	в брой	v broy

Where's a/an …?	Къде има …?	kuh·*de ee·*ma …
ATM	банкомат	ban·ko·*mat*
foreign	бюро за	byoo·*ro* za
exchange	обмяна на	ob·*mya·*na na
office	валута	va·*loo·*ta

What's the …?	Какъв/Каква	ka·*kuhv/*kak·*va*
	е …? **m/f**	e …
charge	таксата **f**	*tak·*sa·ta
exchange	валутният	va·*loot·*nee·yuht
rate	курс **m**	koors

It's …	… е.	… e
(12) lev	(Дванайсет)	(dva·*nai·*set)
	лева	*le·*va
(5) euros	(Пет) евра	(pet) *ev·*ra
free	Безплатно	bez·*plat·*no

How much is	Колко	*kol·*ko
it per …?	струва …?	*stroo·*va …
day	на ден	na den
hour	на час	na chas
(five) minutes	за (пет)	za (pet)
	минути	mee·*noo·*tee
night	една нощ	ed·*na* nosht
person	на човек	na cho·*vek*
week	на седмица	na *sed·*mee·tsa

For more money-related phrases, see **banking**, page 95.

getting around

Which ... goes to (Knyazhevo)?	Кой/Коя е ... за (Княжево)? m/f	koy/ko·*ya* e ... za (*knya*·zhe·vo)
bus	автобусът m	av·to·*boo*·suht
minibus	маршрутката f	marsh·*root*·ka·ta
train	влакът m	*vla*·kuht
Is this the ... to (Varna)?	Това ли е ... за (Варна)?	to·*va* lee e ... za (*var*·na)
boat	корабът	*ko*·ra·buht
train	влакът	*vla*·kuht
When's the ... bus?	Кога тръгва ... автобус?	ko·*ga* truhg·va ... av·to·*boos*
first	първият	*puhr*·vee·yuht
last	последният	po·*sled*·nee·yuht
next	следващият	*sled*·vash·tee·yuht

What time does it leave?
В колко часа тръгва? v *kol*·ko cha·*suh* truhg·va

What time does it get to (Kyustendil)?
В колко часа пристига в (Кюстендил)? v *kol*·ko cha·*suh* prees·*tee*·ga v (kyoo·sten·*deel*)

How long will it be delayed?
Колко е закъснението? *kol*·ko e za·kuhs·*ne*·nee·ye·to

Is this seat available?
Това място свободно ли е? to·*va* *myas*·to svo·*bod*·no lee e

That's my seat.
Това е моето място. to·*va* e *mo*·ye·to *myas*·to

Please tell me when we get to (Plovdiv).
Кажете ми моля когато пристигнем в (Пловдив). ka·*zhe*·te mee *mol*·yuh ko·*ga*·to prees·*teeg*·nem v (*plov*·deev)

Please stop here.

Моля, спрете тук.   *mol·yuh spre·te took*

How long do we stop here?

След колко време   sled *kol·*ko *vre·*me
тръгваме оттук?   *truhg·*va·me ot·*took*

Let's take public transport.

Хайде да отидем с   *hai·*de da o·*tee·*dem s
градския транспорт.   *grad·*skee·yuh trans·*port*

Can we get there by public transport?

Може ли да отидем там   *mo·*zhe lee da o·*tee·*dem tam
с градския транспорт?   s *grad·*skee·yuh trans·*port*

Let's walk there.

Хайде да отидем пеша.   *hai·*de da o·*tee·*dem pe·*sha*

Let's ride there by bike.

Хайде да отидем с колело.   *hai·*de da o·*tee·*dem s ko·le·*lo*

Are you waiting for more people?

Чакате ли още хора?   *cha·*ka·te lee *osh·*te *ho·*ra

Can you take us around the city, please?

Ще можете ли да   shte *mo·*zhe·te lee da
ни разходите из града?   nee raz·*ho·*dee·te eez gra·*duh*

How many people can ride on this?

Колко души могат да   *kol·*ko *doo·*shee *mo·*guht da
се качат на това?   se ka·*chuht* na to·*va*

---

sharing a ride

A popular form of transport in Bulgarian cities is the *маршрутка* marsh·*root·*ka (shared minibus). These operate along fixed routes just like buses, except that you can hail them or ask to be let off at any point along the route. The route is identified by a placard on the dashboard bearing a large number and a few key points along the route. Fares for this mode of transport cost somewhat more than bus or tram fares. You pay a flat rate, whatever the distance, and the money is handed directly to the driver. In the country-side you might see the *каруца* ka·*roo·*tsa (horse-drawn car-riage), used as the traditional way of getting around.

tickets

Where do I buy a ticket?
Къде мога да си купя билет?
kuh·*de mo*·guh da see *koop*·yuh bee·*let*

Do I need to book?
Трябва ли да направя резервация?
tryab·va lee da na·*prav*·yuh re·zer·*va*·tsee·ya

A ... ticket (to Rila).	Един ... билет (за Рила).	e·*deen* ... bee·*let* (za *ree*·la)
1st-class	първокласен	*purh*·vo·kla·sen
2nd-class	второкласен	*vto*·ro·kla·sen
child's	детски	*det*·skee
one-way	еднопосочен	ed·no·po·*so*·chen
return	двупосочен	dvoo·po·*so*·chen
student	студентски	stoo·*dent*·skee

I'd like a/an ... seat.	Искам място ..., моля.	*ees*·kam *myas*·to ... *mol*·yuh
aisle	до коридора	do ko·ree·*do*·ra
nonsmoking	за непушачи	za ne·poo·*sha*·chee
smoking	за пушачи	za poo·*sha*·chee
window	до прозореца	do pro·*zo*·re·tsa

Is there (a) ...?	Има ли ...?	*ee*·ma lee ...
air conditioning	климатик	klee·ma·*teek*
blanket	одеяло	o·de·*ya*·lo
sick bag	торбичка за повръщане	tor·*beech*·ka za po·*vruhsh*·ta·ne
toilet	тоалетна	to·a·*let*·na

How much is it?
Колко струва?
kol·ko *stroo*·va

How long does the trip take?
Колко трае пътуването?
kol·ko *tra*·ye puh·*too*·va·ne·to

Is it a direct route?
Директен ли е?
dee·*rek*·ten lee e

Can I get a couchette/sleeper?

Има ли спален вагон?   ee·ma lee spa·len va·gon

What time should I check in?

Кога е регистрацията?   ko·ga e re·gees·tra·tsee·ya·ta

I'd like to …	Искам да …	ees·kam da …
my ticket,	своя билет,	svo·yuh bee·let
please.	моля.	mol·yuh
cancel	върна	vuhr·nuh
change	сменя	smen·yuh
collect	взема	vze·muh
confirm	потвърдя	pot·vuhr·dyuh

luggage

багаж

Where can I find a/the …?	Къде …?	kuh·de …
baggage claim	се получава багаж	se po·loo·cha·va ba·gazh
left-luggage office	има гардероб	ee·ma gar·de·rob
luggage locker	има гардероб	ee·ma gar·de·rob
trolley	има количка	ee·ma ko·leech·ka

My luggage has been ...	Багажът ми е ...	ba·ga·zhuht mee e ...
damaged	повреден	po·vre·den
lost	загубен	za·goo·ben
stolen	откраднат	ot·krad·nat

That's (not) mine.

Това (не) е мое. to·va (ne) e mo·ye

Can I have some coins/tokens?

Дайте ми моля
монети/жетони. dai·te mee mol·yuh
mo·ne·tee/zhe·to·nee

backpack/rucksack	раница f	ra·nee·tsa
bag	пътна чанта f	puht·na chan·ta
box	кутия f	koo·tee·ya
cosmetic bag	козметична чантичка f	koz·me·teech·na chan·teech·ka
suitcase	куфар m	koo·far

plane

самолет

Where does flight (357) arrive?

Къде пристига полет
номер (три пет седем)? kuh·de pree·stee·ga po·let
no·mer (tree pet se·dem)

Where does flight (357) depart?

Откъде тръгва полет
номер (три пет седем)? ot·kuh·de truhg·va po·let
no·mer (tree pet se·dem)

Where's (the) ...?	Къде се намира ...?	kuh·de se na·mee·ra ...
arrivals hall	терминал 'пристигащи'	ter·mee·nal pree·stee·gash·tee
departures hall	терминал 'заминаващи'	ter·mee·nal za·mee·na·vash·tee
duty-free shop	безмитен магазин	bez·mee·ten ma·ga·zeen
gate (12)	изход (дванайсет)	ees·hod (dva·nai·set)

бордна карта f	*bord*·na *kar*·ta	**boarding pass**
паспорт m	pas·*port*	**passport**
прекачване n	pre·*kach*·va·ne	**transfer**
транзит m	tran·*zeet*	**transit**

bus & coach

автобусите

Is this a bus stop?
Това ли е автобусната
спирка?
to·*va* lee e av·to·*boos*·na·ta
speer·ka

How often do buses come?
Колко често минават
автобусите?
kol·ko *ches*·to mee·*na*·vat
av·to·*boo*·see·te

Does it stop at (Plovdiv)?
Спира ли в (Пловдив)?
spee·ra lee v (*plov*·deev)

What's the next stop?
Коя е следващата спирка?
ko·*ya* e *sled*·vash·ta·ta *speer*·ka

I'd like to get off at (Koprivshtitsa).
Искам да сляза в
(Копривщица).
ees·kam da *slya*·zuh v
(ko·*preev*·shtee·tsa)

bus terminal	депо n	de·*po*
(central) bus	(централната)	(tsen·*tral*·na·ta)
station	автогара f	av·to·*ga*·ra
city bus	градски автобус	*grad*·skee av·to·*boos*
departure bay	платформа f	plat·*for*·ma
intercity bus	междуградски	mezh·doo·*grad*·skee
	автобус	av·to·*boos*
minibus	маршрутка f	marsh·*root*·ka
timetable	разписание n	raz·pee·*sa*·nee·e
trolleybus	тролейбус m	tro·*ley*·boos

For bus numbers, see **numbers & amounts**, page 37.

Забранено за кучета	za·bra·*ne*·no za *koo*·che·ta	**Dogs Not Allowed**
Заминаващи	za·mee·*na*·vash·tee	**Departures**
Коловоз	ko·lo·*voz*	**Track**
Перон	pe·*ron*	**Platform**
Пристигащи	pree·*stee*·gash·tee	**Arrivals**
Пушенето забранено	*poo*·she·ne·to za·bra·*ne*·no	**No Smoking**
Разрешено за кучета	raz·re·*she*·no za *koo*·che·ta	**Dogs Allowed**

train

влакът

What's the next station?
Коя е следващата спирка? ko·*ya* e *sled*·vash·ta·ta *speer*·ka

Does it stop at (Plovdiv)?
Спира ли в (Пловдив)? *spee*·ra lee v (*plov*·deev)

Do I need to change?
Трябва ли да се *tryab*·va lee da se
прехвърля на друг влак? pre·*hvuhr*·lyuh na droog vlak

Which carriage is for dining?
Кой е вагон-ресторант? koy e va·gon·res·to·*rant*

Is it ...?	... ли е?	... lee e
direct	Директен	dee·*rek*·ten
express	Експрес	eks·*pres*
fast	Бърз	buhrz
a passenger (slow) train	Пътнически	puht·*nee*·ches·kee

Which carriage is (for) ...?	Кой вагон е ...?	koy va·*gon* e ...
1st class	от първа класа	ot *puhr*·va *kla*·sa
2nd class	от втора класа	ot *vto*·ra *kla*·sa
Sofia	за София	za *so*·fee·ya

transport

б.в. (бърз влак)	buhrz vlak	**fast train**
Б.Д.Ж. (Български държавни железници)	*buhl*·gar·skee duhr·*zhav*·nee zhe·*lez*·nee·tsee	**Bulgarian State Railways**
екс.в. (експрес влак)	eks·*pres* vlak	**express train**
ж.п. гара (железопътна гара)	zhe·le·zo·*puht*·na *ga*·ra	**train station**
п.в. (пътнически влак)	puht·*nee*·ches·kee vlak	**passenger (slow) train**
р.с.в. (ресторант-спален вагон)	res·to·*rant*·*spa*·len va·*gon*	**restaurant-sleeper car**

boat

корáб

On the Black Sea, a small boat called *гемия* ge·*mee*·ya can be hired for short distances, while longer distances are covered by the *комета* ko·*me*·ta (hydrofoil).

What's the river/sea like today?

Как е реката/морето днес? kak e re·*ka*·ta/mo·*re*·to dnes

Are there life jackets?

Има ли спасителни жилетки? ee·ma lee spa·*see*·tel·nee zhee·*let*·kee

Which island/beach is this?

Кой е този остров/плаж? koy e *to*·zee *os*·trov/plazh

I feel seasick.

Хваща ме морска болест. *hvash*·ta me *mor*·ska *bo*·lest

boat	корáб m	*ko*·rab
cabin	кабина f	ka·*bee*·na
captain	капитан m	kap·ee·*tan*
(car) deck	палуба (за колите) f	*pa*·loo·ba (za ko·*lee*·te)
ferry	ферибот m	*fe*·ree·bot
lifeboat	спасителна лодка f	spa·*see*·tel·na *lod*·ka
life jacket	спасителна жилетка f	spa·*see*·tel·na zhee·*let*·ka

taxi

I'd like a taxi …	Искам да	ees·kam da
	поръчам такси …	po·ruh·cham tak·see …
at (9am)	в (девет часа)	v (de·vet cha·suh
	сутринта)	soo·treen·ta)
now	за сега	za se·ga
tomorrow	за утре	za oot·re

Where's the taxi rank?
Къде е таксиметровата   kuh·de e tak·see·met·ro·va·ta
стоянка?   sto·yan·ka

Is this taxi available?
Таксито свободно ли е?   tak·see·to svo·bod·no lee e

Please take me to (this address).
Моля да ме закарате   mol·yuh da me za·ka·ra·te
до (този адрес).   do (to·zee ad·res)

Please put the meter on.
Моля да включите   mol·yuh da vklyoo·chee·te
таксиметъра.   tak·see·me·tuh·ra

I don't want to pay a flat fare.
Не искам да платя   ne ees·kam da plat·yuh
фиксирана сума.   feek·see·ra·na soo·ma

How much is the flag fall/hiring charge?
Колко е първоначалната   kol·ko e puhr·vo·na·chal·na·ta
такса?   tak·sa

How much is the call-out fee?
Колко струва   kol·ko stroo·va
за повикването?   za po·veek·va·ne·to

How much is it to (the airport)?
Колко струва   kol·ko stroo·va
до (летището)?   do (le·teesh·te·to)

Please …	Моля …	mol·yuh …
come back	върнете се	vuhr·ne·te se
at (10 o'clock)	в (десет часа)	v (de·set cha·suh)
slow down	намалете	na·ma·le·te
stop here	спрете тук	spre·te took
wait here	чакайте тук	cha·kai·te took

57

Благоевград	bla·*go*·ev·grad	**Blagoevgrad**
Бургас	boor·*gas*	**Burgas**
Варна	*var*·na	**Varna**
Велико Търново	ve·*lee*·ko *tuhr*·no·vo	**Veliko Târnovo**
Пловдив	*plov*·deev	**Plovdiv**
Русе	*roo*·se	**Ruse/Rousse**
Сливен	*slee*·ven	**Sliven**
София	so·*fee*·ya	**Sofia**
Стара Загора	*sta*·ra za·*go*·ra	**Stara Zagora**
Шумен	*shoo*·men	**Shumen**

car & motorbike

колите и мотопедите

car & motorbike hire

I'd like to hire a/an ...	Искам да взема под наем ...	*ees*·kam da *vze*·muh pod *na*·em ...
4WD	кола с предаване четири по четири	ko·*la* s pre·*da*·va·ne *che*·tee·ree po *che*·tee·ree
automatic	кола автоматик	ko·*la* av·to·ma·*teek*
car	кола	ko·*la*
manual	кола с ръчни скорости	ko·*la* s *ruhch*·nee *sko*·ros·tee
motorbike	мотопед	mo·to·*ped*
with ...	с ...	s ...
air conditioning	климатик	klee·ma·*teek*
a driver	шофьор	sho·*fyor*
How much for ... hire?	Колко струва ...?	*kol*·ko *stroo*·va ...
daily	на ден	na den
weekly	на седмица	na *sed*·mee·tsa

Does that include insurance?

Включена ли е
застраховката?

vklyoo·che·na lee e
za·stra·hov·ka·ta

Does that include mileage?

Включен ли е
километражът?

vklyoo·chen lee e
kee·lo·me·tra·zhuht

Do you have a guide to the road rules (in English)?

Имате ли правилник
за движението
по пътищата
(на английски)?

ee·ma·te lee pra·veel·neek
za dvee·zhe·nee·e·to
po puh·teesh·ta·ta
(na an·gleey·skee)

Do you have a road map?

Имате ли пътна карта?

ee·ma·te lee puht·na kar·ta

on the road

There are no parking meters in Bulgaria. Instead, you buy a
талон ta·*lon* (coupon with a certain amount of time on it)
from a ticket machine and display it on the dashboard.

What's the speed limit?

Каква е позволената
скорост?

kak·va e poz·vo·le·na·ta
sko·rost

Is this the road to (Blagoevgrad)?

Това ли е пътят за
(Благоевград)?

to·va lee e puht·yuht za
(bla·go·ev·grad)

Where's a petrol/gas station?

Къде има
бензиностанция?

kuh·de ee·ma
ben·zee·no·stan·tsee·ya

Please fill it up.

Моля напълнете
го до края.

mol·yuh na·puhl·ne·te
go do kra·yuh

I'd like (25) litres.

Искам (двайсет и пет)
литра.

ees·kam (dvai·set ee pet)
leet·ra

road signs

Except for *Cmon* stop (Stop) signs, you'll hardly see any written road signs in Bulgaria – pictorial signs are used instead.

безплатно	bez·*plat*·no	**free**
винетка f	vee·*net*·ka	**motorway pass**
регистрационни	re·gee·stra·tsee·o·nee	**registration**
документи m pl	do·koo·*men*·tee	**papers**
шофьорска	sho·*fyor*·ska	**drivers licence**
книжка f	*kneezh*·ka	

diesel	дизел m	*dee*·zel
leaded	оловен бензин m	o·*lo*·ven ben·*zeen*
LPG	газ m	gaz
regular	обикновен	o·beek·no·*ven*
	бензин m	ben·*zeen*
unleaded	безоловен	bez·o·*lo*·ven
super 95/98	супер бензин	*soo*·per ben·*zeen*
	деветдесет и	de·vet·de·*set* ee
	пет/деветдесет	pet/de·vet·de·*set*
	и осем m	ee *o*·sem

Can you check the ...?	Моля да проверите ...	*mol*·yuh da pro·ve·*ree*·te ...
oil	маслото	*mas*·lo·to
tyre pressure	налягането на гумите	na·*lya*·ga·ne·to na *goo*·mee·te
water	водата	vo·*da*·ta

Can I park here?
Мога ли да паркирам тук? *mo*·guh lee da par·*kee*·ram took

How long can I park here?
Колко време мога *kol*·ko *vre*·me *mo*·guh
да паркирам тук? da par·*kee*·ram took

Do I have to pay?
Плаща ли се? *plash*·ta lee se

problems

I need a mechanic.
Трябва ми монтьор. *tryab*·va mee mon·*tyor*

I've had an accident.
Имах злополука. *ee*·mah zlo·po·*loo*·ka

The car/motorbike has broken down (at Knyazhevo).
Колата/Мотопедът   ko·*la*·ta/mo·to·*ped*·uht
претърпя авария   pre·tuhr·*pya* a·*va*·ree·ya
(в Княжево).   (v *knya*·zhe·vo)

The car/motorbike won't start.
Колата/Мотопедът   ko·*la*·ta/mo·to·*pe*·duht
не запалва.   ne za·*pal*·va

I've run out of petrol.
Нямам бензин.   *nya*·mam ben·*zeen*

I have a flat tyre.
Пукна ми се гумата.   *pook*·na mee se *goo*·ma·ta

I've lost my car keys.
Изгубих си   eez·*goo*·beeh see
ключовете на колата.   *klyoo*·cho·ve·te na ko·*la*·ta

I've locked the keys inside.
Заключих си   za·*klyoo*·cheeh see
ключовете в колата.   *klyoo*·cho·ve·te v ko·*la*·ta

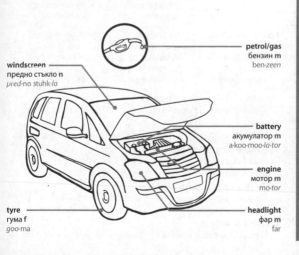

petrol/gas
бензин **m**
ben·*zeen*

windscreen
предно стъкло **n**
pred·no stuhk·*lo*

battery
акумулатор **m**
a·koo·moo·*la*·tor

engine
мотор **m**
mo·*tor*

tyre
гума **f**
goo·ma

headlight
фар **m**
far

transport

Please call roadside assistance.

Моля да позвънете
на пътна помощ.

mol·yuh da poz·*vuh*·ne·te
na *puht*·na po·mosht

Can you fix it (today)?

Ще можете ли да го
поправите (днес)?

shte *mo*·zhe·te lee da go
po·*pra*·vee·te (dnes)

How long will it take?

Колко ще трае поправката? *kol*·ko shte *tra*·ye po·*prav*·ka·ta

bicycle

I'd like ...	Искам да ...	*ees*·kam da ...
my bicycle repaired	ми поправят колелото	mee po·*prav*·yuht ko·le·*lo*·to
to buy a bicycle	си купя колело	see *koop*·yuh ko·le·*lo*
to hire a bicycle	взема под наем едно колело	*vze*·muh pod *na*·em ed·*no* ko·le·*lo*

I'd like a ... bike.	Искам един ... велосипед.	*ees*·kam e·*deen* ... ve·lo·see·*ped*
mountain	планински	pla·*neen*·skee
racing	състезателен	suhs·te·*za*·te·len
secondhand	използван	eez·*polz*·van

How much is it per day/hour?

Колко струва на ден/час? *kol*·ko *stroo*·va na den/chas

Do I need a helmet?

Трябва ли да нося каска? *tryab*·va lee da *nos*·yuh *kas*·ka

Are there bicycle paths?

Има ли алеи за
велосипедисти?

ee·ma lee a·*le*·ee za
ve·lo·see·pe·*dees*·tee

Is there a bicycle-path map?

Има ли карта с алеи
за велосипедисти?

ee·ma lee *kar*·ta s a·*le*·ee
za ve·lo·see·pe·*dees*·tee

I have a puncture.

Пукнала ми се е гумата. *pook*·na·la mee se e *goo*·ma·ta

border crossing

граничен пункт

I'm here in transit.
Аз съм транзитен пътник.   az suhm tran·*zee*·ten *puht*·neek

I'm here …	Тука съм …	*too*·ka suhm …
on business	по работа	po *ra*·bo·ta
on holiday	във	vuhv
	ваканция	va·*kan*·tsee·ya

I'm here for …	Тука съм за …	*too*·ka suhm za …
(10) days	(десет) дена	(*de*·set) *de*·na
(three) weeks	(три) седмици	(tree) *sed*·mee·tsee
(two) months	(два) месеца	(dva) *me*·se·tsa

I'm going to (Shumen).
Отивам в (Шумен).   o·*tee*·vam v (*shoo*·men)

I'm staying at the (Sheraton).
Отседнал/Отседнала съм   ot·*sed*·nal/ot·*sed*·na·la suhm
в (Шератон). m/f   v (she·ra·*ton*)

The children are on this passport.
Децата са записани   de·*tsa*·ta sa za·*pee*·sa·nee
в този паспорт.   v *to*·zee pas·*port*

listen for …		
виза f	*vee*·za	**visa**
група f	*groo*·pa	**group**
паспорт m	pas·*port*	**passport**
печат m	pe·*chat*	**stamp**
сам/сама m/f	sam/sa·*ma*	**alone**
семейство n	se·*meys*·tvo	**family**

border crossing

at customs

I have nothing to declare.
Нямам нищо за
деклар诞иране.
nya·mam *neesh*·to za
dek·la·*ree*·ra·ne

I have something to declare.
Имам какво да
декларирам.
ee·mam kak·*vo* da
dek·la·*ree*·ram

Do I have to declare this?
Трябва ли да
декларирам това?
tryab·va lee da
dek·la·*ree*·ram to·*va*

I didn't know I had to declare it.
Не знаех, че трябва
да се декларира.
ne *zna*·yeh che *tryab*·va
da se dek·la·*ree*·ra

That's (not) mine.
Това (не) е мое.
to·*va* (ne) e *mo*·ye

Do you have this form in (English)?
Имате ли този формуляр
на (английски)?
ee·ma·te lee *to*·zee for·moo·*lyar*
na (an·*gleey*·skee)

Could I please have an (English) interpreter?
Може ли да извикате
преводач (който
говори английски)?
mo·zhe lee da eez·*vee*·ka·te
pre·vo·*dach* (*koy*·to
go·*vo*·ree an·*gleey*·skee)

For phrases on payments and receipts, see **money**, page 47, and the box **paperwork**, page 68.

signs		
Безмитен магазин	bez·*mee*·ten ma·ga·*zeen*	Duty-Free Shop
Карантина	ka·ran·*tee*·na	Quarantine
Митница	*meet*·nee·tsa	Customs
Паспортен контрол	pas·*por*·ten kon·*trol*	Passport Control

Where's a/the ...?	Къде има ...?	kuh·*de ee*·ma ...
bank	банка	*ban*·ka
market	пазар	pa·*zar*
tourist	бюро за	byoo·*ro* za
information	туристическа	too·rees·*tee*·ches·ka
centre	информация	een·for·*ma*·tsee·ya

What's the address?
Какъв е адресът?   ka·*kuhv* e a·*dre*·suht

How do I get there?
Как да стигна дотам?   kak da *steeg*·nuh do·*tam*

How far is it?
На какво растояние е?   na kak·*vo* ras·to·*ya*·nee·e e

Can you show me (on the map)?
Можете ли да ми
покажете (на картата)? pol   *mo*·zhe·te lee da mee po·*ka*·zhe·te (na *kar*·ta·ta)
Можеш ли да ми
покажеш (на картата)? inf   *mo*·zhesh lee da mee po·*ka*·zhesh (na *kar*·ta·ta)

---

listen for ...

In Bulgarian, distance isn't normally measured in terms of time (eg 'an hour's walk from here'), although sometimes the phrase на пет минути оттука na pet mee·*noo*·tee ot·*too*·ka (five minutes away) is used with the meaning 'very close'.

Note that the following nouns are given in the counting form (the one that comes after numbers), so you can just slot in the appropriate number.

... километра	... kee·lo·*me*·tra	**... kilometres**
... метра	... *me*·tra	**... metres**
... преки	... *pre*·kee	**... blocks**

For detached houses, the street name comes first followed by the house number – eg *Оборище 16* o·bo·reesh·te shest·nai·set. In the newer parts of larger cities, most people live in big apartment buildings called *блокове* blo·ko·ve (blocks), which are organised into larger complexes. Each such *жилищен комплекс* zhee·leesh·ten kom·pleks (living complex) – abbreviated to *ЖК* zhe·ka – bears a name, such as *Младост* mla·dost (Youth). Although there are streets among the buildings in a complex, addresses don't refer to the streets, but to the building numbers (which can be in the hundreds). Each building has several entrances, labelled in alphabetical order (*А, Б, В, Г …*). A typical address would look like this:

ЖК Младост	zhe·ka mla·dost	living complex 'Youth'
блок 109	blok sto de·vet	block 109
вх. Б	vhod be	entrance B
5-ти етаж	pe·tee e·tazh	5th floor
ап. 25	a·par·ta·ment dvai·set ee pet	apartment 25

It's …	… е.	… e
behind …	Зад …	zad …
close	Близо	blee·zo
far away	Далече	da·le·che
here	Тука	too·ka
in front of …	Пред …	pred …
near …	Близо до …	blee·zo do …
next to …	До …	do …
on the corner	На ъгъла	na uh·guh·luh
opposite …	Срещу …	sresh·too …
straight ahead	Направо	na·pra·vo
there	Там	tam

by bus	с автобус	s av·to·boos
by taxi	с такси	s tak·see
by train	с влак	s vlak
on foot	пеша	pe·sha

Turn ...	Завийте ... pol	za·*veey*·te ...
	Завий ... inf	za·*veey* ...
at the corner	на ъгъла	na *uh*·guh·luh
at the traffic lights	при светофара	pree sve·to·*fa*·ruh
left	наляво	na·*lya*·vo
right	надясно	na·*dyas*·no
north	север m	*se*·ver
south	юг m	yoog
east	изток m	*eez*·tok
west	запад m	*za*·pad
What ... is this?	Как се казва ...?	kak se *kaz*·va ...
square	този площад	*to*·zee plosh·*tad*
street	тази улица	*ta*·zee oo·lee·tsa
town	този град	*to*·zee grad
village	това село	*to*·va *se*·lo

traffic lights
светофар m
sve·to·*far*

bus
автобус m
av·to·*boos*

shop
магазин m
ma·ga·*zeen*

intersection
пресечка f
pre·*sech*·ka

pedestrian crossing
пешеходна пътека f
pe·she·*hod*·na puh·*te*·ka

corner
ъгъл m
uh·guhl

taxi
такси n
tak·*see*

name/surname	име/презиме n	*ee*·me/*pre*·zee·me
address	адрес m	ad·*res*
date of birth	дата на раждане f	*da*·ta na *razh*·da·ne
place of birth	място на раждане n	*myas*·to na *razh*·da·ne
age	възраст m	*vuhz*·rast
sex	пол m	pol
nationality	националност f	na·tsee·o·*nal*·nost
occupation	професия f	pro·*fe*·see·ya
marital status	семейно положение n	se·*mey*·no po·lo·*zhe*·nee·e
single	неженен m неомъжена f	ne·*zhe*·nen ne·o·*muh*·zhe·na
married	женен m омъжена f	*zhe*·nen o·*muh*·zhe·na
point of departure/ destination	начална/крайна точка на пътуването f	na·*chal*·na/*krai*·na *toch*·ka na puh·*too*·va·ne·to
entry/exit date	дата на влизането/ излизането f	*da*·ta na *vlee*·za·ne·to/ eez·*lee*·za·ne·to
purpose of visit	цел на пътуването f	tsel na puh·*too*·va·ne·to
holiday	ваканция f	va·*kan*·tsee·ya
business	работа f	*ra*·bo·ta
identification	документ за самоличност m	do·koo·*ment* za sa·mo·*leech*·nost
drivers licence	шофьорска книжка f	sho·*fyor*·ska *kneezh*·ka
passport number	номер на паспорта m	*no*·mer na pas·*por*·tuh
work/study permit	разрешително за работа/ обучение n	raz·re·*shee*·tel·no za *ra*·bo·ta/ o·boo·*che*·nee·e

finding accommodation

търсене на стаи

Where's a ...?	Къде има ...?	kuh·de ee·ma ...
camping ground	къмпинг	kuhm·peeng
guesthouse	пансион	pan·see·on
hotel	хотел	ho·tel
motel	мотел	mo·tel
private room	частна квартира	chast·na kvar·tee·ra
subsidised vacation place	почивна станция	po·cheev·na stan·tsee·ya
youth hostel	хостел	hos·tel
Can you recommend somewhere ...?	Можете ли да препоръчате нещо ...? pol	mo·zhe·te lee da pre·po·ruh·cha·te nesh·to ...
	Можеш ли да препоръчаш нещо ...? inf	mo·zhesh lee da pre·po·ruh·chash nesh·to ...
cheap	евтино	ev·tee·no
good	хубаво	hoo·ba·vo
luxurious	разкошно	raz·kosh·no
nearby	наблизо	na·blee·zo
romantic	романтично	ro·man·teech·no

a word of caution

It's not advisable to ask for recommendations to places that are safe (eg for women travellers or someone travelling alone) from people you don't know well. It might provoke a response opposite from the desired one, and you could end up in a *дупка doop*·ka (a 'dive', literally 'pit').

I'd like something near the ...	Искам нещо близо до ...	ees·kam nesh·to blee·zo do ...
beach	плажа	pla·zhuh
city centre	центъра	tsen·tuh·ruh
lake	езерото	e·ze·ro·to
mountains	планината	pla·nee·na·ta
shops	магазините	ma·ga·zee·nee·te
train station	гарата	ga·ra·ta

Are there any ecolodges here?
Има ли тука екохотели? ee·ma lee too·ka e·ko·ho·te·lee

I'd like to stay at a locally run hotel.
Искам да отседна в ees·kam da ot·sed·nuh v
малък частен хотел. ma·luhk chas·ten ho·tel

What's the address?
Какъв е адресът? ka·kuhv e a·dre·suht

For responses, see **directions**, page 65.

booking ahead & checking in

предварителна резервация и регистрация

I'd like to book a room, please.
Искам да взема ees·kam da vze·muh
една стая, моля. ed·na sta·ya mol·yuh

I have a reservation.
Имам резервация. ee·mam re·zer·va·tsee·ya

listen for ...		
За колко нощи?	za kol·ko nosh·tee	**How many nights?**
баня на етажа f	ban·ya na e·ta·zhuh	**shared bathroom**
ключ m	klyooch	**key**
пълен	puh·len	**full**
рецепция f	re·tsep·tsee·ya	**reception**
самостоятелна баня f	sa·mo·sto·ya·tel·na ban·ya	**ensuite bathroom**

My name is …
Казвам се …   *kaz*·vam se …

For (three) nights/weeks.
За (три) нощи/седмици.   za (tree) *nosh*·tee/*sed*·mee·tsee

From (2 July) to (6 July).
От (втори юли) до   ot (*vto*·ree *yoo*·lee) do
(шести юли).   (*shes*·tee *yoo*·lee)

Do I need to pay upfront?
Трябва ли да платя   *tryab*·va lee da plat·*yuh*
предварително?   pred·va·*ree*·tel·no

Can I see it?
Мога ли да я видя?   *mo*·guh lee da ya *veed*·yuh

I'll take it.
Ще я взема.   shte ya *vze*·muh

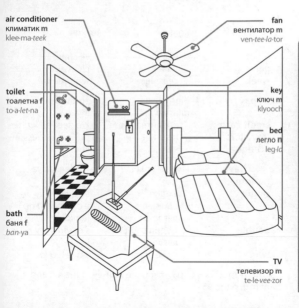

air conditioner
климатик **m**
klee·ma·*teek*

fan
вентилатор **m**
ven·*tee*·la·tor

toilet
тоалетна **f**
to·a·*let*·na

key
ключ **m**
klyooch

bed
легло **n**
leg·*lo*

bath
баня **f**
ban·ya

TV
телевизор **m**
te·le·*vee*·zor

Баня	*ban·*ya	**Bathroom**
Има стаи	*ee·*ma *sta·*ee	**Rooms Available**
Квартирно бюро	kvar·*teer·*no byoo·*ro*	**Accommodation Bureau**
Няма стаи	*nya·*ma *sta·*ee	**No Vacancy**
Пералня	pe·*ral·*nya	**Laundry**
Планинска хижа	pla·*neen·*ska *hee·*zha	**Mountain Hut**
Ресторант	res·to·*rant*	**Restaurant**
Свободни стаи	svo·*bod·*nee *sta·*ee	**Vacancy**
Туристическа спалня	too·rees·*tee·*ches·ka *spal·*nya	**Tourist Bedroom**
Туристически дом	too·rees·*tee·*ches·kee dom	**Tourist Home**

How much is it per ...?	Колко е на ...?	*kol·*ko e na ...
night	вечер	*ve·*cher
person	човек	cho·*vek*
week	седмица	*sed·*mee·tsa
Can I pay by ...?	Мога ли да платя с ...?	*mo·*guh lee da plat·*yuh* s ...
credit card	кредитна карта	*kre·*deet·na *kar·*ta
travellers cheque	пътнически чек	puht·*nee·*ches·kee chek
Do you have a ... room?	Има ли стая ...?	*ee·*ma lee *sta·*ya ...
single	с едно единично легло	s ed·*no* e·dee·*neech·*no *leg·*lo
double	с едно двойно легло	s ed·*no* dvoy·no *leg·*lo
twin	с две легла	s dve leg·*la*

For other methods of payment, see **money**, page 47, and **banking**, page 95.

requests & queries

Is breakfast included?
Включена ли е закуската? *vklyoo·che·na lee e za·koos·ka·ta*

When/Where is breakfast served?
Кога/Къде сервират ko·*ga*/kuh·*de* ser·*vee*·rat
закуската? za·*koos*·ka·ta

Is there hot water all day?
Има ли топла вода *ee*·ma lee *top*·la vo·*da*
през целия ден? prez *tse*·lee·yuh den

Please wake me at (seven).
Моля, събудете *mol*·yuh suh·boo·*de*·te
ме в (седем). me v (*se*·dem)

Can I use the ...? Мога ли да *mo*·guh lee da
използвам ...? eez·*polz*·vam ...
    internet Интернета *een*·ter·ne·tuh
    kitchen кухнята *kooh*·nya·ta
    laundry пералнята pe·*ral*·nya·ta
    telephone телефона te·le·*fo*·nuh

Do you have Има ли ...? *ee*·ma lee ...
a/an ...?
    elevator/lift асансьор a·san·*syor*
    laundry service пералня pe·*ral*·nya
    message board табло за tab·*lo* za
съобщения suh·ob·*shte*·nee·ya
    safe сейф seyf
    swimming pool плувен басейн *ploo*·ven ba·*seyn*

Do you ... here? Има ли при *ee*·ma lee pree
вас ...? vas ...
    arrange tours организирани or·ga·nee·*zee*·ra·nee
екскурзии eks·*koor*·zee·ee
    change money обмяна на ob·*mya*·na na
валута va·*loo*·ta
    offer long-stay намаление за na·ma·*le*·nee·e za
    discounts по-дълъг *po*·duh·luhg
престой pre·*stoy*

73

Could I have ..., please?	Дайте ми ..., моля.	dai·te mee ... mol·yuh
my key	ключа	klyoo·chuh
a receipt	квитанция	kvee·tan·tsee·ya

Is there a message for me?

| Има ли съобщение за мене? | ee·ma lee suh·ob·shte·nee·e za me·ne |

I'm locked out of my room.

| Забравил/Забравила съм си ключа в стаята. m/f | za·bra·veel/za·bra·vee·la suhm see klyoo·chuh v sta·ya·ta |

complaints

оплаквания

It's too ...	Много е ... в стаята.	mno·go e ... v sta·ya·ta
cold	студено	stoo·de·no
dark	тъмно	tuhm·no
noisy	шумно	shoom·no

It's too ...	... ми е.	... mee e
small	Малко	mal·ko
expensive	Скъпо	skuh·po

The ... doesn't work.	... не работи.	... ne ra·bo·tee
air conditioner	Климатикът	klee·ma·tee·kuht
fan	Вентилаторът	ven·tee·la·to·ruht
toilet	Тоалетната	to·a·let·na·ta

Can I get another ...?	Дайте ми моля още ...	dai·te mee mol·yuh osh·te ...
blanket	едно одеяло	ed·no o·de·ya·lo
sheet	един чаршаф	e·deen char·shaf

This ... isn't clean.	Тази ... не е чиста.	ta·zee ... ne e chees·ta
pillow	възглавница	vuhz·glav·nee·tsa
towel	кърпа	kuhr·pa

There's no hot water.

Няма топла вода.   *nya·ma top·la vo·da*

a knock at the door ...		
Who is it?	Кой е?	koy e
Just a moment.	Един момент.	e·deen mo·ment
Come in.	Влезте.	vlez·te
Come back later,	Елате по-късно,	e·la·te po·kuhs·no
please.	моля.	mol·yuh

checking out

What time is checkout?

Кога трябва да   *ko·ga tryab·va da*
освободя стаята?   *os·vo·bo·dyuh sta·ya·ta*

Can I have a late checkout?

Мога ли да остана   *mo·guh lee da o·sta·nuh*
до по-късно?   *do po·kuhs·no*

Can you call a taxi for me (for 11 o'clock)?

Ще ми поръчате ли   *shte mee po·ruh·cha·te lee*
едно такси   *ed·no tak·see*
(за единайсет часа)?   *(za e·dee·nai·set cha·suh)*

I'm leaving now.

Тръгвам сега.   *truhg·vam se·ga*

There's a mistake in the bill.

Има грешка в сметката.   *ee·ma gresh·ka v smet·ka·ta*

Can I leave my bags here?

Мога ли да оставя   *mo·guh lee da os·tav·yuh*
багажа си тук?   *ba·ga·zhuh see took*

Could I have	Дайте ми ...,	*dai·te mee ...*
my ..., please?	моля.	*mol·yuh*
deposit	моя депозит	*mo·yuh de·po·zeet*
passport	моя паспорт	*mo·yuh pas·port*
valuables	моите ценности	*mo·yee·te tsen·nos·tee*

I'll be back … | Ще се върна … | shte se *vurh*·nuh …
  in (three) days | след (три) дена | sled (tree) *de*·na
  on (Thursday) | в (четвъртък) | v (chet·*vurh*·tuhk)

I had a great stay, thanks.
Беше много | *be*·she *mno*·go
приятно, благодаря. | pree·*yat*·no bla·go·dar·*yuh*

camping

Who do I ask to stay here?
Кого да попитам | ko·*go* da po·*pee*·tam
за да остана тука? | za da o·*sta*·nuh *too*·ka

Can I …? | Мога ли да …? | *mo*·guh lee da …
  camp here | лагерувам тук | la·ge·*roo*·vam took
  park next to | паркирам | par·*kee*·ram
  my tent | колата си до | ko·*la*·ta see do
   | палатката | pa·*lat*·ka·ta

Do you have …? | Имате ли …? | *ee*·ma·te lee …
  bungalows | бунгала | boon·ga·*la*
  electricity | електричество | e·lek·*tree*·chest·vo
  a laundry | пералня | pe·*ral*·nya
  a tent site | свободно | svo·*bod*·no
   | място за | *myas*·to za
   | палатката | pa·*lat*·ka·ta
  shower facilities | душове | doo·*sho*·ve
  tents for hire | палатки | pa·*lat*·kee
   | под наем | pod *na*·em

Is it coin-operated?
Работи ли с монети? | ra·*bo*·tee lee s mo·*ne*·tee

Is the water drinkable?
Водата може ли | vo·*da*·ta *mo*·zhe lee
да се пие? | da se *pee*·e

Could I borrow …?
Мога ли да взема | *mo*·guh lee da *vze*·muh
под наем …? | pod *na*·em …

PRACTICAL

How much is it per ...?	Колко струва на ...?	kol·ko stroo·va na ...
caravan	каравана	ka·ra·va·na
person	човек	cho·vek
tent	палатка	pa·lat·ka
vehicle	кола	ko·la

renting

I'm here about the ... for rent.	Дойдох да попитам за ... под наем.	doy·doh da po·pee·tam za ... pod na·em
apartment	апартамента	a·par·ta·men·tuh
cabin	бунгалото	boon·ga·lo·to
house	къщата	kuhsh·ta·ta
(private) room	стая (в частно жилище)	sta·ya (v chast·no zhee·leesh·te)

Do you have a/an ... for rent?	Давате ли ... под наем?	da·va·te lee ... pod na·em
apartment	апартамент	a·par·ta·ment
cabin	бунгало	boon·ga·lo
house	къща	kuhsh·ta
room	стая	sta·ya

furnished	мебелиран	me·be·lee·ran
partly furnished	отчасти мебелиран	ot·chas·tee me·be·lee·ran
unfurnished	без мебели	bez me·be·lee

Is a deposit required?
Необходим ли е депозит? ne·ob·ho·deem lee e de·po·zeet

Are bills extra?
Режийните включени ли са в цената? re·zheey·nee·te vklyoo·che·nee lee suh v tse·na·ta

accommodation

staying with locals

Bulgarians sincerely love entertaining guests and are always delighted when they arrive. Allow your hosts to indicate where you should sit. It's also best to let them direct the topics of conversation. The usual gifts are flowers (just make sure it's an uneven number of stems, as even numbers are for funerals), a bottle of alcohol and sweets (eg chocolates) for the children.

Can I stay at your place?

| Може ли да остана | mo·zhe lee da o·sta·nuh |
| да спя у вас? | da spyuh oo vas |

Is there anything I can do to help?

| Да ви помогна с нещо? | da vee po·mog·nuh s nesh·to |

Can I bring anything for dinner/lunch?

| Какво да донеса за | kak·vo da do·ne·suh za |
| вечеря/обяд? | ve·che·rya/o·byad |

I have my own ...	Нося своя ...	nos·yuh svo·yuh ...
mattress	дюшек	dyoo·shek
sleeping bag	спален чувал	spa·len choo·val

Can I ...?	Може ли да ...?	mo·zhe lee da ...
do the dishes	измия	eez·mee·yuh
	съдовете	suh·do·ve·te
set/clear the table	сложа/	slo·zhuh/
	прибера	pree·be·ruh
	масата	ma·sa·ta
take out the rubbish	изхвърля	eez·hvuhr·lyuh
	боклука	bok·loo·kuh

Thanks for your hospitality.

| Благодаря ви за | bla·go·dar·yuh vee za |
| гостоприемството. | gos·to·pree·ems·tvo·to |

To compliment your hosts' cooking, see **eating out**, page 168.

looking for ...

Are shops open on (24 May)?
Магазините отворени
ли са на (двайсет и
четвърти май)?
ma·ga·*zee*·nee·te ot·*vo*·re·nee
lee suh na (*dvai*·set ee
chet·*vuhr*·tee mai)

What hours are shops open?
Какво е работното
време на магазините?
kak·vo e ra·*bot*·no·to
vre·me na ma·ga·*zee*·nee·te

Where can I buy (a padlock)?
Къде мога да си
купя (катинар)?
kuh·*de mo*·guh da see
koop·yuh (ka·tee·*nar*)

Where can I buy locally produced goods?
Къде мога да си купя
нещо направено тук?
kuh·*de mo*·guh da see *koop*·yuh
nesh·to na·*pra*·ve·no took

Where can I buy locally produced souvenirs?
Къде мога да си купя
сувенири направени
тук?
kuh·*de mo*·guh da see *koop*·yuh
soo·ve·*nee*·ree na·*pra*·ve·nee
took

Where's a ...?	**Къде има ...?**	kuh·*de ee*·ma ...
department	универсален	oo·nee·ver·*sa*·len
store	магазин	ma·ga·*zeen*
market	пазар	pa·*zar*
supermarket	супермаркет	soo·per·mar·ket

For more items and shopping locations, see the **dictionary**.

making a purchase

I'm just looking.
Само разгледам.   *sa*·mo raz·*gle*·dam

I'd like to buy (an adaptor plug).
Искам да си купя   *ees*·kam da see *koop*·yuh
(адаптор).   (a·*dap*·tor)

How much is it?
Колко струва?   *kol*·ko *stroo*·va

Can you write down the price?
Моля, напишете цената.   *mol*·yuh na·pee·*she*·te tse·*na*·ta

Do you have any others?
Имате ли други от   *ee*·ma·te lee *droo*·gee ot
този вид?   *to*·zee veed

Can I look at it?
Мога ли да го видя?   *mo*·guh lee da go *veed*·yuh

Is this (220) volts?
Това на (двеста двайсет)   to·*va* na (*dve*·sta *dvai*·set)
волта ли е?   *vol*·ta lee e

street-side shopping

In Bulgaria, many things (both new and secondhand) are
sold by street vendors. They display their wares in various
ways, ranging from a simple *маса ma*·sa (table) to a
серия ser·*gee*·ya (more extended display area), to a *пазар*
pa·*zar* (an established set of tables) or a *будка bood*·ka (an
enclosed kiosk). The latter can be small, selling newspapers,
magazines etc, or large, effectively functioning as a one-
room store. These displays can be set up on the pavement,
set back from the street in what used to be a garage, or
in *подлези pod*·le·zee (underground walkways helping
pedestrians cross major intersections).

PRACTICAL

The acquisition of new possessions is often accompanied by the following good wishes:

Със здраве да го носите/носиш! pol/inf
suhs *zdra*·ve da go   May you wear it in good health!
no·see·te/*no*·seesh   (for clothing)

Със здраве да го използвате/използваш! pol/inf
suhs *zdra*·ve da go   May you use it in good health!
eez·*polz*·va·te/   (for appliances, cars, utensils etc)
eez·*polz*·vash

Do you accept ...?	Приемате ли ...?	pree·*e*·ma·te lee ...
credit cards	кредитни карти	kre·*deet*·nee *kar*·tee
debit cards	дебитни карти	de·beet·nee *kar*·tee
travellers	пътнически	*puht*·nee·ches·kee
cheques	чекове	*che*·ko·ve

Could I have a ..., please?	Дайте ми моля ...	*dai*·te mee *mol*·yuh ...
bag	плик	pleek
receipt	квитанция	kvee·*tan*·tsee·ya

I don't need a bag, thanks.
Не ми трябва плик,   ne mee *tryab*·va pleek
благодаря.   bla·go·dar·*yuh*

Could I have it wrapped?
Моля да го опаковате.   *mol*·yuh da go o·pa·*ko*·va·te

Does it have a guarantee?
Има ли гаранция?   ee·ma lee ga·*ran*·tsee·ya

Can I have it sent abroad?
Можете ли да го   *mo*·zhe·te lee da go
изпратите в чужбина?   eez·*pra*·tee·te v choozh·*bee*·na

Can you order it for me?
Можете ли да го   *mo*·zhe·te lee da go
поръчате за мене?   po·*ruh*·cha·te za *me*·ne

Can I pick it up later?
Мога ли да го взема   *mo*·guh lee da go *vze*·muh
по-късно?   po·kuhs·no

The quality isn't good.
    Качеството не е добро.   *ka*·chest·vo·to ne e do·*bro*

I'd like my change, please.
    Дайте ми моля ресто.   *dai*·te mee *mol*·yuh *res*·to

I'd like ..., please.	Искам да ...	*ees*·kam da ...
a refund	ми върнете	mee *vurh*·ne·te
	парите	pa·*ree*·te
to return this	върна това	*vuhr*·nuh to·*va*

bargaining

That's too expensive.
    Много е скъпо.   *mno*·go e *skuh*·po

Can you lower the price?
    Можете ли да свалите   *mo*·zhe·te lee da sva·*lee*·te
    цената?   tse·*na*·ta

Do you have something cheaper?
    Имате ли нещо   *ee*·ma·te lee *nesh*·to
    по-евтино?   *po*·ev·tee·no

What's your final price?
    Каква е най-ниската   kak·*va* e *nai*·nees·ka·ta
    ви цена?   vee tse·*na*

I'll give you (five lev/euros).
    Ще ви дам (пет лева/евра).   shte vee dam (pet *le*·va/*ev*·ra)

---

faulty things

Има дефект.	*ee*·ma de·*fekt*	It's faulty.
(lit: there's a defect)		(clothes, shoes)
Не работи.	ne ra·*bo*·tee	It's faulty.
(lit: it doesn't work)		(electrical goods, etc)
Развалено е.	raz·va·*le*·no e	It's faulty.
(lit: it's spoiled)		(general: no good, etc)
Повредено е.	po·*vre*·de·no e	It's faulty.
(lit: it's broken)		(general: no good, etc)

bargain	изгодно n	eez-*god*-no
sale n	разпродажба f	raz-pro-*dazh*-ba
specials	стоки с	*sto*-kee s
	намаление f pl	na-ma-*le*-nee-e
(straight-out)	(пладнешки)	(plad-*nesh*-kee)
rip-off n	обир m	*o*-beer

books & reading

книги и четене

Do you have ...?	Имате ли ...?	*ee*-ma-tee lee ...
a book by	някоя книга	*nya*-ko-ya *knee*-ga
(Elin Pelin)	на (Елин Пелин)	na (e-*leen* pe-*leen*)
an entertainment	справочник	*spra*-voch-neek
guide	за културни	za kool-*toor*-nee
	събития	suh-*bee*-tee-ya
Is there an	Има ли ...	*ee*-ma lee ...
English-	с книги на	s *knee*-gee na
language ...?	английски?	an-*gleey*-skee
bookshop	книжарница	knee-*zhar*-nee-tsa
section	отделение	ot-de-*le*-nee-e
I'd like a ...	Търся ...	*tuhr*-syuh ...
dictionary	речник	*rech*-neek
newspaper	вестник	*vest*-neek
(in English)	(на английски)	(na an-*gleey*-skee)
notepad	бележник	be-*lezh*-neek

Can you recommend a book for me?

Можете ли да ми	*mo*-zhe-te lee da mee
препоръчате някоя	pre-po-*ruh*-cha-te *nya*-ko-ya
книга?	*knee*-ga

Do you have Lonely Planet guidebooks/phrasebooks?

Имате ли пътеводители/	*ee*-ma-te lee puh-te-vo-*dee*-te-lee/
разговорници на фирма	raz-go-*vor*-nee-tsee na *feer*-ma
'Лонли Планет'?	*lon*-lee *pla*-net

clothes

My size is ...	Моят номер е ...	mo·yuht no·mer e ...
(40)	(четирийсет)	(chet·tee·ree·set)
small (S)	малък (S)	ma·luhk (es)
medium (M)	среден (M)	sre·den (em)
large (L)	голям (L)	go·lyam (el)

Can I try it on?
Мога ли да го пробвам?   mo·guh lee da go prob·vam

It doesn't fit.
Не ми става.   ne mee sta·va

hairdressing

I'd like (a) ...	Искам да ...	ees·kam da ...
colour	ми боядисате косата	mee bo·ya·dee·sa·te ko·sa·ta
foils/streaks	ми направите кичури	mee na·pra·vee·te kee·choo·ree
haircut	ме подстрижете	me pod·stree·zhe·te
my beard trimmed	ми подстрижете брадата	mee pod·stree·zhe·te bra·da·ta
my hair washed/ dried	ми измиете/ изсушите косата	mee eez·mee·e·te/ eez·soo·shee·te ko·sa·ta
shave	ме обръснете	me o·bruhs·ne·te
trim	ми подстрижете крайчетата на косата	mee pod·stree·zhe·te krai·che·ta·ta na ko·sa·ta

Don't cut it too short.
Да не е много късо.   da ne e mno·go kuh·so

Please use a new blade.
Моля, използвайте ново ножче за бръснене.   mol·yuh eez·polz·vai·te no·vo nozh·che za bruhs·ne·ne

Shave it all off!
Обръснете я цялата! o·bruhs·*ne*·te ya *tsa*·la·ta

I don't like this!
Не ми харесва! ne mee ha·*res*·va

I should never have let you near me!
Не трябваше да се ne *tryab*·va·she da se
оставям в ръцете ви! os·*tav*·yam v ruh·*tse*·te vee

music & DVD

музика и дивиди

I'd like a ...	Искам ...	*ees*·kam ...
blank tape	една празна касета	ed·*na praz*·na ka·*se*·ta
CD	едно сиди	ed·*no* see·*dee*
DVD	едно дивиди	ed·*no* dee·vee·*dee*
video	едно видео	ed·*no* vee·de·o

I'm looking for something by (Teodosi Spassov).
Търся изпълнение *turh*·syuh eez·puhl·*ne*·nee·e
на (Теодоси Спасов). na (te·o·*do*·see *spa*·sov)

What's his best recording?
Кой е най-добрият koy e *nai*·do·bree·yuht
му запис? moo *za*·pees

Can I listen to this?
Мога ли да чуя това? *mo*·guh lee da *choo*·yuh to·*va*

Will this work on any DVD player?
Това ще работи ли на to·*va* shte ra·*bo*·tee lee na
всеки дивиди-плейър? *vse*·kee dee·vee·*dee* *ple*·yuhr

video & photography

Can you ...?	Можете ли да ...?	*mo*·zhe·te lee da ...
develop this film	проявите този филм	pro·ya·*vee*·te *to*·zee feelm
load my film	ми заредите филма	mee za·re·*dee*·te *feel*·muh
recharge the battery for my digital camera	презаредите батерията на цифровия ми фотоапарат	pre·za·re·*dee*·te ba·*te*·ree·ya·ta na *tsee*·fro·vee·yuh mee fo·to·a·pa·*rat*
transfer photos from my camera to CD	прехвърлите снимките от фотоапарата ми на едно сиди	pre·*hvuhr*·lee·te *sneem*·kee·te ot fo·to·a·pa·*ra*·tuh mee na ed·*no* see·*dee*

Do you have (a) ... for this camera?	Имате ли ... за този фотоапарат?	*ee*·ma·te lee ... za *to*·zee fo·to·a·pa·*rat*
batteries	батерии	ba·*te*·ree·ee
flash (bulb)	(крушка за) светкавица	(*kroosh*·ka za) svet·*ka*·vee·tsa
(zoom) lens	(варио-) обектив	(*va*·ree·o·) o·bek·*teev*
light meter	светломер	svet·lo·*mer*
memory cards	памет	*pa*·met

Can I connect my ... to this computer?	Мога ли да свържа моя ... към този компютър?	*mo*·guh lee da *svuhr*·zhu *mo*·yuh ... kuhm *to*·zee kom·*pyoo*·tuhr
camera	фотоапарат	fo·to·a·pa·*rat*
media player	плейър	*ple*·yuhr
portable hard drive	портативен харддиск	por·ta·*tee*·ven *hard*·deesk
USB flash drive	USB флаш памет	yoo·es·*bee* flash *pa*·met

I need a/an ... film for this camera.	Трябва ми ... филм за този фотоапарат.	*tryab*·va mee ... feelm za *to*·zee fo·to·a·pa·*rat*
APS	APS	a·pe·*es*
B&W	черно-бял	cher·no·*byal*
colour	цветен	*tsve*·ten
slide	диапозитивен	dee·a·po·zee·*tee*·ven

I need a (200)-speed film for this camera.

Трябва ми филм от скорост (двеста) за този фотоапарат.	*tryab*·va mee feelm ot *sko*·rost (*dve*·sta) za *to*·zee fo·to·a·pa·*rat*

I need a cable to recharge this battery.

Трябва ми кабел да презаредя тази батерия.	*tryab*·va mee *ka*·bel da pre·za·red·*yuh ta*·zee ba·*te*·ree·ya

I need a video cassette for this camera.

Трябва ми видеокасета за тази камера.	*tryab*·va mee vee·dee·o·ka·*se*·ta za *ta*·zee *ka*·me·ra

shopping

I need a passport photo taken.
Трябва ми снимка
за паспорт.
tryab·va mee *sneem*·ka
za pas·*port*

I'm not happy with these photos.
Не ми харесват тези
снимки.
ne mee ha·*res*·vat *te*·zee
sneem·kee

I don't want to pay the full price.
Не искам да платя
цялата цена.
ne *ees*·kam da plat·*yuh*
tsya·la·ta tse·*na*

repairs

Can I have my … repaired here?
Можете ли да
поправите … тук?
mo·zhe·te lee da
po·*pra*·vee·te … took

**When will my …
be ready?**
    **backpack/
    rucksack**
    bag
    camera

Кога ще бъде
готов моята …?
    раница

    чанта
    фотоапарат

ko·*ga* shte *buh*·de
go·tov mo·ya·ta …
    ra·nee·tsa

    chan·ta
    fo·to·a·pa·*rat*

souvenirs		
бродерия f	bro·*de*·ree·ya	**embroidery**
губери m pl	*goo*·be·ree	**tufted rugs**
дърворезба f	duhr·vo·rez·*ba*	**woodcarving**
икони f pl	ee·*ko*·nee	**icons**
килими m pl	kee·*lee*·mee	**carpets**
китеници f pl	*kee*·te·nee·tsee	**fleecy rugs**
розово масло n	ro·zo·vo *mas*·lo	**rose products (eg oil and perfume)**
торби f pl	tor·*bee*	**bags**
Троянска керамика f	tro·*yan*·ska ke·*ra*·mee·ka	**Troyan pottery**
черги f pl	*cher*·gee	**rugs**

communications

коммуникации

the internet

интернет

Where's the local internet café?
Къде се намира
най-близкото
Интернет-кафе?

kuh·*de* se na·*mee*·ra
nai·bleez·ko·to
een·ter·net·ka·fe

Do you have English-language keyboards?
Имате ли английска
клавиатура?

ee·ma·te lee ang·*lees*·ka
kla·vee·a·*too*·ra

Please change it to the English-language setting.
Моля да смените
настройката на
английски език.

mol·yuh da sme·*nee*·te
na·*stroy*·ka·ta na
an·*gleey*·skee e·*zeek*

I'd like to ...
  check my
    email
  burn a CD

  download my
    photos
  get internet
    access
  use a printer/
    scanner

Искам да ...
проверя
своя е-мейл
изгоря едно
сиди
сваля
снимките си
вляза в
Интернета
използвам
принтер/скенер

ees·kam da ...
pro·ver·*yuh*
svo·yuh *ee*·meyl
eez·gor·*yuh* ed·*no*
see·*dee*
sval·*yuh*
sneem·kee·te see
vlya·zuh v
een·ter·ne·tuh
eez·*polz*·vam
preen·ter/*ske*·ner

Do you have ...?
  Macs
  PCs
  a Zip drive

Имате ли ...?
мак
писи
зип драйв

ee·ma·te lee ...
mak
pee·*see*
zeep draiv

Can I connect my ... to this computer?	Мога ли да свържа своя ... към този компютър?	*mo*·guh lee da *svuhr*·zhuh svo·yuh ... kuhm *to*·zee kom·*pyoo*·tuhr
camera	фотоапарат	fo·to·a·pa·*rat*
iPod	iPod	*ai*·pod
media player (MP3)	плейър (ем-пи-три)	*ple*·yuhr (em·pee·*tree*)
portable hard drive	портативен харддиск	por·ta·*tee*·ven *hard*·deesk
USB flash drive (memory stick)	USB флаш драйв (памет)	yoo·es·*bee* flash draiv (*pa*·met)
How much per ...?	Колко струва ...?	*kol*·ko *stroo*·va ...
hour	на час	na chas
(five) minutes	за (пет) минути	za (pet) mee·*noo*·tee
page	на страница	na *stra*·nee·tsa
How do I log on?	Как да вляза?	kak da *vlya*·zuh
It's crashed.	Счупи се.	s·*choo*·pee se
I've finished.	Свърших.	*svuhr*·sheeh

mobile/cell phone

GSM

I'd like a ...	Искам ...	*ees*·kam ...
charger for my phone	зарядно устройство за моя GSM	zar·*yad*·no oo·*stroys*·tvo za *mo*·yuh dzhee·es·*em*
mobile/cell phone for hire	да взема под наем GSM	da *vze*·muh pod *na*·em dzhee·es·*em*
prepaid mobile/cell phone	GSM с предплатена карта	dzhee·es·*em* s pred·pla·*te*·na *kar*·ta
SIM card for your network	сим-карта за вашата мрежа	seem *kar*·ta za *va*·sha·ta *mre*·zha

What are the call rates?
Какви са тарифите?   kak·*vee* sa ta·*ree*·fee·te

(40 stotinki) per minute.
(Четирийсет стотинки)   (che·*tee*·ree·set sto·*teen*·kee)
на минута.   na mee·*noo*·ta

(20 cents) per minute.
(Двадесет цента)   (*dva*·de·set *tsen*·ta)
на минута.   na mee·*noo*·ta

phone

телефон

What's your phone number?
Какъв е вашият   ka·*kuhv* e *va*·shee·yuht
телефонен номер?   te·le·*fo*·nen *no*·mer

Where's the nearest telephone centre?
Къде се намира   kuh·*de* se na·*mee*·ra
най-близката телефонна   *nai*·bleez·ka·ta te·le·*fon*·na
централа?   tsen·*tra*·la

Where's the nearest public phone?
Къде се намира   kuh·*de* se na·*mee*·ra
най-близкият   *nai*·bleez·kee·yuht
телефонен автомат?   te·le·*fo*·nen av·to·*mat*

Can I look at a phone book?
Мога ли да погледна   *mo*·guh lee da po·*gled*·nuh
телефонния указател?   te·le·*fon*·nee·yuh oo·ka·*za*·tel

Can I have some coins, please?
Дайте ми моля монети.   *dai*·te mee *mol*·yuh mo·*ne*·tee

How much does ... cost?	Колко струва ...?	*kol*·ko *stroo*·va ...
a (three)-minute call	разговор от (три) минути	*raz*·go·vor ot (tree) mee·*noo*·tee
each extra minute	всяка допълнителна минута	*vsya*·ka do·puhl·*nee*·tel·na mee·*noo*·ta

communications

I want to ...	Искам да ...	*ees*·kam da ...
buy a	си купя	see *koop*·yuh
phonecard	една фонокарта	ed·*na* fo·no·*kar*·ta
call (Singapore)	се обадя в (Сингапур)	se o·*bad*·yuh v (seen·ga·*poor*)
make a call	се обадя по телефона	se o·*bad*·yuh po te·le·*fo*·na
make a local call	се обадя в града	se o·*bad*·yuh v gra·*duh*
reverse the charges	се обадя за тяхна сметка	se o·*bad*·yuh za *tyah*·na *smet*·ka
speak for (three) minutes	говоря (три) минути	go·*vor*·yuh (tree) mee·*noo*·tee

The number is ...
Номерът е ...   *no*·me·ruht e ...

What's the code for (New Zealand)?
Какъв е кодът за (Нова Зеландия)?   ka·*kuhv* e *ko*·duht za (*no*·va ze·*lan*·dee·ya)

It's engaged.
Дава заето.   *da*·va za·*e*·to

I've been cut off.
Прекъснаха ни.   pre·*kuhs*·na·ha nee

The connection's bad.
Връзката е лоша.   *vruhz*·ka·ta e *lo*·sha

---

dial me up

In Bulgarian, phone numbers with an even number of digits are pronounced in pairs – eg 42 56 21 is che·*tee*·ree·set ee dve pet·de·*set* ee shest *dvai*·set ee ed·*no* (forty-two, fifty-six, twenty-one). If there's an uneven number of digits, either the first number is pronounced separately or the first three digits are rolled into one number, and the other numbers are pronounced in pairs – eg 3 57 21 34 is tree pet·de·*set* ee se·dem *dvai*·set ee ed·*no* *tree*·set ee che·tee·ree (three, fifty-seven, twenty-one, thirty-four) or tree sto pet·de·*set* ee se·dem *dvai*·set ee ed·*no* *tree*·set ee che·tee·ree (three hundred and fifty-seven, twenty-one, thirty-four).

Имате грешка.	ee·ma·te gresh·ka	**Wrong number.**
Кой е на телефона?	koy e na te·le·fo·na	**Who's calling?**
Кого търсите?	ko·go tuhr·see·te	**Who do you want to speak to?**
Един момент, моля.	e·deen mo·ment mol·yuh	**One moment, please.**
Няма го/я.	nya·ma go/ya	**He/She isn't here.**

Hello.
Алло.   al·lo

Can I speak to ...?
Може ли да говоря с ...?   mo·zhe lee da go·vor·yuh s ...

It's ...
На телефона е ...   na te·le·fo·na e ...

Can I leave a message?
Мога ли да оставя бележка?   mo·guh lee da o·stav·yuh be·lezh·ka

My number is ...
Моят телефонен номер е ...   mo·yuht te·le·fo·nen no·mer e ...

I don't have a contact number.
Нямам връзка с телефон.   nya·mam vruhz·ka s te·le·fon

I'll call back later.
Ще се обадя по-късно.   shte se o·ba·dyuh po·kuhs·no

What time should I call?
В колко часа да се обадя?   v kol·ko cha·suh da se o·bad·yuh

Please tell (him/her) I called.
Моля, кажете (му/й), че съм се обаждал/обаждала. **m/f**   mol·yuh ka·zhe·te (mu/ee) che suhm se o·bazh·dal/o·bazh·da·la

For telephone numbers, see **numbers & amounts**, page 37.

communications

93

post office

I want to send a ...	Искам да изпратя ...	*ees*·kam da eez·*prat*·yuh ...
fax	един факс	e·*deen* faks
letter	едно писмо	ed·*no* pees·*mo*
parcel	един колет	e·*deen* ko·*let*

I want to buy a/an ...	Искам да си купя ...	*ees*·kam da see *koop*·yuh ...
envelope	един плик	e·*deen* pleek
stamp	една марка	ed·*na* mar·ka

customs declaration	митническа декларация f	meet·*nee*·ches·ka de·kla·*ra*·tsee·ya
domestic mail	вътрешна поща f	vuh·tresh·na *posh*·ta
fragile	чуплив	choop·*leev*
international mail	международна поща f	mezh·doo·na·*rod*·na *posh*·ta
PO box	П.К. f	puh·*kuh*
postcode	пощенски код m	*posh*·ten·skee kod

Please send it by airmail/surface mail to (Australia).
Моля да го изпратите с въздушна/обикновена поща в (Австралия).
mol·yuh da go eez·*pra*·tee·te s vuhz·*doosh*·na/o·beek·no·*ve*·na *posh*·ta v (av·*stra*·lee·ya)

It contains (souvenirs).
Съдържа (сувенири).
suh·*duhr*·zha (soo·ve·*nee*·ree)

Is there any mail for me?
Има ли поща за мене?
ee·ma lee *posh*·ta za *me*·ne

snail mail

by ...	с ... поща	s ... *posh*·ta
airmail	въздушна	vuhz·*doosh*·na
express mail	бърза	*buhr*·za
sea/surface mail	обикновена	o·beek·no·*ve*·na
by registered mail	препоръчано	pre·po·*ruh*·cha·no

94

What times is the bank open?

Какво е работното време на банката?

kak·vo e ra·bot·no·to vre·me na ban·ka·ta

What days is the bank open?

В кои дни работи банката?

v ko·yee dnee ra·bo·tee ban·ka·ta

I'd like to …	Искам да …	ees·kam da …
Where can I …?	Къде мога да …?	kuh·de mo·guh da …
cash a cheque	осребря чек	o·sreb·ruh chek
change a travellers cheque	осребря пътнически чек	o·sreb·ruh puht·nee·ches·kee chek
change money	обменя пари	ob·men·yuh pa·ree
get a cash advance	изтегля пари от кредитната си карта	eez·teg·lyuh pa·ree ot kre·deet·na·ta see kar·ta
get change for this note	разваля тази банкнота	raz·va·lyuh ta·zee bank·no·ta
withdraw money	изтегля пари	eez·teg·lyuh pa·ree

What's the …?	Какъв/Каква е …? m/f	ka·kuhv/kak·va e …
charge for that	таксата f	tak·sa·ta
exchange rate	обменният курс на валутата m	ob·men·nee·yuht koors na va·loo·ta·ta

Where's a/an…?	Къде има …?	kuh·de ee·ma …
ATM	банкомат	ban·ko·mat
bank	банка	ban·ka
foreign exchange office	пункт за обмяна на валута	poonkt za ob·mya·na na va·loo·ta

The ATM took my card.
Банкоматът ми взе
картата.
ban·ko·*ma*·tuht mee vze
kar·ta·ta

I've forgotten my PIN.
Забравих си пин-кода.
za·*bra*·veeh see *peen*·ko·da

Can I use my credit card to withdraw money?
Мога ли да изтегля
пари от кредитната си
карта?
mo·guh lee da eez·*teg*·lyuh
pa·*ree* ot kre·*deet*·na·ta see
kar·ta

Has my money arrived yet?
Моите пари
пристигнаха ли вече?
mo·yee·tee pa·*ree*
pree·*steeg*·na·ha lee *ve*·che

How long will it take to arrive?
След колко време ще
пристигнат?
sled *kol*·ko *vre*·me shte
pree·*steeg*·nuht

For other useful phrases, see **money**, page 47.

---

listen for ...

документ за самоличност m	do·koo·*ment* za sa·mo·*leech*·nost	**identification**
паспорт m	pas·*port*	**passport**
твърда валута f	*tvuhr*·da va·*loo*·ta	**hard currency**

Има проблем.
ee·ma prob·*lem* — **There's a problem.**

На вашата сметка няма пари.
na *va*·sha·ta *smet*·ka *nya*·ma pa·*ree* — **You have no funds left.**

Не можем да направим това.
ne *mo*·zhem da na·*pra*·veem to·*va* — **We can't do that.**

Подпишете тука.
pod·pee·*she*·te *too*·ka — **Sign here.**

sightseeing

разглеждане на забележителности

I'd like a/an ...	Искам ...	*ees*·kam ...
audio set	аудио-гид	*a*·oo·dee·o·geed
catalogue	каталог	ka·ta·*log*
guide	пътеводител	puh·te·vo·*dee*·tel
(in English)	(на английски)	(na an·*gleey*·skee)
(local) map	карта	*kar*·ta
	(на района)	(na ra·*yo*·nuh)

Do you have	Имате ли	*ee*·ma·te lee
information	информация	een·for·*ma*·tsee·ya
on ... sights?	за ... забеле-	za ... za·be·le·
	жителности?	*zhee*·tel·nos·tee
cultural	културните	kool·*toor*·nee·te
historical	историческите	ees·to·*ree*·ches·kee·te
natural	природните	pree·*rod*·nee·te
religious	религиозните	re·lee·gee·*oz*·nee·te

I'd like to go somewhere off the beaten track.

Искам да отида
някъде, където ходят
малко хора.

ees·kam da o·*tee*·duh
nya·kuh·de kuh·*de*·to ho·dyuht
mal·ko ho·ra

I'd like to see ...

Искам да видя ...

ees·kam da *vee*·dyuh ...

What's that?

Какво е това?

kak·*vo* e to·*va*

Who built/made it?

Кой го е построил/
направил?

koy go e po·stro·*yeel*/
na·*pra*·veel

How old is it?

Колко е старо?

kol·ko e *sta*·ro

Could you take a photo (of me/us)?
Можете ли да (ме/ни)   *mo*·zhe·te lee da (me/nee)
снимате? **pol**   *snee*·ma·te

Could you take a photo (of me/us)?
Можеш ли да (ми/ни)   *mo*·zhesh lee da (mee/nee)
снимаш? **inf**   *snee*·mash

Can I take a photo (of you)?
Може ли да (ви/те)   *mo*·zhe lee da (vee/te)
снимам? **pol/inf**   *snee*·mam

I'll send you the photo.
Ще ви/ти изпратя   shte vee/tee eez·*pra*·tyuh
снимката. **pol/inf**   *sneem*·ka·ta

getting in

What time does it open/close?
В колко часа отварят/   v *kol*·ko cha·*suh* ot·*var*·yuht/
затварят?   zat·*var*·yuht

What's the admission charge?
Каква е входната такса?   kak·*va* e *vhod*·na·ta *tak*·sa

Is there a discount for …?	Има ли намаление за …?	*ee*·ma lee na·ma·*le*·nee·e za …
children	деца	de·*tsa*
families	семейства	se·*meys*·tva
groups	групи	*groo*·pee
military personnel	войници	voy·*nee*·tsee
older people	възрастни хора	vuhz·*rast*·nee *ho*·ra
pensioners	пенсионери	pen·see·o·*ne*·ree
pupils	ученици	oo·che·*nee*·tsee
students	студенти	stoo·*den*·tee

tours

Can you recommend a ...?	Можете ли да ми препоръчате ...?	*mo*·zhe·te lee da mee pre·po·*ruh*·cha·te ...
When's the next ...?	Кога е следващата ...?	ko·*ga* e *sled*·vash·ta·ta ...
boat trip	лодка	*lod*·ka
day trip	екскурзия с гид	eks·*koor*·zee·ya s geed
(sightseeing) tour	обиколка (на забележителностите)	o·bee·*kol*·ka (na za·be·le·*zhe*·tel·nos·tee·te)
Is ... included?	Включен/ Включена ли е ...? m/f	*vklyoo*·chen/ *vklyoo*·che·na lee e ...
accommodation	нощувката f	nosh·*toov*·ka·ta
food	храната f	hra·*na*·ta
transport	транспортът m	trans·*por*·tuht
Are there any ... tours?	Организирате ли ...?	or·ga·nee·*zee*·ra·te lee ...
cultural	културен туризъм	kool·*too*·ren too·*ree*·zuhm
ecotourism	екотуризъм	e·ko·too·*ree*·zuhm

Do you employ local guides?

Местни екскурзоводи ли използвате?
mest·nee eks·koor·zo·*vo*·dee lee eez·*polz*·va·te

I'd like to hire a local guide.

Искам да наемам местен екскурзовод.
ees·kam da na·*e*·mam *mes*·ten eks·koor·zo·*vod*

Does the guide speak the local dialect?

Екскурзоводът разбира ли местния диалект?
eks·koor·zo·*vo*·duht raz·*bee*·ra lee *mest*·nee·yuh dee·a·*lekt*

The guide will pay.

Екскурзоводът ще плати.
eks·koor·zo·*vo*·duht shte pla·*tee*

How long is the tour?

Колко трае екскурзията? *kol·ko tra·ye eks·koor·zee·ya·ta*

What time should we be back?

В колко часа ще се *v kol·ko cha·suh shte se*
върнем? *vuhr·nem*

I'm with them.

Аз съм с тях. *az suhm s tyah*

I've lost my group.

Загубих си групата. *za·goo·beeh see groo·pa·ta*

---

signs

Авариен изход	a·va·*ree*·en *eez*·hod	**Emergency Exit**
Вход	vhod	**Entrance**
Вход безплатен	vhod bez·*pla*·ten	**Free Admission**
Жени	zhe·*nee*	**Women**
Забранено	za·bra·*ne*·no	**Prohibited**
Запазено	za·*pa*·ze·no	**Reserved**
Затворено	zat·*vo*·re·no	**Closed**
Изход	*eez*·hod	**Exit**
Информация	een·for·*ma*·tsee·ya	**Information**
Мъже	muh·*zhe*	**Men**
Отворено	ot·*vo*·re·no	**Open**
Пушенето	*poo*·she·ne·to	**No Smoking**
забранено	za·bra·*ne*·no	
Студено	stoo·*de*·no	**Cold**
Телефон	te·le·*fon*	**Telephone**
Тоалетни	to·a·*let*·nee	**Toilets**
Топло	*top*·lo	**Hot**
Фотографирането	fo·to·gra·*fee*·ra·ne·to	**No Photography**
забранено	za·bra·*ne*·no	

doing business

търговия

I'm attending a …	На … съм.	na … suhm
business meeting	деловата среща	de·lo·va·ta sresh·ta
conference	конференция	kon·fe·ren·tsee·ya
course	курс	koors
trade fair	търговски панаир	tuhr·gov·skee pa·na·eer

I'm with …	Тука съм с …	too·ka suhm s …
the EU	Европейския съюз	ev·ro·pey·skee·yuh suh·yooz
my colleague/ colleagues	колегата/ колегите си	ko·le·ga·ta/ ko·le·gee·te see
some others	другите	droo·gee·te
(two) others	още (двама) души	osh·te (dva·ma) doo·shee

I'm alone.
Сам/Сама съм. m/f
sam/sa·ma suhm

I have an appointment with …
Имам среща с …
ee·mam sresh·ta s …

I'm staying at the (Ganesh), room (205).
Отседнал/Отседнала съм в (Ганеш), стая (двеста и пет). m/f
ot·sed·nal/ot·sed·na·la suhm v (ga·nesh) sta·ya (dve·sta ee pet)

I'm here for (two) days.
Тука съм за (два) дена.
too·ka suhm za (dva) de·na

I'm here for (two) weeks.
Тука съм за (две) седмици.
too·ka suhm za (dve) sed·mee·tsee

Can I please have your business card?

| Дайте ми моля вашата | *dai*·te mee *mol*·yuh *va*·sha·ta |
| визитна картичка. | vee·*zeet*·na *kar*·teech·ka |

Here's my business card.

| Заповядайте моята | za·po·*vya*·dai·te *mo*·ya·ta |
| визитна картичка. | vee·*zeet*·na *kar*·teech·ka |

Here's my …	Заповядайте	za·po·*vya*·dai·te
	моя …	*mo*·yuh …
What's your …?	Какъв е	ka·*kuhv* e
	вашият …?	*va*·shee·yuht …
(email) address	(и-мейл) адрес	(*ee*·meyl) ad·*res*
fax number	номер на факса	*no*·mer na *fak*·suh
mobile/cell	номер на	*no*·mer na
phone number	GSM-а	dzhee·es·*em*·uh
pager number	номер на	*no*·mer na
	пейджъра	*pey*·dzhuh·ruh
work number	служебен	sloo·*zhe*·ben
	телефон	te·le·*fon*
Where's the …?	Къде е…?	kuh·*de* e …
business	бизнес	*beez*·nes
centre	центърът	*tsen*·tuh·ruht
conference	конференцията	kon·fe·*ren*·tsee·a·ta
meeting	срещата	*sresh*·ta·ta
I need (a/an) …	Трябва ми …	*tryab*·va mee …
computer	компютър	kom·*pyoo*·tuhr
internet	Интернет	*een*·ter·net
connection	връзка	*vruhz*·ka
interpreter	преводач	pre·vo·*dach*
who speaks	говорещ	go·vo·*resht*
(English)	(английски)	(an·*gleey*·skee)
space to set	място да	*myas*·to da
up my	подредя	pod·re·*dyuh*
presentation	презентацията	pre·zen·*ta*·tsee·ya·ta
	си	see

I need more business cards.
    Трябват ми още   *tryab*·vat mee *osh*·te
    визитни картички.   vee·*zeet*·nee *kar*·teech·kee

I need to send a fax.
    Трябва да изпратя факс.   *tryab*·va da eez·*prat*·yuh faks

That went very well.
    Това мина много добре.   to·*va mee*·na *mno*·go do·*bre*

Thank you for your time.
    Благодаря за вашето   bla·go·da·*ryuh* za *va*·she·to
    време.   *vre*·me

Shall we go for a drink/meal?
    Хайде да пийнем/хапнем *hai*·de da *peey*·nem/*hap*·nem
    нещо.   *nesh*·to

It's on me.
    Аз черпя.   az *cher*·pyuh

looking for a job

търсене на работа

Where are jobs advertised?
    Къде се обявяват   kuh·*de* se ob·ya·*vya*·vat
    работните места?   ra·*bot*·nee·te mes·*ta*

I'm enquiring about the position advertised.
    Интересува мс   een·te·re·*soo*·va me
    обявеното място.   ob·ya·*ve*·no·to *myas*·to

What's the wage?
    Каква е надницата?   kak·*va* e *nad*·nee·tsa·ta

I'm looking for … work.	Търся работа като …	*tuhr*·syuh *ra*·bo·ta *ka*·to …
bar	барман	bar·*man*
English-teaching	преподавател по английски	pre·po·da·*va*·tel po an·*gleey*·skee
fruit-picking	берач на плодове	be·*rach* na plo·do·*ve*
labouring	работник	ra·*bot*·neek
waitering	сервитьор	ser·vee·*tyor*

Do I need to ...?	Трябва ли да ...?	*tryab·va lee da ...*
complete	попълня	*po·puhl·nyuh*
paperwork	документи	*do·koo·men·tee*
have insurance	имам	*ee·mam*
	застраховка	*za·stra·hov·ka*
provide my	имам собствен	*ee·mam sobs·tven*
own transport	транспорт	*trans·port*
sign a contract	подпиша	*pod·pee·shuh*
	трудов договор	*troo·dov do·go·vor*
Here is/are my ...	Заповядайте ...	*za·po·vya·dai·te ...*
bank account	информаци-	*een·for·ma·tsee·*
details	ята за моята	*ya·ta za mo·ya·ta*
	банкова сметка	*ban·ko·va smet·ka*
CV	моята авто-	*mo·ya·ta av·to·*
	биография	*bee·o·gra·fee·ya*
visa	моята виза	*mo·ya·ta vee·za*
I can start ...	Мога да	*mo·guh da*
	започна ...	*za·poch·nuh ...*
at (eight) o'clock	в (осем) часа	*v (o·sem) cha·suh*
today	днес	*dnes*
tomorrow	утре	*oo·tre*
next week	следващата	*sled·vash·ta·ta*
	седмица	*sed·meet·tsa*
What time do I ...?	В колко часа ...?	*v kol·ko cha·suh ...*
start	започвам	*za·poch·vam*
	работа	*ra·bo·ta*
have a break	имам	*ee·mam*
	почивка	*po·cheev·ka*
finish	свършвам	*svuhr·shvam*
	работния ден	*ra·bot·nee·ya den*
advertisement	обява f	*ob·ya·va*
contract n	трудов договор m	*troo·dov do·go·vor*
employee	служител m	*sloo·zhee·tel*
	служителка f	*sloo·zhee·tel·ka*
employer	работодател m	*ra·bo·to·da·tel*
job	работа f	*ra·bo·ta*
work experience	професионален	*pro·fe·see·o·na·len*
	опит m	*o·peet*

104

senior & disabled travellers
ъзрастни пътници и пътници инвалиди

I have a disability.
Аз съм инвалид.   az suhm een·va·*leed*

I need assistance.
Трябва ми помощ.   *tryab*·va mee *po*·mosht

I'm deaf.
Глух/Глуха съм. m/f   glooh/*gloo*·ha suhm

I have a hearing aid.
Имам слухов апарат.   ee·mam *sloo*·hov a·pa·*rat*

My travelling companion's blind.
Моят съпътник е сляп. m   *mo*·yuht suh·*puht*·neek e slyap
Моята съпътница   *mo*·ya·ta suh·*puht*·nee·tsa
е сляпа. f   e *slya*·pa

What services do you have for people with a disability?
Какви услуги   kak·*vee* oo·*sloo*·gee
предлагате за инвалиди?   pred·*la*·ga·te za een·va·*lee*·dee

Are guide dogs permitted?
Разрешени ли са   raz·re·*she*·nee lee sa
кучетата водачи?   *koo*·che·ta·ta vo·*da*·chee

Are there disabled parking spaces?
Има ли места за   *ee*·ma lee mes·*ta* za
паркиране за инвалиди?   par·*kee*·ra·ne za een·va·*lee*·dee

Is there wheelchair access?
Има ли достъп за   *ee*·ma lee *do*·stuhp za
инвалидни колички?   een·va·*leed*·nee ko·*leech*·kee

How wide is the entrance?
Каква е ширината   kak·*va* e shee·ree·*na*·ta
на входа?   na *vho*·duh

How many steps are there?
Колко стъпала има?   *kol*·ko stuh·pa·*la ee*·ma

Is there an elevator/lift?
Има ли асансьор?   *ee*·ma lee a·san·*syor*

Are there disabled toilets?
Има ли тоалетни
за инвалиди?
ee·ma lee to·a·*let*·nee
za een·va·*lee*·dee

Are there rails in the bathroom?
Има ли парапети
в банята?
ee·ma lee pa·ra·*pe*·tee
v *ban*·ya·ta

Could you call me a disabled taxi?
Можете ли да ми
поръчате такси за
инвалида?
mo·zhe·te lee da mee
po·*ruh*·cha·te tak·*see* za
een·va·*lee*·duh

Could you help me cross the street safely?
Можете ли да ми
помогнете да
пресека улицата?
mo·zhe·te lee da mee
po·*mog*·ne·te da
pre·se·*kuh* oo·lee·tsa·ta

Is there somewhere I can sit down?
Има ли място където
мога да седна?
ee·ma lee *myas*·to kuh·*de*·to
mo·guh da *sed*·nuh

guide dog	куче водач m	*koo*·che vo·*dach*
older man	възрастен човек m	*vuhz*·ras·ten cho·*vek*
older woman	възрастна жена f	*vuhz*·rast·na zhe·*na*
person with a disability	инвалид m	een·va·*leed*
ramp	склон m	sklon
walking frame	помощна рамка за ходене f	po·*mosht*·na *ram*·ka za *ho*·de·ne
walking stick	бастун m	bas·*toon*
wheelchair	инвалидна количка f	een·va·*leed*·na ko·*leech*·ka

animal talk

бау-бау	*ba*·oo·*ba*·oo	(dog)
бе-е	be·*e*	(sheep)
грох-грох	*groh*·groh	(pig)
кукуригу	koo·koo·ree·*goo*	(rooster)
ме-е	me·*e*	(goat)
му-у	moo·*oo*	(cow)
мяу	*mya*·oo	(cat)
па-па-па	*pa*·pa·pa	(duck)

PRACTICAL

travelling with children

пътуване с деца

Is there a …?	Има ли …?	*ee*·ma lee …
baby change room	стая за преобличане на бебета	*sta*·ya za pre·o·*blee*·cha·ne na *be*·be·ta
child-minding service	служба осигуряваща услуги на бавачки	*sloozh*·ba o·see·goor·*ya*·vash·ta oo·*sloo*·gee na ba·*vach*·kee
child's portion	детска порция	*det*·ska *por*·tsee·ya
children's menu	детско меню	*det*·sko men·*yoo*
crèche	детски ясли	*det*·skee *yas*·lee
discount for children	намаление за децата	na·ma·*le*·nee·e za de·*tsa*·ta
family ticket	семеен билет	se·*me*·en bee·*let*

Do you sell …?	Продавате ли …?	pro·*da*·va·te lee …
baby wipes	мокри кърпички за бебета	*mo*·kree *kuhr*·peech·kee za *be*·be·ta
disposable nappies	пелени за еднократка употреба	pe·le·*nee* za ed·no·*krat*·ka oo·po·tre·ba
painkillers for babies	болкоуспо- коутелни лекарства за бебета	bol·ko·oos·po· ko·*ee*·tel·nee le·*kars*·tva za *be*·be·ta
tissues	хартиени кърпички	har·*tee*·e·nee *kuhr*·peech·kee

I need a/an ...	Трябва ми ...	*tryab*·va mee ...
baby seat (for the car)	детска седалка (за кола)	*det*·ska se·*dal*·ka (za ko·*la*)
(English-speaking) babysitter	бавачка (говореща английски)	ba·*vach*·ka (go·vo·*resh*·ta an·*gleey*·skee)
booster seat	детска седалка	*det*·ska se·*dal*·ka
cot	детско легло	*det*·sko leg·*lo*
highchair	високо детско столче за хранене	vee·*so*·ko *det*·sko *stol*·che za *hra*·ne·ne
plastic bag	найлонова торбичка	nai·*lo*·no·va tor·*beech*·ka
plastic sheet	найлонов чаршаф	nai·*lo*·nov char·*shaf*
potty	гърне	guhr·*ne*
pram	бебешка количка	be·besh·ka ko·*leech*·ka
pushchair/stroller	детска количка	*det*·ska ko·*leech*·ka
sick bag	торбичка за повръщане	tor·*beech*·ka za po·*vruh*·shta·ne
Where's the nearest ...?	Къде е найблизкият/найблизката ...? m/f	kuh·*de* e *nai*·bleez·kee·yuht/ *nai*·bleez·ka·ta ...
drinking fountain	чешма f	chesh·ma
playground	детска площадка f	*det*·ska plosh·*tad*·ka
puppet theatre	куклен театър m	*kook*·len te·*a*·tuhr
swimming pool	плувен басейн m	*ploo*·ven ba·*seyn*
tap	чешма f	chesh·ma
theme park	детски универсален парк m	*det*·skee oo·nee·ver·*sa*·len park
toyshop	магазин за детски играчки m	ma·ga·*zeen* za *det*·skee ee·*grach*·kee

Are there any good places to take children around here?

Има ли в района добри   *ee·ma lee v ra·yo·nuh do·bree*
места за разходка с деца?   *mes·ta za raz·hod·ka s de·tsa*

Are children allowed?

Разрешено ли е за деца?   *raz·re·she·no lee e za de·tsa*

Is there space for a pram?

Има ли място за   *ee·ma lee myas·to za*
бебешка количка?   *be·besh·ka ko·leech·ka*

Where can I change a nappy?

Къде мога да сменя   *kuh·de mo·guh da smen·yuh*
бебешките пелени?   *be·besh·kee·te pe·le·nee*

Could I have some paper and pencils, please?

Ще ми дадете/дадеш ли   *shte mee da·de·te/da·desh lee*
моля хартия и   *mol·yuh har·tee·ya ee*
моливи? **pol/inf**   *mo·lee·vee*

Is this suitable for (six)-year-old children?

Това подходящо ли е   *to·va pod·hod·yash·to lee e*
за (шест)годишни деца?   *za (shest·)go·deesh·nee de·tsa*

Do you know a dentist/doctor who is good with children?

Можете ли да   *mo·zhe·te lee da*
препоръчате детски   *pre·po·ruh·cha·te det·skee*
зъболекар/лекар?   *zuh·bo·le·kar/le·kar*

If your child is sick, see **health**, page 193.

talking with children

разговор с деца

In this section, phrases are in the informal 'you' form only. For more information, see the box **all about you**, page 138.

What's your name?

Как се казваш?   *kak se kaz·vash*

How old are you?

На колко си години?   *na kol·ko see go·dee·nee*

Do you go to school?

Ходиш ли на училище?   *ho·deesh lee na oo·chee·leesh·te*

What grade are you in?
В кой клас си?   v koy klas see

Do you learn (English)?
Учиш ли (английски)?   oo·cheesh lee (an·gleey·skee)

What do you do after school?
Какво правиш след   kak·vo pra·veesh sled
училище?   oo·chee·leesh·te

talking about children

разговор за децата

Avoid complimenting children, as it's believed to bring bad luck. For the same reason, Bulgarians don't bring gifts for unborn children.

When's the baby due?
Кога очаквате/   ko·ga o·chak·va·te/
очакваш да се роди   o·chak·vash da se ro·dee
бебето? **pol/inf**   be·be·to

What are you going to call the baby?
Как ще кръстите/   kak shte kruh·stee·te/
кръстиш бебето? **pol/inf**   kruh·steesh be·be·to

Is this your first child?
Това вашето/твоето   to·va va·she·to/tvo·ye·to
първо дете ли е? **pol/inf**   puhr·vo de·te lee e

How many children do you have?
Колко деца имате/   kol·ko de·tsa ee·ma·te/
имаш? **pol/inf**   ee·mash

What's his/her name?
Как се казва?   kak se kaz·va

How old is he/she?
На колко години е?   na kol·ko go·dee·nee e

Does he/she go to school?
Ходи ли на училище?   ho·dee lee na oo·chee·leesh·te

He/She looks like you.
Прилича на вас. **pol**   pree·lee·cha na vas
Прилича на тебе. **inf**   pree·lee·cha na te·be

basics

основни неща

Yes.	Да.	da
No.	Не.	ne
Please.	Моля.	*mol*·yuh
Thank you (very much).	(Много) Благодаря.	(*mno*·go) bla·go·dar·*yuh*
You're welcome.	Няма защо.	*nya*·ma zash·*to*
Excuse me. (to get attention)	Моля.	*mol*·ya
Excuse me. (to get past)	Извинете.	eez·vee·*ne*·te
Sorry.	Съжалявам.	suh·zhal·*ya*·vam

hello goodbye

The greeting extended to a new arrival is *Добре дошли!* do·bre dosh·lee (welcome) to a group or in the polite form, and *Добре дошъл!* do·bre do·*shuhl* (to a man) or *Добре дошла!* do·bre dosh·la (to a woman) in the informal form. The response, less commonly used, is *Добре заварили!* do·bre za·va·ree·lee (lit: well met), spoken in the polite form or on behalf of a group. In the informal form, the equivalent is *Добре заварила!* do·bre za·va·ree·la (said by a woman) or *Добре заварил!* do·bre za·va·reel (said by a man). When someone departs on a long trip it's traditional to throw water in front of them and say *Да ви/ти върви по вода!* pol/inf da vee/tee vuhr·*vee* po vo·da (May all go smoothly for you!).

greetings & goodbyes

It's customary to shake hands when introduced. Old friends hug each other and kiss on both cheeks.

Hello.	Здравейте. pol	zdra·*vey*·te
Hi.	Здравей. inf	zdra·*vey*
Good morning.	Добро утро.	dob·*ro* oot·ro
Good day.	Добър ден.	*do*·buhr den
Good afternoon.	Добър ден.	*do*·buhr den
Good evening.	Добър вечер.	*do*·buhr ve·cher

How are you?
Как сте/си? pol/inf — kak ste/see

Fine, thanks. And you?
Добре, благодаря. — dob·*re* bla·go·dar·*yuh*
А вие/ти? pol/inf — a *vee*·e·tee

What's your name?
Как се казвате/казваш? pol/inf — kak se *kaz*·va·te/*kaz*·vash

My name is …
Казвам се … — *kaz*·vam se …

I'd like to introduce you to (Petar Petrov).
Искам да ви/ти — *ees*·kam da vee/tee
представя (Петър — pred·*stav*·yuh (*pe*·tuhr
Петров). pol/inf — pet·*rov*)

I'm pleased to meet you.
Приятно ми е да се — pree·*yat*·no mee e da se
запозная с вас/тебе. pol/inf — za·poz·*na*·yuh s vas/te·be

This is my …	Това е … ми.	to·*va* e … mee
child	детето	de·*te*·to
colleague	колегата	ko·*le*·ga·ta
friend	приятелят m	pree·*ya*·tel·yuht
	приятелката f	pree·*ya*·tel·ka·ta
husband	мъжът	muh·*zhuht*
partner	приятелят m	pree·*ya*·tel·yuht
(romantic)	приятелката f	pree·*ya*·tel·ka·ta
wife	жена	zhe·*na*

See you later.	До скоро виждане.	do *sko*·ro *veezh*·da·ne
Bye.	Чао.	*cha*·o
Goodbye.	Довиждане.	do·*veezh*·da·ne
Good night.	Лека нощ.	*le*·ka nosht
Bon voyage!	Приятно пътуване!	pree·*yat*·no puh·*too*·va·ne

addressing people

обръщения

The words for 'Sir/Madam' are given below in the vocative form, which is the form used when addressing someone. The other words are given in the neutral form, used when talking about a person. The term *госпожице* gos·po·zhee·tse ('Miss' in the vocative form) should be avoided if the female in question looks over 20 or so, as it implies you think that the woman isn't married, which is considered impolite. The phrase *Дами и господа* da·mee ee gos·po·da (Ladies and gentlemen) is also used as a form of address, just like in English.

Sir	Господине	gos·po·*dee*·ne
Madam	Госпожо	gos·*po*·zho
Mr	Господин	gos·po·*deen*
Mrs/Ms	Госпожа	gos·po·*zha*
Ms/Miss	Госпожица	gos·po·zhee·tsa

hey there!

The words *колега* ko·*le*·ga (colleague), *приятел* pree·*ya*·tel (friend) and *мой човек* moy cho·*vek* (my man) are often used as neutral forms of address (without implying that the person is a colleague or a friend). The latter two are only for men, whereas the first one can be used for both men and women. The colloquial term *бе* be (buddy, mate) is often used in expressions such as *Хайде бе!* hai·de be (Come on, pal!) or *Стига бе!* stee·ga be (That's enough, mate!). It refers to both men and women. The phrase *моето момиче* mo·e·to mo·mee·che (my girl) can be used for addressing women, but only if you know them relatively well.

meeting people

113

making conversation

What's new?
Какво ново?   kak·vo no·vo

What's up?
Какво правиш?   kak·vo pra·veesh

What a beautiful day!
Какъв прекрасен ден!   ka·kuhv pre·kra·sen den

Nice/Awful weather, isn't it?
Хубаво/Ужасно време,   hoo·ba·vo/oo·zhas·no vre·me
нали?   na·lee

Do you live here?
Вие тука ли живеете? pol   vee·e too·ka lee zhee·ve·e·te
Ти тука ли живееш? inf   tee too·ka lee zhee·ve·esh

Where are you going?
Къде отивате/   kuh·de o·tee·va·te/
отиваш? pol/inf   o·tee·vash

What are you doing?
Какво правите/   kak·vo pra·vee·te/
правиш? pol/inf   pra·veesh

Do you like it here?
Харесва ли ви/ти   ha·res·va lee vee/tee
тука? pol/inf   too·ka

I love it here.
Много ми харесва тука.   mno·go mee ha·res·va too·ka

---

etiquette tips

- Wait to be invited before sitting down, taking food or drinking (even when it's clearly meant for consumption).
- Maintain eye contact during conversation. Keep your hands in view, especially when in small towns.
- Lively facial expressions and frequent touching on the shoulder are a normal part of conversation.
- Avoid asking personal questions about religion, finances or family. It's also impolite to ask a woman's age.

SOCIAL

Hey!	Хей!	hey
Great!	Супер!	*soo*·per
Sure.	Естествено.	es·*test*·ve·no
Maybe.	Може би.	*mo*·zhe bee
No way!	Няма начин!	*nya*·ma *na*·cheen
Just a minute.	Един момент.	e·*deen* mo·*ment*
Just joking.	Шегувам се.	she·*goo*·vam se
It's OK.	Добре.	do·*bre*
No problem.	Няма проблем.	*nya*·ma prob·*lem*

What's this called?

Това как се казва?	to·*va* kak se *kaz*·va

That's (beautiful), isn't it?

Това е (хубаво), нали?	to·*va* e (*hoo*·ba·vo) na·*lee*

Can I take a photo (of you)?

Мога ли да (ви/те) снимам? pol/inf	*mo*·guh lee da (vee/te) *snee*·mam

I'll send you the photo.

Ще ви/ти изпратя снимката. pol/inf	shte vee/tee eez·*prat*·yuh *sneem*·ka·ta

How long are you here for?

Колко ще останете/ останеш тук? pol/inf	*kol*·ko shte o·*sta*·ne·te/ o·*sta*·nesh took

I'm here for (four) weeks/days.

Тука съм (четири) седмици/дена.	*too*·ka suhm (*che*·tee·ree) *sed*·mee·tsee/*de*·na

Are you here on holiday?

Вие във ваканция ли сте тука? pol	*vee*·e vuhv va·*kan*·tsee·ya lee ste *too*·ka
Ти във ваканция ли си тука? inf	tee vuhv va·*kan*·tsee·ya lee see *too*·ka

I'm here ...

	Тука съм ...	*too*·ka suhm ...
for a holiday	във ваканция	vuhv va·*kan*·tsee·ya
on business	по работа	po *ra*·bo·ta
to study	за да уча	za da *oo*·chuh

meeting people

115

nationalities

Where are you from?
Откъде сте/си? pol/inf   ot·kuh·*de* ste/see

I'm from …	Аз съм от …	az suhm ot …
Australia	Австралия	av·*stra*·lee·ya
Canada	Канада	ka·*na*·da
Ireland	Ирландия	eer·*lan*·dee·ya
New Zealand	Нова	*no*·va
	Зеландия	ze·*lan*·dee·ya
the UK	Велико-	ve·lee·ko·
	британия	bree·*ta*·nee·ya
the USA	САЩ	sasht

age

възраст

How old …?	На колко	na *kol*·ko
	години …?	go·*dee*·nee …
are you	сте/си pol/inf	ste/see
is your	е дъщеря	e duhsh·ter·*ya*
daughter	ви/ти pol/inf	vee/tee
is your son	е синът	e see·*nuht*
	ви/ти pol/inf	vee/tee

I'm … years old.
Аз съм на … години.   az suhm na … go·*dee*·nee

He/She is … years old.
Той/Тя е на … години.   toy/tya e na … go·*dee*·nee

Too old!
Прекалено стар/стара! m/f   pre·ka·*le*·no star/*sta*·ra

I'm younger than I look.
По-млад/По-млада съм   *po*·mlad/*po*·mla·da suhm
отколкото изглеждам. m/f   ot·*kol*·ko·to eez·*glezh*·dam

For your age, see **numbers & amounts**, page 37.

occupations & studies

What's your occupation?

Какво работите/	kak·vo ra·bo·tee·te/	
работиш? pol/inf	ra·bo·teesh	

I'm a ...	Аз съм ...	az suhm ...
chef	готвач	got·vach
journalist	журналист m	zhoor·na·leest
	журналистка f	zhoor·na·leest·ka
teacher	учител m	oo·chee·tel
	учителка f	oo·chee·tel·ka

I work in ...	Работя в ...	ra·bo·tyuh v ...
banking	банка	ban·ka
education	учебно	oo·cheb·no
	заведение	za·ve·de·nee·e
sales & marketing	търговията	tuhr·go·vee·ya·ta
transport	транспорта	trans·por·tuh

I'm ...	Аз съм ...	az suhm ...
retired	пенсионер m	pen·see·o·ner
	пенсионерка f	pen·see·o·ner·ka
unemployed	без работа	bez ra·bo·ta

I'm self-employed.

Имам частен бизнис.	ee·mam chas·ten beez·nees

What are you studying?

Какво следвате/	kak·vo sled·va·te/
следваш? pol/inf	sled·vash

I'm studying ...	Следвам ...	sled·vam ...
Bulgarian	български	buhl·gar·skee
	език	e·zeek
chemistry	химия	hee·mee·ya
history	история	ees·to·ree·ya
philology	филология	fee·lo·lo·gee·ya
physics	физика	fee·zee·ka

family

Do you have a ...?	Имате/Имаш ли ...? pol/inf	ee·ma·te/ee·mash lee ...
I have a ...	Имам ...	ee·mam ...
I don't have a ...	Нямам ...	nya·mam ...
brother	брат	brat
daughter	дъщеря	duhsh·te·rya
granddaughter	внучка	vnooch·ka
grandson	внук	vnook
husband	мъж	muhzh
partner (romantic)	приятел m приятелка f	pree·ya·tel pree·ya·tel·ka
sister	сестра	ses·tra
son	син	seen
wife	жена	zhe·na

Are you married?

Женен ли сте/си? m pol/inf	zhe·nen lee ste/see
Омъжена ли сте/си? f pol/inf	o·muh·zhe·na lee ste/see

I live with someone.

Живея с някого.	zhee·ve·ya s nya·ko·go

I'm ...	Аз съм ...	az suhm ...
divorced	разведен m разведена f	raz·ve·den raz·ve·de·na
married	женен m омъжена f	zhe·nen o·muh·zhe·na
single	неженен m неомъжена f	ne·zhe·nen ne·o·muh·zhe·na

family tree

The system of names for family members in Bulgarian is very complex, reflecting the norm, in the past, of large extended families. There are a number of different terms for both 'aunt' and 'uncle', depending on whether it's the father's or the mother's sibling, and on whether the relationship is by blood or by marriage. As family units become increasingly nuclear, the system of names is becoming simpler. Everyone distinguishes the names for mother-in-law and father-in-law – although both bride and groom are expected to call their mother-in-law simply *майка mai·*ka (mother).

father-in-law and mother-in-law:

свекър	*sve·*kuhr	**husband's father**
свекърва	*sve·kuhr·*va	**husband's mother**
тъст	tuhst	**wife's father**
тъща	*tuhsh·*ta	**wife's mother**

brother-in-law:

баджанак	bad·zha·*nak*	**wife's sister's husband**
девер	*de·*ver	**husband's brother**
зет	zet	**sister's husband**
шурей	*shoo·*rey	**wife's brother**

sister-in-law:

балдъза	bal·*duh·*za	**wife's sister**
етърва	e·*tuhr·*va	**husband's brother's wife**
зълва	*zuhl·*va	**husband's sister**
снаха	sna·*ha*	**brother's wife**
шуренайка	shoo·re·*nai·*ka	**wife's brother's wife**

uncle:

вуйчо	*vooy·*cho	**mother's brother**
свако	*sva·*ko	**mother's or father's sister's husband**
чичо	*chee·*cho	**father's brother**

aunt:

вуйна	*vooy·*na	**mother's brother's wife**
леля	*lel·*ya	**father's or mother's sister**
стринка	*streen·*ka	**father's brother's wife**

meeting people

farewells

Tomorrow is my last day here.

Утре ми е последният
ден тука.

oo·tre mee e po·*sled*·nee·yuht
den *too*·ka

If you come to (Scotland), you can stay with me.

Ако дойдете в
(Шотландия), ще можете
да отседнете при мен. **pol**

a·ko doy·de·te v
(shot·*lan*·dee·ya) shte mo·zhe·te
da ot·*sed*·ne·te pree men

Ако дойдеш в
(Шотландия), ще можеш
да отседнеш при мен. **inf**

a·ko doy·desh v
(shot·*lan*·dee·ya) shte mo·zhesh
da ot·*sed*·nesh pree men

Keep in touch!

Да поддържаме връзка!

da pod·*durh*·zha·me *vruhz*·ka

It's been great meeting you.

Много ме беше приятно
да се запознаем.

mno·go mee *be*·she pree·*yat*·no
da se za·po·*zna*·yem

Here's my ...	Заповядайте/ Заповядай моя ... **pol/inf**	za·po·*vya*·dai·te/ za·po·*vya*·dai *mo*·yuh ...
What's your ...?	Какъв е вашият/ твоят ...? **pol/inf**	ka·*kuhv* e *va*·shee·yuht/ *tvo*·yuht ...
(email) address	(и-мейл) адрес	(*ee*·meyl) ad·*res*
phone number	телефонен номер	te·le·*fo*·nen *no*·mer

---

well-wishing

Bless you!	Наздраве!	na·*zdra*·ve
Congratulations!	Честито!	ches·*tee*·to
Good luck!	Успех!	oo·*speh*
Happy birthday!	Честит рожден ден!	ches·*teet* rozh·*den* den
Happy holiday!	Честит празник!	ches·*teet* *praz*·neek
Happy name day!	Честит имен ден!	ches·*teet* *ee*·men den

In this chapter, phrases are in the informal *mu* tee (you) form only. For more information, see the box **all about you**, page 138.

common interests

общи интереси

What do you do in your spare time?

Какво правиш в
свободното си време?

kak·*vo pra*·veesh v
svo·*bod*·no·to see *vre*·me

Do you like ...?	Обичаш ли ...?	o·*bee*·chash lee ...
I (don't) like ...	(Не) Обичам ...	(ne) o·*bee*·cham ...
computer	компютър-	kom·*pyoo*·tuhr·
games	ните игри	nee·te ee·*gree*
cooking	готвенето	*got*·ve·ne·to
gardening	градинарството	gra·dee·*narst*·vo·to
music	музиката	*moo*·zee·ka·ta
photography	фотографията	fo·to·*gra*·fee·ya·ta
sport	спорта	*spor*·tuh

Do you like ...?	Обичаш ли да ...?	o·*bee*·chash lee da ...
dancing	танцуваш	tan·*tsoo*·vash
drawing	рисуваш	ree·*soo*·vash
films	гледаш филми	*gle*·dash *feel*·mee
painting	рисуваш	ree·*soo*·vash
reading	четеш	che·*tesh*
shopping	пазаруваш	pa·za·*roo*·vash
socialising	си сред хората	see sred *ho*·ra·ta
surfing the	сърфираш	suhr·*fee*·rash
internet	Интернета	*een*·ter·ne·tuh
travelling	пътуваш	puh·*too*·vash
watching TV	гледаш	*gle*·dash
	телевизия	te·le·*vee*·zee·ya

I (don't) like ...	(Не) Обичам да ...	(ne) o·*bee*·cham da ...
dancing	танцувам	tan·*tsoo*·vam
drawing	рисувам	ree·*soo*·vam
films	гледам филми	*gle*·dam *feel*·mee
painting	рисувам	ree·*soo*·vam
reading	чета	che·*tuh*
shopping	пазарувам	pa·za·*roo*·vam
socialising	съм сред	suhm sred
	хората	*ho*·ra·ta
surfing the	сърфирам	suhr·*fee*·ram
internet	интернета	een·ter·ne·tuh
travelling	пътувам	puh·*too*·vam
watching TV	гледам	*gle*·dam
	телевизия	te·le·*vee*·zee·ya

For types of sport, see **sport**, page 149, and the **dictionary**.

traditional pastimes

Older men in Bulgaria frequently play games such as *табла tab*·la (backgammon) and *карти kar*·tee (cards), while older women often entertain themselves by doing *ръкоделие* ruh·ko·*de*·lee·e (needlework).

music

музика

Do you ...?		
dance	Танцуваш ли?	tan·*tsoo*·vash lee
go to concerts	Ходиш ли на	*ho*·deesh lee
	концерти?	na kon·*tser*·tee
listen to music	Слушаш ли	*sloo*·shash lee
	музика?	*moo*·zee·ka
play an	Свириш ли	*svee*·reesh lee
instrument	някакъв	*nya*·ka·kuhv
	инструмент?	een·stroo·*ment*
sing	Пееш ли?	*pe*·esh lee

in the folk groove

Bulgarian traditional music presents a contrast between the Byzantine elements found in Orthodox church music and the Turkish influence evident in the folk songs and dances of the villages. Here are some traditional folk instruments:

гъдулка f	guh·*dool*·ka	small pear-shaped fiddle, also known as *ребек* m *re*·bek
гайда f	*gai*·da	goatskin bagpipe
даире n	dai·*re*	similar to a tambourine
кавал m	ka·*val*	long, open flute, held diagonally when played
тамбура f	tam·boo·*ra*	four-stringed, long-necked lute, also called *дрънка* f *druhn*·ka
тъпан m	*tuh*·pan	large, cylindrical, double-headed drum

Which ... do you like?	Какви ... харесваш?	kak·*vee* ... ha·*res*·vash
bands	оркестри	or·*kes*·tree
performers	изпълнители	eez·puhl·*nee*·te·lee
singers	певци	pev·*tsee*
choral music	хорова музика f	*ho*·ro·va *moo*·zee·ka
classical music	класическа музика f	kla·*see*·ches·ka *moo*·zee·ka
contemporary music	съвременна музика f	suh·*vre*·men·na *moo*·zee·ka
electronic music	електронна музика f	e·lek·*tron*·na *moo*·zee·ka
folk music	народна музика f	na·*rod*·na *moo*·zee·ka
pop	естрадна музика f	es·*trad*·na *moo*·zee·ka
world music	музика на други народи f	*moo*·zee·ka na *droo*·gee na·*ro*·dee

Planning to go to a concert? See **tickets**, page 51, and **going out**, page 133.

interests

123

cinema & theatre

I feel like going to a/an ...	Ходи ми се на ...	*ho*·dee mee se na ...
ballet	балет	ba·*let*
film	кино	*kee*·no
opera	опера	*o*·pe·ra
performance	представление	pred·stav·*le*·nee·e
play	театър	te·*a*·tuhr

Did you like the ...?	Хареса ли ти ...?	ha·*re*·sa lee tee ...
ballet	балетът	ba·*le*·tuht
film	филмът	*feel*·muht
opera	операта	*o*·pe·ra·ta
performance	представле-нието	pred·stav·*le*·nee·e·to
play	пиесата	pee·*e*·sa·ta

What's showing at the cinema/theatre tonight?
Какво дават в киното/театъра довечера? — kak·*vo da*·vat v *kee*·no·to/te·*a*·tuh·ruh do·*ve*·che·ra

Is it in (English)?
На (английски) ли е? — na (an·*gleey*·skee) lee e

Does it have (English) subtitles?
Има ли субтитри (на английски)? — *ee*·ma lee *soob*·tee·tree (na an·*gleey*·skee)

Is it dubbed?
Дублиран ли е? — doob·*lee*·ran lee e

Is this seat taken?
Това място заето ли е? — to·*va myas*·to za·*e*·to lee e

Do you have tickets for ...?
Имате ли билети за ...? — *ee*·ma·te lee bee·*le*·tee za ...

Are there any extra tickets?
Има ли още билети? — *ee*·ma lee *osh*·te bee·*le*·tee

I'd like cheap/the best tickets.
Искам евтини/най-хубавите билети. — *ees*·kam *ev*·tee·nee/*nai*·hoo·ba·vee·te bee·*le*·tee

Is there a matinée show?

Има ли дневно
представление?

ee·ma lee *dnev*·no
pred·stav·*le*·nee·e

Have you seen (The Peach Thief)?

Гледал/Гледала ли си
(Крадецът на праскови)? **m/f**

gle·dal/*gle*·da·la lee see
(kra·*de*·tsuht na *pras*·ko·vee)

Who's in it?

Кой играе в него?

koy ee·*gra*·ye v *ne*·go

It stars (Hristo Shopov).

В главната роля е
(Христо Шопов).

v *glav*·na·ta *rol*·ya e
(*hrees*·to sho·*pov*)

I thought it was …	Мисля, че беше …	*mees*·lya che *be*·she …
excellent	страхотно	stra·*hot*·no
long	много дълго	*mno*·go *duhl*·go
OK	добре	do·*bre*

I (don't) like …	(Не) Харесвам …	(ne) ha·*res*·vam …
action movies	приключенски филми	pree·*klyoo*·chen·skee *feel*·mee
animated films	анимационни филми	a·nee·ma·tsee·*on*·nee *feel*·mee
(Bulgarian) cinema	(българското) кино	(*buhl*·gar·sko·to) *kee*·no
comedies	комедии	ko·*me*·dee·ee
documentaries	документални филми	do·koo·men·*tal*·nee *feel*·mee
drama	драма	*dra*·ma
horror movies	филми на ужасите	*feel*·mee na oo·zha·*see*·te
sci-fi	фантастични филми	fan·tas·*teech*·nee *feel*·mee
short films	кратко-метражни филми	krat·ko-me·*trazh*·nee *feel*·mee
thrillers	криминални филми	kree·mee·*nal*·nee *feel*·mee
war movies	военни филми	vo·*yen*·nee *feel*·mee

interests

125

words of wisdom

Like father, like son.
Крушата не пада   *kroo*·sha·ta ne *pa*·da
по-далеч от дървото.   *po*·da·lech ot duhr·*vo*·to
(lit: The pear doesn't fall any further than the tree.)

Talk is cheap.
Дума дупка не прави.   *doo*·ma *doop*·ka ne *pra*·vee
(lit: A word doesn't make a hole.)

Best to keep your head down.
Преклонена глава   prek·lo·*ne*·na gla·*va*
сабя не я сече.   sab·*ya* ne ya se·*che*
(lit: Swords don't cut off the bowed head.)

Mind your own business.
Всяка жаба да си   *vsya*·ka *zha*·ba da see
знае гьола.   *zna*·e *gyo*·la
(lit: Each frog needs to know its own pond.)

There's strength in numbers.
Сговорна дружина   sgo·*vor*·na droo·*zhee*·na
планина повдига.   pla·nee·*na* pov·*dee*·ga
(lit: A harmonious group can raise a mountain.)

A bad penny always turns up.
Черен гологан   *che*·ren go·lo·*gan*
не се губи.   ne se *goo*·bee
(lit: A black coin doesn't get lost.)

Every dog has its day.
Всяко чудо за три дена.   *vsya*·ko *choo*·do za tree *de*·na
(lit: Each miracle lasts three days.)

feelings

чувства

In this section, phrases are in the informal *mu tee* (you) form only. For more information, see the box **all about you**, page 138.

Are you …?	… ли си?	… lee see
I'm (not) …	Аз (не) съм …	az (ne) suhm …
annoyed	раздразнен m	raz-*draz*-nen
	раздразнена f	raz-*draz*-ne-na
disappointed	разочарован m	ra-zo-cha-*ro*-van
	разочарована f	ra-zo-cha-*ro*-va-na
embarrassed	притеснен m	pree-tes-*nen*
	притеснена f	pree-tes-*ne*-na
happy	щастлив m	shtast-*leev*
	щастлива f	shtast-*lee*-va
homesick	обзет/обзета от	ob-*zet*/ob-*ze*-ta ot
	носталгия m/f	nos-*tal*-gee-ya
hungry	гладен m	*gla*-den
	гладна f	*glad*-na
surprised	изненадан m	eez-ne-*na*-dan
	изненадана f	eez-ne-*na*-da-na
sad	тъжен m	*tuh*-zhen
	тъжна f	*tuhzh*-na
thirsty	жаден m	*zha*-den
	жадна f	*zhad*-na
tired	уморен m	oo-mo-*ren*
	уморена f	oo-mo-*re*-na

Are you worried?	Притесняваш ли се?	pree-tes-*nya*-vash lee se
I'm worried.	Притеснявам се.	pree-tes-*nya*-vam se
I'm not worried.	Не се притеснявам.	ne se pree-tes-*nya*-vam

Are you ...?	... ли ти е?	... lee tee e
I'm ...	... ми е.	... mee e
cold	Студено	stoo·*de*·no
hot	Горещо	go·*resh*·to
I'm not ...	Не ми е ...	ne mee e ...
cold	студено	stoo·*de*·no
hot	горещо	go·*resh*·to

If you're not feeling well, see **health**, page 193.

mixed emotions

not at all	никак	*nee*·kak
I don't care at all.		
Никак не ме вълнува.		*nee*·kak ne me vuhl·*noo*·va
a little	малко	*mal*·ko
I'm a little sad.		
Малко съм тъжен/		*mal*·ko suhm *tuh*·zhen/
тъжна. **m/f**		*tuhzh*·na
very	много	*mno*·go
I feel very happy.		
Чувствам се много		*chuvs*·tvam se *mno*·go
щастлив/щастлива. **m/f**		shtast·*leev*/shtast·*lee*·va
extremely	страшно	*strash*·no
I'm extremely sorry.		
Страшно съжалявам.		*strash*·no suh·zhal·*ya*·vam

opinions

мнения

Did you like it?
Това хареса ли ви/ти? **pol/inf**   to·*va* ha·*re*·sa lee vee/tee

What do you think of it?
Какво мислите/мислиш   kak·*vo mees*·lee·te/*mees*·leesh
за това? **pol/inf**   za to·*va*

I thought it	Мисля, че	*mees*·lyuh che
was …	беше …	*be*·she …
It's …	Това е …	to·*va* e …
awful	ужасно	oo·*zhas*·no
beautiful	много хубаво	*mno*·go *hoo*·ba·vo
boring	досадно	do·*sad*·no
(too) expensive	(много) скъпо	(*mno*·go) *skuh*·po
great	чудесно	choo·*des*·no
interesting	интересно	een·te·*res*·no
OK	добре	do·*bre*
strange	странно	*stran*·no

politics & social issues

политика и обществени проблеми

Tread carefully when discussing politics in Bulgaria – it's best not to ask which political party someone belongs to or how they vote. The issue of ethnic minorities, especially *Рома ro*·ma (the Roma people) but also *Помаци po*·*ma*·tsee (Bulgarian Muslims, or Pomaks), is a sensitive one.

I support the …	Подкрепям …	pod·*krep*·yam …
party.	партия.	*par*·tee·ya
I'm a member	Член съм на	chlen suhm na
of the … party.	… партия.	… *par*·tee·ya
communist	комунисти-	ko·moo·nees·*tee*·
	ческата	*ches*·ka·ta
conservative	консерватив-	kon·ser·va·*teev*·
	ната	na·ta
democratic	демократи-	de·mo·kra·*tee*·
	ческата	*ches*·ka·ta
green	зелената	ze·*le*·na·ta
liberal	либералната	lee·be·*ral*·na·ta
social	социал-демо-	so·tsee·yal·de·mo·
democratic	кратическата	kra·*tee*·ches·ka·ta
socialist	социалисти-	so·tsee·a·lees·*tee*·
	ческата	*ches*·ka·ta

I'm (Australian), but I didn't vote for …

Аз съм (австралиец/
австралийка), но не
гласувах за … m/f

az suhm (av·stra·*lee*·ets/
av·stra·*leey*·ka) no ne
gla·*soo*·vah za …

Did you hear about …?

Чухте/Чу ли за …? pol/inf

chooh·te/choo lee za …

Do you agree with …?

Съгласни ли сте с …? pol

suh·*glas*·nee lee ste s …

Съгласен/Съгласна
ли си с …? inf m/f

suh·*gla*·sen/suh·*glas*·na
lee see s …

I (don't) agree with …

Аз (не) съм съгласен/
съгласна с … m/f

az (ne) suhm suh·*gla*·sen/
suh·*glas*·na s …

How do people feel about …?

Какво мислят хората
за …?

kak·*vo mees*·lyuht *ho*·ra·ta
za …

How can we protest against …?

Как можем да
протестираме против …?

kak *mo*·zhem da
pro·tes·*tee*·ra·me pro·*teev* …

How can we support …?

Как можем да
подкрепим …?

kak *mo*·zhem da
pod·*kre*·peem …

abortion	абортите m pl	a·*bor*·tee·te
animal rights	закрилата на	za·*kree*·la·ta na
	животните f pl	zhee·*vot*·nee·te
civil liberties	гражданските	grazh·*dan*·skee·te
	права n pl	pra·*va*
corruption	корупцията f	ko·*roop*·tsee·ya·ta
crime	престъпността f	pre·stuhp·*nost*·*ta*
drugs	наркотиците m pl	nar·ko·*tee*·tsee·te
the economy	икономиката f	ee·ko·*no*·mee·ka·ta
education	образованието n	o·bra·zo·*va*·nee·e·to
the EU	Европейският	ev·ro·*pey*·skee·yuht
	съюз m	suh·*yooz*

euthanasia	евтаназията f	ev·ta·*na*·zee·ya·ta
freedom of the press	свободата на печата f	svo·bo·*da*·ta na pe·*cha*·tuh
globalisation	глобализацията f	glo·ba·lee·*za*·tsee·ya·ta
human rights	човешките права n pl	cho·*vesh*·kee·te pra·*va*
immigration	имиграцията f	ee·mee·*gra*·tsee·ya·ta
party politics	партийната политика f	par·*teey*·na·ta po·*lee*·tee·ka
poverty	бедността f	bed·nost·*ta*
privatisation	приватизацията f	pree·va·tee·*za*·tsee·ya·ta
racism	расизмът m	ra·*seez*·muht
sexism	сексизмът m	sek·*seez*·muht
social welfare	социалното обезпечаване n	so·tsee·*yal*·no·to o·bez·pe·*cha*·va·ne
terrorism	тероризмът m	te·ro·*reez*·muht
tourism	туризмът m	too·*reez*·muht
unemployment	безработицата f	bez·ra·*bo*·tee·tsa·ta
the war (in …)	войната (в …) f	voy·*na*·ta (v …)

Is there help for (the) …?	Отпускат ли се помощи за …?	ot·*poos*·kat lee se po·*mosh*·tee za …
aged	възрастните	vuhz·*rast*·nee·te
beggars	просяците	pros·ya·tsee·te
disabled	инвалидите	een·va·*lee*·dee·te
homeless	бездомните	bez·*dom*·nee·te
street kids	безпризорните деца	bez·pree·*zor*·nee·te de·*tsa*
unemployed	безработните	bez·ra·*bot*·nee·te

the environment

околната среда

Is there a … problem here?
Има ли тук проблеми
с …?

ee·ma lee took pro·*ble*·mee
s …

What should be done about …?
Какво трябва да се
направи за …?

kak·*vo tryab*·va da se
na·*pra*·vee za …

alternative	алтернативните	al·ter·na·*teev*·nee·te
energy	източници	eez·*toch*·nee·tsee
sources	на енергия m pl	na e·*ner*·gee·ya
climate	промяната	pro·*mya*·na·ta
change	на климата f	na *klee*·ma·ta
conservation	опазването на	o·*paz*·va·ne·to na
	околната среда n	o·*kol*·na·ta sre·*da*
deforestation	изсичането	eez·*see*·cha·ne·to
	на горите n	na go·*ree*·te
drought	сушата f	*soo*·sha·ta
ecosystem	екосистемата f	e·ko·sees·*te*·ma·ta
endangered	застрашените	za·*stra*·she·nee·te
species	видове m pl	*vee*·do·ve
genetically	генетически	ge·ne·*tee*·ches·kee
modified	модифицира-	mo·dee·fee·*tsee*·ra-
food	ните храни f pl	nee·te hra·*nee*
global	глобалното	glo·*bal*·no·to
warming	затопляне n	za·top·*le*·nee·e
hunting	ловът m	lo·*vuht*
hydroelectricity	токът от водно-	to·*kuht* ot vod·no-
	електрическите	e·lek·*tree*·ches·kee·te
	централи m	tsen·*tra*·lee
irrigation	напояването n	na·po·*ya*·va·ne·to
nuclear	атомната	*a*·tom·na·ta
energy	енергия f	e·*ner*·gee·ya
nuclear	ядрените	*ya*·dre·nee·te
testing	опити m pl	o·pee·tee
ozone layer	озоновият слой m	o·*zo*·no·vee·yuht sloy
pesticides	пестицидите m pl	pes·tee·*tsee*·dee·te
pollution	замърсяването n	za·muhr·*sya*·va·ne·to
recycling	програмата за	pro·*gra*·ma·ta za
programme	преработване на	pre·ra·*bot*·va·ne na
	отпадъците f	ot·*pa*·duh·tsee·te
toxic waste	токсичните	tok·*seech*·nee·te
	отпадъци m pl	ot·*pa*·duh·tsee
water supply	водоизточ-	vo·do·eez·*toch*-
	ниците m pl	nee·tsee·te

In this chapter, phrases are in the informal *mu* tee (you) form only. For more information, see the box **all about you**, page 138.

where to go

къде да отидем

What's there to do in the evenings?

Какво се прави тука вечер?	kak·*vo* se *pra*·vee *too*·ka *ve*·cher	

What's on ...?	Какво се предлага ...?	kak·*vo* se pred·*la*·ga ...
locally	наоколо	na·o·*ko*·lo
today	днес	dnes
tonight	довечера	do·*ve*·che·ra
this weekend	този уикенд	*to*·zee oo·*ee*·kend

Where can I find ...?	Къде има ...?	kuh·*de* ee·ma ...
clubs	клубове	*kloo*·bo·ve
gay/lesbian venues	гей клубове	gey *kloo*·bo·ve
music venues	музикални клубове	moo·zee·*kal*·nee *kloo*·bo·ve
places to eat	места за хапване	mes·*ta* za *hap*·va·ne
pubs	кръчми	kruhch·*mee*

Is there a local ... guide?	Има ли програма на ...?	*ee*·ma lee pro·*gra*·ma na ...
entertainment	развлеченията	raz·vle·*che*·nee·ya·ta
film	филмите	*feel*·mee·te
gay/lesbian	гей клубовете	gey *kloo*·bo·ve·te
music	концертите	kon·*tser*·tee·te

I feel like going to a/an ...	Ходи ми се на ...	ho·dee mee se na ...
ballet	балет	ba·let
bar	бар	bar
café	кафене	ka·fe·ne
concert	концерт	kon·tsert
film	кино	kee·no
karaoke bar	кариоки	ka·ree·o·kee
nightclub	нощен клуб	nosh·ten kloob
opera	опера	o·pe·ra
party	купон	koo·pon
(folk) performance	концерт (на народна музика)	kon·tsert (na na·rod·na moo·zee·ka)
play	театър	te·a·tuhr
pub	кръчма	kruhch·ma
restaurant	ресторант	res·to·rant

For more on bars, drinks and partying, see **romance**, page 139, and **eating out**, page 163.

invitations

покани

What are you doing now?
Какво правиш сега?　　　kak·vo pra·veesh se·ga

What are you doing ...?	Какво ще правиш ...?	kak·vo shte pra·veesh ...
tonight	довечера	do·ve·che·ra
this weekend	този уикенд	to·zee oo·ee·kend

Would you like to go (for a) ...?	Искаш ли да излезем ...?	ees·kash lee da eez·le·zem ...
I feel like going (for a) ...	Иска ми се да изляза ...	ees·ka mee se da eez·lya·zuh ...
dancing	на танци	na tan·tsee
out somewhere	някъде	nya·kuh·de
walk	на разходка	na raz·hod·ka

Would you like to go for a …?	Искаш ли да излезем …?	*ees*·kash lee da eez·*le*·zem …
coffee	за по едно кафе	za po ed·*no* ka·*fe*
drink	да пийнем по нещо	da *peey*·nem po *nesh*·to
meal	да хапнем по нещо	da *hap*·nem po *nesh*·to

I feel like going for a …	Иска ми се да изляза …	*ees*·ka mee se da eez·*lya*·zuh …
coffee	за едно кафе	za ed·*no* ka·*fe*
drink	да пийна нещо	da *peey*·nuh *nesh*·to
meal	да хапна нещо	da *hap*·nuh *nesh*·to

Do you know a good restaurant?
Знаеш ли някой
добър ресторант?
zna·yesh lee *nya*·koy
do·*buhr* res·to·*rant*

Do you want to come to the concert with me?
Искаш ли да дойдеш
с мен на концерт?
ees·kash lee da *doy*·desh
s men na kon·*tsert*

We're having a party.
Ще правим купон.
shte *pra*·veem koo·*pon*

You should come.
Ела непременно.
e·*la* ne·pre·*men*·no

what's in a name?

Luckily for modern-day travellers, Bulgarian nouns have lost nearly all elements of the case system (ie endings on nouns which indicate their role in a sentence). The only exception is the vocative – the noun form used for addressing people. It still remains in men's names, which change form when used to address a person. As for women's names, using them in the vocative form is avoided as it's considered archaic and even rude. Here are some common men's names, in the subject form followed by the vocative:

Петър	*pe*·tuhr	Петре	*pe*·tre
Димитър	dee·*mee*·tuhr	Димитре	dee·*mee*·tre
Иван	ee·*van*	Иване	ee·*va*·ne

going out

135

responding to invitations

Sure!
Разбира се!   raz·*bee*·ra se

Yes, I'd love to.
Да, с удоволствие.   da s oo·do·*vols*·tvee·e

That's very kind of you.
Това е много мило   to·*va* e *mno*·go *mee*·lo
от твоя страна.   ot *tvo*·ya stra·*na*

Where shall we go?
Къде ще отидем?   kuh·*de* shte o·*tee*·dem

No, I'm afraid I can't.
Съжалявам, не мога.   suh·zhal·*ya*·vam ne *mo*·guh

Sorry, I can't sing/dance.
Съжалявам, не мога   suh·zhal·*ya*·vam ne *mo*·guh
да пея/танцувам.   da *pe*·yuh/tan·*tsoo*·vam

What about tomorrow?
А утре?   a *oo*·tre

I'm looking forward to it.
Радвам се.   *rad*·vam se

---

colourful bulgarian

Nonsense!
Вятър и мъгла!   *vya*·tuhr ee muh·*gla*
(lit: wind and fog)

on occasion
от дъжд на вятър   ot duhzhd na *vya*·tuhr
(lit: from rain to wind)

completely
от глава до пети   ot gla·*va* do pe·*tee*
(lit: from head to heels)

from the frying pan into the fire
от трън та на глог   ot truhn ta na glog
(lit: from the thorn
into the bush)

arranging to meet

What time will we meet?
По кое време ще се
срещнем?
po ko·ye vre·me shte se
sresht·nem

Where will we meet?
Къде ще се срещнем?
kuh·de shte se sresht·nem

Let's meet at … Нека да се
срещнем …
ne·ka da se
sresht·nem …
  (eight) o'clock в (осем) часа v (o·sem) cha·suh
  the entrance при входа pree vho·da

I'll pick you up.
Ще те взема.
shte te vze·muh

Are you ready?
Готов/Готова ли си? m/f
go·tov/go·to·va lee see

I'm ready.
Готов/Готова съм. m/f
go·tov/go·to·va suhm

I'll be coming later.
Ще дойда по-късно.
shte doy·duh po·kuhs·no

Where will you be?
Къде ще бъдеш?
kuh·de shte buh·desh

OK!
Добре!
do·bre

I'll see you then.
Ще те видя тогава.
shte te vee·dyuh to·ga·va

See you later/tomorrow.
Ще се видим
по-късно/утре.
shte se vee·deem
po·kuhs·no/oo·tre

Sorry I'm late.
Съжалявам, че
закъснях.
suh·zhal·ya·vam che
za·kuhs·nyah

Never mind.
Няма защо.
nya·ma zash·to

drugs

I don't take drugs.
Аз не взимам наркотици.   az ne *vzee*·mam nar·*ko*·tee·tsee

I take ... occasionally.
Използвам ... понякога.   eez·*polz*·vam ... po·*nya*·ko·ga

Do you want to have a smoke?
Искаш ли да ходим   *ees*·kash lee da *ho*·deem
да пушим?   da *poo*·sheem

Do you have a light?
Имаш ли огънче?   *ee*·mash lee o·*guhn*·che

If the police are talking to you about drugs, see **police**, page 190, for useful phrases.

---

all about you

In Bulgarian, the informal form of address is used when speaking to children, animals, God, among students and with those you know well. It's appropriate to use the polite form with people older than you, and with those you don't know well. However, the informal mode of address is becoming more common. It's always been the norm in rural settings, where the polite form is rarely used.

The two forms are reflected in the use of the pronoun 'you' – *mu* tee inf or *вие* vee·e pol – and the verb endings accompanying them. For more information on pronouns and verbs, see the **phrasebuilder**.

In this book we've given the appropriate form for the situation that the phrase is used in – this is normally the polite form, unless marked otherwise. For phrases where either form might be suitable, we've given both.

In this chapter, phrases are in the informal *mu* tee (you) form only. For more information, see the box **all about you**, page 138.

asking someone out

да поканиш някого

Where would you like to go (tonight)?

Къде искаш да отидем (довечера)?

kuh·*de* ees·kash da o·*tee*·dem (do·*ve*·che·ra)

Would you like to do something (tomorrow)?

Искаш ли (утре) да отидем някъде заедно?

ees·kash lee (*oo*·tre) da o·*tee*·dem *nya*·kuh·de za·*ed*·no

Yes, I'd love to.

Да, с удоволствие.

da s oo·do·*vols*·tvee·e

Sorry, I can't.

Съжалявам, не мога.

suh·zhal·*ya*·vam ne *mo*·guh

local talk		
He's a babe.	Той е много готин.	toy e *mno*·go *go*·teen
She's a babe.	Тя е много готина.	tya e *mno*·go *go*·tee·na
	Тя е голямо маце.	tya e go·*lya*·mo *ma*·tse
He/She is hot.	Той/Тя е секси.	toy/tya e *sek*·see
He's a bastard.	Той е копиле.	toy e *ko*·pee·le
She's a bitch.	Тя е кобра.	tya e *ko*·bra
He gets around.	Той е коцкар.	toy e kots·*kar*
She gets around.	Тя много кръшка.	tya *mno*·go *kruh*·shka

pick-up lines

Would you like a drink?
Да ти почерпя едно   da tee po·*cher*·pyuh ed·*no*
питие?   pee·tee·*e*

Don't I know you from somewhere?
Не се ли познаваме   ne se lee poz·*na*·va·me
от някъде?   ot *nya*·kuh·de

You're a fantastic dancer.
Страхотно танцуваш.   stra·*hot*·no tan·*tsoo*·vash

Can I ...?	Може ли да ...?	*mo*·zhe lee da ...
dance with you	танцувам с теб	tant·*soo*·vam s teb
sit here	седна тука	*sed*·nuh *too*·ka
take you home	те изпратя	te eez·*prat*·yuh

rejections

I'm here with my girlfriend/boyfriend.
Тука съм с приятелката/   *too*·ka suhm s pree·*ya*·tel·ka·ta/
приятеля си.   pree·*ya*·tel·ya see

I'd rather not.
Не трябва.   ne *tryab*·va

No, thank you.
Не, благодаря.   ne bla·go·da·*ryuh*

Excuse me, I have to go now.
Извинявай, трябва   eez·vee·*nya*·vai *tryab*·va
да си тръгвам.   da see *truhg*·vam

Here are some phrases that might come in handy if you're being hassled.

Leave me alone, please.

Ако обичаш, остави   a·ko o·bee·chash o·sta·vee

ме на мира.   me na mee·ra

Leave me alone!

Остави ме на мира!   o·sta·vee me na mee·ra

Go away!	Разкарай се!	raz·ka·rai se
Get lost!	Махай се!	ma·hai se
Piss off!	Чупката!	choop·ka·ta

getting closer

сближаване

I really like you.

Много те харесвам.   mno·go te ha·res·vam

You're great.

Чудесен/Чудесна си. m/f   choo·de·sen/choo·des·na see

Can I kiss you?

Може ли да те целуна?   mo·zhe lee da te tse·loo·nuh

Do you want to come inside for a while?

Искаш ли да влезеш   ees·kash lee da vle·zesh

за малко?   za mal·ko

Do you want a massage?

Искаш ли да ти   ees·kash lee da tee

направя масаж?   na·prav·yuh ma·sazh

Would you like to stay over?

Искаш ли да останеш   ees·kash lee da o·sta·nesh

да спиш тука?   da speesh too·ka

Can I stay over?

Може ли да остана   mo·zhe lee da o·sta·nuh

да спа тука?   da spuh too·ka

romance

sex

Kiss me.	Целуни ме.	tse·loo·*nee* me
I want you.	Желая те.	zhe·*la*·yuh te
Let's go to bed.	Да си лягаме.	da see *lya*·ga·me
Touch me here.	Докосни ме тук.	do·kos·*nee* me took
Do you like this?	Харесва ли	ha·*res*·va lee
	ти това?	tee to·*va*
I like that.	Харесва ми.	ha·*res*·va mee
I don't like that.	Не ми харесва.	ne mee ha·*res*·va
I think we should stop now.	Стига толкова.	*stee*·ga *tol*·ko·va

Do you have a (condom)?
Имаш ли (презерватив)?   *ee*·mash lee (pre·zer·va·*teev*)

Let's use a (condom).
Нека да използваме   *ne*·ka da eez·*polz*·va·me
(презерватив)   (pre·zer·va·*teev*)

I won't do it without protection.
Не искам да го правим   ne *ees*·kam da go *pra*·veem
без предпазни мерки.   bez pred·*paz*·nee *mer*·kee

It's my first time.
Това ми е за първи път.   to·*va* mee e za *puhr*·vee puht

It helps to have a sense of humour.
Хубаво е, човек да   *hoo*·ba·vo e cho·*vek* da
има чувство за хумор.   *ee*·ma *choovs*·tvo za *hoo*·mor

Is that why you're single?
Това ли е причината   to·*va* lee e pree·*chee*·na·ta
да си сам/сама? m/f   da see sam/*sa*·ma

Oh my god!	О боже!	o *bo*·zhe
That's great.	Това е върха.	to·*va* e vuhr·*huh*
Easy tiger!	Полека!	po·*le*·ka

That was …	Това беше …	to·*va* be·she …
amazing	страхотно	stra·*hot*·no
romantic	романтично	ro·man·*teech*·no
wild	диво	*dee*·vo

love

любов

I think we're good together.
Мисля, че се разбираме
добре.
mees·lyuh che se raz·*bee*·ra·me
do·*bre*

I love you.
Обичам те.
o·*bee*·cham te

Will you go out with me?
Ще излезеш ли с мен?
shte eez·*le*·zesh lee s men

Will you marry me? (to a man)
Ще се ожениш ли за мен?
shte se o·*zhe*·neesh lee za men

Will you marry me? (to a woman)
Ще се омъжеш ли за мен?
shte se o·*muh*·zhesh lee za men

Will you meet my parents?
Съгласен/Съгласна ли
си да те представя
на родителите си? m/f
suh·*gla*·sen/suh·*glas*·na lee
see da te pred·*stav*·yuh
na ro·*dee*·te·lee·te see

sweet talk		
бубенце n	*boo*·ben·tse	**little bug**
котенце n	*ko*·ten·tse	**kitten**
маце n	*ma*·tse	**dear cat**
миличко n	*mee*·leech·ko	**dear little one**
пиленце n	*pee*·len·tse	**little chick**
слънчице n	*sluhn*·chee·tse	**little sun**

romance

problems

I don't think it's working out.
Нещо не върви   *nesh*·to ne vuhr·*vee*
между нас.   mezh·*doo* nas

Are you seeing another man/woman?
С друг/друга ли   s droog/droo·*ga* lee
излизаш? m/f   eez·*lee*·zash

He's just a friend.
Той е само добър познат.   toy e *sa*·mo do·*buhr* poz·*nat*

She's just a friend.
Тя е само добра позната.   tya e *sa*·mo dob·*ra* poz·*na*·ta

You're just using me for sex.
Използваш ме само   eez·*polz*·vash me *sa*·mo
за секс.   za seks

I never want to see you again.
Не искам да те видя   ne *ees*·kam da te *vee*·dyuh
повече.   *po*·ve·che

We'll work it out.
Ще намерим решение.   shte na·*me*·reem re·*she*·nee·e

leaving

I have to leave (tomorrow).
(Утре) Трябва да тръгвам.   (*oo*·tre) *tryab*·va da *truhg*·vam

I'll ...	Ще ...	shte ...
keep in touch	поддържам	pod·*duhr*·zham
	връзка с теб	*vruhz*·ka s teb
miss you	ми липсваш	mee *leeps*·vash
visit you	ти дойда на	tee *doy*·duh na
	гости	*gos*·tee

religion

религия

What's your religion?
Каква вяра изповядвате/ kak·*va vya*·ra ees·pov·*yad*·va·te/
изповядваш? pol/inf ees·pov·*yad*·vash

I'm not religious.
Не съм религиозен/ ne suhm re·lee·gee·*o*·zen/
религиозна. m/f re·lee·gee·*oz*·na

I'm (a/an) …	Аз съм …	az suhm …
agnostic	агностик m	ag·nos·*teek*
	агностичка f	ag·nos·*teech*·ka
atheist	атеист m	a·te·*eest*
	атеистка f	a·te·*eest*·ka
Catholic	католик m	ka·to·*leek*
	католичка f	ka·to·*leech*·ka
Christian	християнин m	hrees·tee·*ya*·neen
	християнка f	hrees·tee·*yan*·ka
Dunovist	дъновист m	duh·no·*veest*
	дъновистка f	duh·no·*veest*·ka
Jewish	евреин m	ev·*re*·yeen
	еврейка f	ev·*rey*·ka
Muslim	мохамеданин m	mo·ha·me·*da*·neen
	мохамеданка f	mo·ha·me·*dan*·ka
Orthodox	православен m	pra·vo·*sla*·ven
	православна f	pra·vo·*slav*·na
Protestant	протестант m	pro·tes·*tant*
	протестантка f	pro·tes·*tant*·ka

I (don't) believe in …	(Не) Вярвам в …	(ne) *vyar*·vam v …
astrology	астрологията	as·tro·*lo*·gee·ya·ta
fate	съдбата	suhd·*ba*·ta
God	Бога	*bo*·ga

Where can I ...?	Къде мога да ...?	kuh·de mo·guh da ...
attend a service	посетя църковна служба	po·set·yuh tsuhr·kov·na sloozh·ba
pray	се помоля	se po·mol·yuh

cultural differences

културни различия

I didn't mean to do/say anything wrong.
Аз нямах предвид да направя/кажа нищо нередно.
az *nya*·mah pred·*veed* da na·*prav*·yuh/*ka*·zhuh *neesh*·to ne·*red*·no

I don't want to offend you.
Не искам да ви/те обидя. pol/inf
ne *ees*·kam da vee/te o·*bee*·dyuh

I respect your beliefs.
Уважавам вашата/ твоята вяра. pol/inf
oo·va·*zha*·vam *va*·sha·ta/ *tvo*·ya·ta *vya*·ra

I'm not used to this.
Не съм свикнал/ свикнала с това. m/f
ne suhm *sveek*·nal/ *sveek*·na·la s to·*va*

I'd rather not join in.
Предпочитам да не участвам.
pred·po·*chee*·tam da ne oo·*chast*·vam

I'm sorry, it's against my ...	Съжалявам, но това е против ...	suh·zhal·*ya*·vam no to·*va* e pro·*teev*...
beliefs	моите вярвания	*mo*·yee·te *vyar*·va·nee·ya
religion	моята религия	*mo*·ya·ta re·*lee*·gee·ya

This is ...	Това е ...	to·*va* e ...
different	различно	raz·*leech*·no
fun	забавно	za·*bav*·no
interesting	интересно	een·te·*res*·no

When's the gallery/museum open?

Какво е работното време
на галерията/музея?

kak·*vo* e ra·*bot*·no·to *vre*·me
na ga·*le*·ree·ya·ta/moo·*ze*·yuh

What kind of art are you interested in?

От какво изкуство се
интересувате/
интересуваш? **pol/inf**

ot kak·*vo* eez·*koost*·vo se
een·te·re·*soo*·va·te/
een·te·re·*soo*·vash

What's in the collection?

Какво има в колекцията?

kak·*vo* ee·ma v ko·*lek*·tsee·ya·ta

What do you think of …?

Какво мислите/
мислиш за …? **pol/inf**

kak·*vo* *mees*·lee·te/
mees·leesh za …

It's an exhibition of …

Това е изложба на …

to·*va* e eez·*lozh*·ba na …

I'm interested in …

Интересувам се от …

een·te·re·*soo*·vam se ot …

I like the works of …

Харесвам работите на …

ha·*res*·vam *ra*·bo·tee·te na …

It reminds me of …

Това ми напомня за …

to·*va* mee na·*pom*·nya za …

… art	… изкуство	… eez·*koost*·vo
abstract	абстрактното	ab·*strakt*·no·to
contemporary	съвременното	suh·*vre*·men·no·to
modern	модерното	mo·*der*·no·to
performance	изпълнител-ното	eez·puhl·*nee*·tel·no·to
religious	религиозното	re·lee·gee·*oz*·no·to

... art		
graphic	графиката f	gra·fee·ka·ta
icon painting	иконописът m	ee·ko·no·pee·suht
impressionist	импресио-	eem·pre·see·o·
	низмът m	neez·muht
inlaid	инкрус-	een·kroos·
	тацията f	ta·tsee·ya·ta
Renaissance	ренесансът m	re·ne·san·suht
textiles	текстилът m	teks·tee·luht
architecture	архитектура f	ar·hee·tek·too·ra
artwork	произведение	pro·eez·ve·de·nee·e
	на изкуството n	na eez·koost·vo·to
curator	куратор m	koo·ra·tor
design n	дизайн m	dee·zain
embroidery	бродерия f	bro·de·ree·ya
etching	гравюра f	grav·yoo·ra
exhibit n	изложба f	eez·lozh·ba
exhibition hall	изложбена	eez·lozh·be·na
	галерия f	ga·le·ree·ya
installation	инсталация f	een·sta·la·tsee·ya
opening	откриване n	ot·kree·va·ne
painter	художник m	hoo·dozh·neek
	художничка f	hoo·dozh·neech·ka
painting (artwork)	картина f	kar·tee·na
painting (technique)	живопис n	zhee·vo·pees
period	период m	pe·ree·od
permanent collection	постоянна	po·sto·yan·na
	експозиция f	eks·po·zee·tsee·ya
pottery	керамика f	ke·ra·mee·ka
print n	копие n	ko·pee·e
sculptor	скулптор m	skoolp·tor
	скулпторка f	skoolp·tor·ka
sculpture	скулптура f	skoolp·too·ra
statue	статуя f	sta·too·a
studio	ателие n	a·te·lee·e
style n	стил m	steel
technique	техника f	teh·nee·ka
weaving	тъкан m	tuh·kan
woodcarving n	дърворезба f	duhr·vo·rez·ba

sporting interests

спортни интереси

Popular sports in Bulgaria, in addition to those given in the list below, are *художествена гимнастика* hoo·do·zhest·ve·na geem·nas·tee·ka (rhythmic gymnastics), *фигурно пързаляне* fee·goor·no puhr·za·lya·ne (figure skating), as well as *борба* bor·ba (wrestling) and *вдигане на тежести* vdee·ga·ne na te·zhes·tee (weightlifting). For more sports, see the **dictionary**.

What sport do you follow?

От какъв спорт се интересувате/ интересуваш? pol/inf	ot ka·*kuhv* sport se een·te·re·*soo*·va·te/ een·te·re·*soo*·vash

What sport do you play?

С какъв спорт се занимавате/ занимаваш? pol/inf	s ka·*kuhv* sport se za·nee·*ma*·va·te/ za·nee·*ma*·vash

I follow athletics.

Интересувам се от лека атлетика.	een·te·re·*soo*·vam se ot *le*·ka at·*le*·tee·ka

I do athletics.

Занимавам се с лека атлетика.	za·nee·*ma*·vam se s *le*·ka at·*le*·tee·ka

I follow ...	Интересувам се от ...	een·te·re·*soo*·vam se ot ...
I play/do ...	Играя ...	ee·*gra*·yuh ...
basketball	баскетбол	*bas*·ket·bol
boxing	бокс	boks
football (soccer)	футбол	*foot*·bol
karate	карате	ka·*ra*·te
tennis	тенис	*te*·nees
volleyball	волейбол	*vo*·ley·bol

I ...	Аз ...	az ...
cycle	карам колело	*ka*·ram ko·le·*lo*
run	бягам	*bya*·gam

Who's your favourite ...?	Кой е любимия ви/ти ...? pol/inf	koy e lyoo·*bee*·mee·yuh vee/tee ...
sportsperson	спортист m	spor·*teest*
	спортистка f	spor·*teest*·ka
team	отбор	ot·*bor*

Do you like (basketball)?
Обичате/Обичаш ли (баскетбол)? pol/inf
o·*bee*·cha·te/o·*bee*·chash lee (*bas*·ket·bol)

Yes, very much.
Да, много.
da *mno*·go

Not really.
Не особено.
ne o·*so*·be·no

going to a game

Would you like to go to a game?
Искате/Искаш ли да отидем на мач? pol/inf
ees·ka·te/*ees*·kash lee da o·*tee*·dem na mach

Who are you supporting?
Кого подкрепяте/ подкрепяш? pol/inf
ko·*go* pod·*kre*·pya·te/ pod·*kre*·pyash

Who's playing/winning?
Кой играе/печели?
koy ee·*gra*·ye/pe·*che*·lee

What's the score?
Какъв е резултатът?
ka·*kuhv* e re·zool·*ta*·tuht

scoring		
draw/even	равен резултат	*ra*·ven re·zool·*tat*
love (zero)	нула на нула	*noo*·la na *noo*·la
match-point	мач-пойнт	*mach*·poynt
nil (zero)	нулев резултат	*noo*·lev re·zool·*tat*

sports talk

What a …!	Какъв …!	ka·*kuhv* …
goal	гол	gol
hit	удар	*oo*·dar
kick	шут	shoot
pass	пас	pas

That was a …	Това беше …	to·*va* be·she …
game!	мач!	mach
bad	лош	losh
great	страхотен	stra·*ho*·ten

playing sport

спортуване

Do you want to play?
Искате ли да играете? pol   *ees*·ka·te lee da ee·*gra*·ye·te
Искаш ли да играеш? inf   *ees*·kash lee da ee·*gra*·yesh

Can I join in?
Може ли да участвам?   *mo*·zhe lee da oo·*chast*·vam

That would be great.
Това би било чудесно.   to·*va* bee bee·*lo* choo·*des*·no

I can't.
Не мога.   ne *mo*·guh

I have an injury.
Имам контузия.   *ee*·mam kon·*too*·zee·ya

Kick/Pass it to me!
Подай ми го! inf   po·*dai* mee go

Your/My point.
Точка за теб/мен. inf   *toch*·ka za teb/men

You're a good player.
Вие сте добър играч. pol   *vee*·e ste do·*buhr* ee·*grach*
Ти си добър играч. inf   tee see do·*buhr* ee·*grach*

Thanks for the game.
Благодаря за играта.   bla·go·dar·*yuh* za ee·*gra*·ta

Where's a good place to …?	Къде има хубаво място за …?	kuh·de ee·ma hoo·ba·vo myas·to za …
fish	риболов	ree·bo·lov
go hiking	туризъм	too·ree·zuhm
go horse riding	конна езда	kon·na ez·da
paraglide	летене с делтапланер	le·te·ne s del·ta·pla·ner
run	бягане	bya·ga·ne
scuba dive	гмуркане	gmoor·ka·ne
ski	каране на ски	ka·ra·ne na skee
windsurf	уиндсърфинг	oo·eend·suhr·feeng

Where's the nearest …?	Къде е най-близкият/най-близкото …? m/n	kuh·de e nai·bleez·kee·yuht/nai·bleez·ko·to …
gym	фитнес център m	feet·nes·tsen·tuhr
swimming pool	плувен басейн m	ploo·ven ba·seyn
tennis court	тенискорт m	te·nees·kort

Do I have to be a member to attend?

Трябва ли да съм член
за да мога да участвам?
tryab·va lee da suhm chlen
za da mo·guh da oo·chast·vam

Is there a women-only session?

Има ли женска секция?
ee·ma lee zhen·ska sek·tsee·ya

Where are the changing rooms?

Къде са съблекалните?
kuh·de suh suh·ble·kal·nee·te

Can I hire a court?

Мога ли да си запазя
час за корта?
mo·guh lee da see za·paz·yuh
chas za kor·tuh

Can I hire a …?	Мога ли да взема под наем …?	mo·guh lee da vze·muh pod na·em …
ball	една топка	ed·na top·ka
bicycle	едно колело	ed·no ko·le·lo
racquet	една ракета	ed·na ra·ke·ta

What's the charge per ...?	Колко струва ...?	kol·ko stroo·va ...
day	на ден	na den
game	за една игра	za ed·na ee·gra
hour	на час	na chas

fishing

риболов

Where are the good spots?
Рибата къде кълве? — ree·ba·ta kuh·de kuhl·ve

Do I need a fishing permit?
Нужен ли е риболовен билет? — noo·zhen lee e ree·bo·lo·ven bee·let

Do you do fishing tours?
Правите ли риболовни излети? — pra·vee·te lee ree·bo·lov·nee eez·le·tee

What's the best bait?
Коя е най-добрата стръв? — ko·ya e nai·do·bra·ta struhv

What kind of fish are you landing?
Какво ловите/ловиш? pol/inf — kak·vo lo·vee·te/lo·veesh

How much does it weigh?
Колко тежи? — kol·ko te·zhee

bait	стръв f	struhv
fishing line	корда f	kor·da
float n	плувка f	ploov·ka
hooks	въдици f pl	vuh·dee·tsee
lures	мамки f pl	mam·kee
rod	прът m	pruht
sinkers	оловни тежести f pl	o·lov·nee te·zhes·tee

skiing

How much is a pass?
Колко струва един абонамент?
kol·ko *stroo*·va e·*deen* a·bo·na·*ment*

Can I take lessons?
Може ли да взимам уроци?
mo·zhe lee da *vzee*·mam oo·ro·tsee

I'd like to hire ...	Искам да взема под наем ...	*ees*·kam da *vze*·muh pod *na*·em ...
boots	скиорски обувки	skee·*or*·skee o·*boov*·kee
goggles	скиорски очила	skee·*or*·skee o·chee·*la*
poles	щеки	*shte*·kee
a ski suit	скиорски костюм	skee·*or*·skee kos·*tyoom*

Is it possible to go ...?	Може ли тука да ...?	*mo*·zhe lee *too*·ka da ...
Alpine skiing	карам ски	*ka*·ram skee
cross-country skiing	се занимавам със ски-бягане	se za·nee·*ma*·vam suhs *skee*·bya·ga·ne
snowboarding	се пързалям със сноуборд	se puhr·*za*·lyam suhs *sno*·oo·bord
tobogganing	спускам с тобоган	*spoos*·kam s to·bo·*gan*

What are the conditions like ...?	Какви са условията ...?	kak·*vee* suh oo·*slo*·vee·ya·ta ...
higher up	по-нагоре	*po*·na·go·re
on that run	на онази писта	na o·*na*·zee *pees*·ta

Which are the ... slopes?	Кои са пистите за ...?	koy·*ee* suh *pees*·tee·te za ...
beginner	начинаещи	na·chee·*na*·esh·tee
intermediate	средно-напреднали	*sred*·no·na·*pred*·na·lee
advanced	напреднали	na·*pred*·na·lee

cable car	кабинков лифт m	ka·*been*·kov leeft
chairlift	седалков лифт m	se·*dal*·kov leeft
instructor	инструктор m	een·*strook*·tor
resort	курорт m	koo·*rort*
ski lift	лифт m	leeft
sled	шейна f	shey·*na*

soccer/football

футбол

Who plays for (Levski)?
Кой играе за (Левски)?   koy ee·*gra*·ye za (*lev*·skee)

He's a great (player).
Той е страхотен (играч).   toy e stra·*ho*·ten (ee·*grach*)

Which team is at the top of the league?
Кой отбор е лидер   koy ot·*bor* e lee·der
в групата?   v *groo*·pa·ta

What a great/terrible team!
Какъв чудесен/ужасен   ka·*kuhv* choo·*de*·sen/oo·*zha*·sen
отбор!   ot·*bor*

ball	топка f	*top*·ka
coach n	треньор m	tre·*nyor*
expulsion	изгонване n	Iz·*gon*·va·ne
fan	запалянко m	za·pa·*lyan*·ko
free kick	свободен удар m	svo·*bo*·den oo·dar
goal (structure)	врата f	vra·*ta*
goalkeeper	вратар m	vra·*tar*
offside	засада f	za·*sa*·da
penalty (kick)	наказателен удар m	na·ka·*za*·te·len oo·dar
player	играч m	ee·*grach*
red card	червен картон m	cher·*ven* kar·*ton*
referee	съдия m	suh·dee·*ya*
striker	нападател m	na·pa·*da*·tel
throw in v	хвърлям тъч	*hvuhr*·lyam tuhch
yellow card	жълт картон m	zhuhlt kar·*ton*

Off to see a match? Check out **going to a game**, page 150.

water sports

Can I book a lesson?

Мога ли да си запиша
време за инструкция?

*mo·guh lee da see za·pee·shuh
vre·me za een·strook·tsee·ya*

Can I hire (a) …?	Мога ли да взема под наем …?	*mo·guh lee da vze·muh pod na·em …*
boat	лодка	*lod·ka*
life jacket	спасителна жилетка	*spa·see·tel·na zhee·let·ka*
snorkelling gear	екипировка със шнорхел	*e·kee·pee·rov·ka suhs shnor·hel*
water-skis	водни ски	*vod·nee skee*
wetsuit	неопренов костюм	*ne·o·pre·nov kos·tyoom*

Are there any …?	Има ли …?	*ee·ma lee …*
reefs	рифове	*ree·fo·ve*
rips	мъртво вълнение	*muhrt·vo vuhl·ne·nee·e*
water hazards	подводни опасности	*pod·vod·nee o·pas·nos·tee*

guide n	водач m	*vo·dach*
motorboat	моторница f	*mo·tor·nee·tsa*
oars	гребла n pl	*greb·la*
sailboard	сърф m	*suhrf*
sailboarding	каране на сърф n	*ka·ra·ne na suhrf*
sailing boat	платноходка f	*plat·no·hod·ka*
surfboard	сърф m	*suhrf*
surfing	сърфиране n	*suhr·fee·ra·ne*
wave n	вълна f	*vuhl·na*

hiking

туризъм

Where can I ...?	Къде мога да ...?	kuh·de mo·guh da ...
buy supplies	си купя	see koop·yuh
	всичко	vseech·ko
	необходимо	ne·ob·ho·dee·mo
find someone	намеря	na·mer·yuh
who knows	човек, който	cho·vek koy·to
this area	знае околността	zna·e o·kol·nost·ta
get a map	взема карта	vze·muh kar·ta
hire hiking	взема под наем	vze·muh pod na·em
gear	туристическа	too·ree·stee·ches·ka
	екипировка	e·kee·pee·rov·ka

Do we need a guide?
Трябва ли водач?   tryab·va lee vo·dach

Are there guided treks?
Има ли групови   ee·ma lee groo·po·vee
екскурзии?   eks·koor·zee·ee

Is it safe?
Безопасно ли е?   be·zo·pas·no lee e

Is there a hut?
Има ли хижа?   ee·ma lee hee·zha

When does it get dark?
В колко часа се мръква?   v kol·ko cha·suh se mruhk·va

How high is the climb?
Каква височина ще   kak·va vee·so·chee·na shte
вземем?   vze·mem

How long is the trail?
Колко дълга е пътеката?   kol·ko duhl·ga e puh·te·ka·ta

Is the track well marked?
Пътеката добре ли   puh·te·ka·ta do·bre lee
е означена?   e o·zna·che·na

Is the track ...?	Пътеката ... ли е?	puh·*te*·ka·ta ... lee e
open	открита	ot·*kree*·ta
scenic	с изгледи	s *eez*·gle·dee

Which is the ... route?	Кой е ... път?	koy e ... puht
easiest	най-лекият	*nai*·le·kee·yuht
most interesting	най-интересният	*nai*· een·te·res·nee·yuht
shortest	най-краткият	*nai*·krat·kee·yuht

Do we need to take ...?	Тряба ли да носим ...?	*tryab*·va lee da *no*·seem ...
food	храна	hra·*na*
water	вода	vo·*da*

Where can I find the ...?	Къде се намира ...?	kuh·*de* se na·*mee*·ra ...
camping ground	къмпингът	*kuhm*·peeng·uht
nearest village	най-близкото село	*nai*·bleez·ko·to se·lo

Where can I find the ...?	Къде се намират ...?	kuh·*de* se na·*mee*·rat ...
showers	душовете	*doo*·sho·ve·te
toilets	тоалетните	to·a·*let*·nee·te

Where have you come from?
Откъде идвате/идваш? **pol/inf** ot·kuh·*de* eed·va·te/*eed*·vash

How long did it take you?
За колко време взехте/взе прехода? **pol/inf** za *kol*·ko *vre*·me *vzeh*·te/ vze pre·*ho*·duh

Does this path go to (Knyazhevo)?
Тази пътека води ли до (Княжево)? *ta*·zee puh·*te*·ka *vo*·dee lee do (*knya*·zhe·vo)

beach & pool signs		
Плуването забранено	*ploo*·va·ne·to za·bra·*ne*·no	**No Swimming**
Скачането забранено	*ska*·cha·ne·to za·bra·*ne*·no	**No Diving**

SOCIAL

Can I go through here?
Мога ли да мина оттук?   *mo*·guh lee da *mee*·nuh ot·*took*

Is the water OK to drink?
Тази вода може ли да   *ta*·zee vo·*da* mo·zhe lee da
се пие?   se *pee*·e

beach

на плажа

Where's the …	Къде се намира	kuh·*de* se na·*mee*·ra
beach?	… плаж?	… plazh
best	най-хубавият	*nai*·hoo·ba·vee·yuht
nearest	най-близкият	*nai*·bleez·kee·yuht
nudist	нудисткият	noo·*deest*·kee·yuht
public	общественият	ob·*shtest*·ve·nee·yuht

Внимавайте/Внимавай мъртво вълнение! **pol/inf**
vnee·*ma*·vai·te/vnee·*ma*·vai
muhr·tvo vuhl·*ne*·nee·e

Be careful of the undertow!

Опасно е!
o·*pas*·no e

It's dangerous!

Is it safe to dive/swim here?

Безопасно ли е
гмуркането/плуването
тук?

be·zo·*pas*·no lee e
gmoor·ka·ne·to/*ploo*·va·ne·to
took

What time is high/low tide?

В колко часа е
приливът/отливът?

v *kol*·ko cha·*suh* e
pree·lee·vuht/*ot*·lee·vuht

Do we have to pay?

Плаща ли се?

plash·ta lee se

How much to rent a/an ...?	Колко струва да се наеме ...?	*kol*·ko *stroo*·va da se na·*e*·me ...
chair	столче	*stol*·che
hut	бунгало	boon·*ga*·lo
umbrella	чадър	cha·*duhr*

weather

времето

What's the weather like?

Какво е времето?

kak·*vo* e *vre*·me·to

What will the weather be like tomorrow?

Какво ще бъде
времето утре?

kak·*vo* shte *buh*·de
vre·me·to *oo*·tre

It's freezing.

Много е студено.

mno·go e stoo·*de*·no

It's raining/snowing.

Вали дъжд/сняг.

va·*lee* duhzhd/snyag

It's ...	... е.	... e
cloudy	Облачно	*o*·blach·no
cold	Студено	stoo·*de*·no
fine	Хубаво	*hoo*·ba·vo
hot	Горещо	go·*resh*·to
sunny	Слънчево	*sluhn*·che·vo
warm	Топло	*top*·lo
windy	Ветровито	ve·tro·*vee*·to
Where can I buy a/an ...?	Къде мога да си купя ...?	kuh·*de* mo·guh da see *koop*·yuh ...
rain jacket	дъждобран	duhzh·do·*bran*
umbrella	чадър	cha·*duhr*

flora & fauna

растения и животни

What ... is that?	Какво е това ...?	kak·*vo* e to·*va* ...
animal	животно	zhee·*vot*·no
flower	цвете	*tsve*·te
plant	растение	ras·*te*·nee·e
tree	дърво	duhr·*vo*

local plants & animals

chamomile	лайка f	*lai*·ka
fir	елха f	el·*ha*
(Bulgarian) geranium	здравец m	*zdra*·vets
marigold	невен m	ne·*ven*
rose	роза f	*ro*·za
summer savoury	чубрица f	*choo*·bree·tsa
bear	мечка f	*mech*·ka
eagle	орел m	o·*rel*
ferret	пор m	por
fox	лисица f	lee·*see*·tsa
stork	щъркел m	*shtuhr*·kel
wolf	вълк m	vuhlk

Is it …?	… ли е?	… lee e
common	Разпространено	ras·pros·tra·*ne*·no
dangerous	Опасно	o·*pas*·no
endangered	Застрашено	za·stra·*she*·no
poisonous	Отровно	o·*trov*·no
protected	Защитено	zash·tee·*te*·no

Is this a protected …?	Това защитен/ защитена	to·*va* zash·tee·*ten*/ zash·tee·*te*·na
	… ли е? m/f	… lee e
forest	гора f	go·*ra*
park	парк m	park
species	вид m	veed

What's it used for?

За какво се използва? za kak·*vo* se eez·*polz*·va

Can you eat the fruit?

Яде ли се плодът му? ya·*de* lee se plo·*duht* moo

For geographical and agricultural terms and names of animals and plants, see the **dictionary**.

---

names across borders

Many 'international' names are also found in Bulgaria, but the local version has a distinctively Bulgarian flavour (especially considering the written, Cyrillic, form). If you'd like to adopt the Bulgarian version of your name while travelling, here are some equivalents:

Andrew	Андрей	an·*drey*
George	Георги	ge·*or*·gee
John	Иван	ee·*van*
Michael	Михаил	mee·ha·*eel*
Paul	Павел	*pa*·vel
Barbara	Варвара	var·*va*·ra
Elizabeth	Елисавета	e·lee·sa·*ve*·ta
Helen	Елена	e·*le*·na
Irene	Ирина	ee·*ree*·na
Katherine	Екатерина	e·ka·te·*ree*·na

FOOD > eating out

ходене по ресторанти

basics

основни неща

breakfast	закуска f	za·*koos*·ka
lunch	обед m	o·bed
dinner	вечеря f	ve·*cher*·ya
snack	закуска f	za·*koos*·ka
eat v	ям	yam
drink v	пия	*pee*·yuh
I'd like …	Искам …	*ees*·kam …
Please.	Моля.	*mol*·yuh
Thank you.	Благодаря.	bla·go·dar·*yuh*
I'm starving!	Много съм гладен/гладна. m/f	*mno*·go suhm *gla*·den/*glad*·na

the meal deal

A typical Bulgarian breakfast consists of sweet pastries and/or bread, butter and jam, *сирене see*·re·ne (soft white cheese) or *кашкавал* kash·ka·*val* (hard yellow cheese), sliced ham and coffee or tea.

The main meal can be taken either at lunchtime or at dinnertime. If lunch is the main meal, it begins with salad, often accompanied by *ракия* ra·*kee*·ya (grape brandy), followed by soup, then a cooked main dish usually containing meat and vegetables, and either a sweet or fruit for dessert. If lunch is the lighter meal, it's frequently a sandwich.

If dinner is the main meal, it follows the model above. If it's the lighter meal, it's either cheese, yogurt and bread, *баница* ba·*nee*·tsa (savoury cheese pastry), eggs and tomatoes, a toasted sandwich or something similar. Classic snacks are sandwiches or small savoury pastries.

eating out

163

finding a place to eat

Can you recommend a ...?	Можете ли да препоръчате ...? pol	mo·zhe·te lee da pre·po·ruh·cha·te ...
	Можеш ли да препоръчаш ...? inf	mo·zhesh lee da pre·po·ruh·chash ...
bar	бар	bar
café	кафене	ka·fe·ne
pub	кръчма	kruhch·ma
restaurant	ресторант	res·to·rant
tavern	механа	me·ha·na

Where would you go for ...?	Къде ходите да ...?	kuh·de ho·dee·te da ...
a celebration	опразнувате нещо	o·praz·noo·va·te nesh·to
a cheap meal	хапнете евтино	hap·ne·te ev·tee·no
local specialities	опитате местните специалитети	o·pee·ta·te mest·nee·te spe·tsee·a·lee·te·tee

I'd like to reserve a table for ...	Искам да запазя една маса за ...	ees·kam da za·paz·yuh ed·na ma·sa za ...
(two) people	(двама) души	(dva·ma) doo·shee
(eight) o'clock	(осем) часа	(o·sem) cha·suh

Are you still serving food?
Сервирате ли все още?   ser·vee·ra·te lee vse osh·te

How long is the wait?
Колко се чака?   kol·ko se cha·ka

---

listen for ...

Затворено е.	zat·vo·re·no e	We're closed.
Няма места.	nya·ma mes·ta	We're full.
Един момент.	e·deen mo·ment	One moment.

at the restaurant

Summon the waiter using the phrase *ако обичате* a·ko o·bee·cha·te (lit: if you like). To ask for the bill, say *сметката, моля* smet·ka·ta mol·yuh (lit: the bill, please) – the waiter will not bring the bill until it's specifically requested. Tips are normally minimal. Unless the service has been exceptional, or you wish to make a gesture for some other reason, just round the bill off slightly upwards.

What would you recommend?
Какво ще препоръчате? kak·vo shte pre·po·ruh·cha·te

What's in that dish?
Какво има в това блюдо? kak·vo ee·ma v to·va blyoo·do

What's that called?
Как се казва това? kak se kaz·va to·va

I'll have that.
Ще го взема. shte go vze·muh

Does it take long to prepare?
Дълго ли се готви? *duhl*·go lee se *got*·vee

Is it self-serve?
На самообслужване ли е? na sa·mo·ob·*sloozh*·va·ne lee e

Is there a cover/service charge?
Плаща ли се кувертът/ *plash*·ta lee se koo·*ver*·tuht/
обслужването? ob·*sloozh*·va·ne·to

Is service included in the bill?
Обслужването ob·*sloozh*·va·ne·to
включено ли е в сметката? *vklyoo*·che·no lee e v *smet*·ka·ta

Are these complimentary?
Тези безплатни ли са? *te*·zee bez·*plat*·nee lee suh

Could I see the wine list, please?
Моля, дайте ми *mol*·yuh *dai*·te mee
листата с вината. *lees*·ta·ta s vee·*na*·ta

Can you recommend a good local wine?
Можете ли да ми *mo*·zhe·te lee da mee
препоръчате някое pre·po·*ruh*·cha·te *nya*·koy·e
хубаво местно вино? *hoo*·ba·vo *mest*·no *vee*·no

I'd like (a/the) ..., please.	Дайте ми ..., моля.	dai·te mee ... mol·yuh
children's menu	детското меню	det·sko·to me·nyoo
drink list	листата с напитките	lees·ta·ta s na·peet·kee·te
half portion	половин порция	po·lo·veen por·tsee·ya
local speciality	някой местен специалитет	nya·koy mes·ten spe·tsee·a·lee·tet
meal fit for a king	царска трапеза	tsar·ska tra·pe·za
menu (in English)	менюто (на английски)	me·nyoo·to (na an·gleey·skee)
(non)smoking section	маса за (не)пушачи	ma·sa za (ne·)poo·sha·chee
table for (five)	маса за (пет) човека	ma·sa za (pet) cho·ve·ka
that dish	онова блюдо	o·no·va blyoo·do

listen for ...

Къде искате да седнете? kuh·de ees·ka·te da sed·ne·te	Where would you like to sit?
Какво ще желаете? kak·vo shte zhe·la·ye·te	What can I get for you?
Заповядайте! za·po·vya·dai·te	Here you go!
Добър апетит. do·buhr a·pe·teet	Enjoy your meal.
Обичате ли ...? o·bee·cha·te lee ...	Do you like ...?
Препоръчвам ... pre·po·ruhch·vam ...	I suggest the ...
Как искате да го приготвим? kak ees·ka·te da go pree·got·veem	How would you like that cooked?

FOOD

166

Предястия	pred·*yas*·tee·ya	Appetisers
Ордьоври	or·*dyo*·vree	Entrées
Супи	*soo*·pee	Soups
Салати	sa·*la*·tee	Salads
Основни ястия	os·*nov*·nee *yas*·tee·ya	Main Courses
Аламинути	a·la·mee·*noo*·tee	Prepared to Order
Скара	*ska*·ra	From the Grill
Гарнитури	gar·nee·*too*·ree	Side Dishes
Десерти	de·*ser*·tee	Desserts
Аперитиви	a·pe·ree·*tee*·vee	Apéritifs
Безалкохолни напитки	bez·al·ko·*hol*·nee na·*peet*·kee	Soft Drinks
Алкохолни напитки	al·ko·*hol*·nee na·*peet*·kee	Spirits
Бири	*bee*·ree	Beers
Шумящи вина	shoo·*myash*·tee vee·*na*	Sparkling Wines
Бели вина	*be*·lee vee·*na*	White Wines
Червени вина	cher·*ve*·nee vee·*na*	Red Wines
Десертни вина	de·*sert*·nee vee·*na*	Dessert Wines

For additional items, see the **menu decoder**, page 181.

I'd like it with/ without ...	Моля, дайте ми го с/без ...	*mol*·yuh *dai*·te mee go s/bez ...
cheese	кашкавал	kash·ka·*val*
chilli	люти чушки	*lyoo*·tee *choosh*·kee
chilli sauce	чили сос	*chee*·lee sos
garlic	чесън	*che*·suhn
ketchup	кетчуп	*ket*·choop
nuts	ядки	*yad*·kee
oil	олио	o·lee·o
pepper	пипер	pee·*per*
salt	сол	sol
tomato sauce	доматен сос	do·*ma*·ten sos
vinegar	оцет	o·*tset*

For other specific meal requests, see **vegetarian & special meals**, page 179.

at the table

Please bring a/the ...	Моля, донесете ...	*mol*·yuh *do*·ne·*se*·te ...
bill	сметката	*smet*·ka·ta
cutlery	прибори	*pree*·bo·ree
(wine)glass	чаша (за вино)	*cha*·sha (za *vee*·no)
serviette	салфетка	sal·*fet*·ka
tablecloth	покривка	po·*kreev*·ka

I didn't order this.

Аз не съм поръчвал/   az ne suhm po·*ruhch*·val/
поръчвала това. m/f   po·ruhch·*va*·la to·*va*

There's a mistake in the bill.

В сметката има грешка.   v *smet*·ka·ta *ee*·ma *gresh*·ka

street eats

баnички f pl	*ba*·neech·kee	cheese pastries
гевреци m pl	ge·*vre*·tsee	large pretzels
дюнер кебаб m	dyoo·*ner* ke·*bab*	doner kebab
палачинки f pl	pa·la·*cheen*·kee	pancakes
сладолед m	sla·do·*led*	ice cream
слънчогледови семки f pl	sluhn·cho·*gle*·do·vee *sem*·kee	sunflower seeds
тиквени семки f pl	*teek*·ve·nee *sem*·kee	pumpkin seeds
фъстъци m pl	fuh·*stuh*·tsee	peanuts
царевица f	*tsa*·re·vee·tsa	corn on the cob

talking food

That was delicious!

Това беше много вкусно!   to·*va* be·she *mno*·go vkoos·no

I'm full.

Преядох.   pre·*ya*·doh

I love this dish.
Много харесвам това
ястие.

mno·go ha·res·vam to·va
yas·tee·e

I love the local cuisine.
Много харесвам
местната кухня.

mno·go ha·res·vam
mest·na·ta kooh·nya

My compliments to the chef.
Моите поздравления
за готвача.

mo·yee·te poz·drav·le·nee·ya
za got·va·chuh

This is stale.
Това не е прясно.

to·va ne e pryas·no

This is …	Това е …	*to·va e …*
burnt	изгорено	*eez·go·re·no*
(too) cold	(прекалено)	*(pre·ka·le·no)*
	студено	*stoo·de·no*
(too) spicy	(прекалено)	*(pre·ka·le·no)*
	люто	*lyoo·to*
superb	отлично	*ot·leech·no*

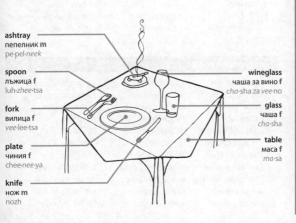

ashtray
пепелник **m**
pe·pel·neek

spoon
лъжица **f**
luh·zhee·tsa

fork
вилица **f**
vee·lee·tsa

plate
чиния **f**
chee·nee·ya

knife
нож **m**
nozh

wineglass
чаша за вино **f**
cha·sha za vee·no

glass
чаша **f**
cha·sha

table
маса **f**
ma·sa

methods of preparation

I'd like it …	Предпочитам да е …	pred·po·chee·tam da e …
I don't want it …	Предпочитам да не е …	pred·po·chee·tam da ne e …
boiled	варено	va·re·no
broiled	печено	pe·che·no
deep-fried	пържено	puhr·zhe·no
fried	пържено	puhr·zhe·no
grilled	на скара	na ska·ra
mashed	на пюре	na pyoo·re
medium	средно изпечено	sred·no eez·pe·che·no
rare	алангле	a·lan·gle
reheated	претоплено	pre·top·le·no
steamed	варено на пара	va·re·no na pa·ra
well-done	добре изпечено	do·bre eez·pe·che·no
without …	без …	bez …
with the dressing on the side	със соса отделно	suhs so·sa ot·del·no

coffee, anyone?

black coffee	кафе без мляко n	ka·fe bez mlya·ko
cappuccino	капучино n	ka·poo·chee·no
decaffeinated	без кофеин	bez ko·fe·een
espresso	еспресо n	es·pre·so
iced coffee	айскафе n	ais·ka·fe
instant coffee	нескафе n	nes·ka·fe
strong coffee	силно кафе n	seel·no ka·fe
Turkish coffee	турско кафе n	toor·sko ka·fe
Viennese coffee	виенско кафе n	vee·en·sko ka·fe
weak coffee	слабо кафе n	sla·bo ka·fe
white coffee	кафе с мляко n	ka·fe s mlya·ko

nonalcoholic drinks

безалкохолни напитки

(cup of) coffee …	(чаша) кафе …	(cha·sha) ka·fe …
(cup of) tea …	(чаша) чай …	(cha·sha) chai …
with (milk)	с (мляко)	s (mlya·ko)
without (sugar)	без (захар)	bez (za·har)
… mineral water	… минерална вода	… mee·ne·ral·na vo·da
sparkling	газирана	ga·zee·ra·na
still	негазирана	ne·ga·zee·ra·na
(orange) juice	(портокалов) сок m	(por·to·ka·lov) sok
soft drink	безалкохолна напитка f	bez·al·ko·hol·na na·peet·ka
(boiled) water	(преварена) вода f	(pre·va·re·na) vo·da

alcoholic drinks

алкохолни напитки

beer	бира f	bee·ra
(local) brandy	ракия f	ra·kee·ya
champagne	шампанско n	sham·pan·sko
a shot of whisky	едно малко уиски	ed·no mal·ko oo·ees·kee
a shot of …	един малък …	e·deen ma·luhk …
gin	джин	dzheen
rum	ром	rom
a shot of …	една малка …	ed·na mal·ka …
tequila	текила	te·kee·la
vodka	водка	vod·ka

171

a bottle/glass	бутилка/чаша	boo·*teel*·ka/*cha*·sha
of … wine	… вино	… *vee*·no
dessert	десертно	de·*sert*·no
red	червено	cher·*ve*·no
sparkling	шумящо	shoo·*myash*·to
white	бяло	*bya*·lo
a … of beer	… бира	… *bee*·ra
glass	чаша	*cha*·sha
jug	кана	*ka*·na
large bottle	голяма	go·*lya*·ma
	бутилка	boo·*teel*·ka
small bottle	малка бутилка	*mal*·ka boo·*teel*·ka

For additional items, see the **menu decoder**, page 181, and the **dictionary**.

local drinks

Bulgarians' favourite alcoholic drinks are beer, wine and *ракия* ra·*kee*·ya (brandy usually made from grapes, but sometimes from plums or apricots). Red wines from Melnik and Asenovgrad are made from the *мавруд* mav·*rood* and *гъмза* *guhm*·za grapes, which aren't found anywhere else in the world. Vodka, whisky, gin, *мента* *men*·ta (crème de menthe) and *мастика* mas·*tee*·ka (ouzo) are also popular.

in the bar

в бара

Before taking a sip, wait until everyone in the group is served and someone offers a toast, either in spoken form or by means of eye contact and a raised glass. Common toasts are *Да сме живи и здрави!* da sme *zhee*·vee ee *zdra*·vee (May we live in health!) and *За много години!* za *mno*·go go·*dee*·nee (To many years!). 'Topping up' isn't done in Bulgaria: a glass should be drained before it's refilled.

Excuse me!
Моля.   *mol*·yuh

I'm next.
Аз съм на ред.   az suhm na red

I'll have a brandy.
За мене ракия.   za *me*·ne ra·*kee*·ya

Same again, please.
Същото, моля.   *suhsh*·to·to *mol*·yuh

No ice, thanks.
Без лед, моля.   bez led *mol*·yuh

I'll buy you a drink.
Аз черпя.   az *cher*·pyuh

What would you like?
Какво ще пиете/пиеш? **pol/inf**   kak·*vo* shte *pee*·e·te/*pee*·esh

I don't drink alcohol.
Не пия алкохол.   ne *pee*·yuh al·ko·*hol*

It's my round.
Сега е моят ред   se·*ga* e *mo*·yuht red
да почерпя.   da po·*cherp*·yuh

How much is that?
Колко струва?   *kol*·ko *stroo*·va

Do you serve meals here?
Тука сервирате ли храна?   *too*·ka ser·*vee*·ra·te lee hra·*na*

eating out

---

ready to order?

Beer and wine are ordered either by the glass or by the bottle. Spirits are ordered according to standard sizes – 50 grams (small), 100 grams (large), 200 grams (double) – eg *една малка/голяма/двойна ракия* ed·*na* mal·ka/go·*lya*·ma/*dvoy*·na ra·*kee*·ya (a small/large/double brandy) or *един малък/голям/двоен джин* e·*deen* ma·luhk/go·*lyam*/*dvo*·yen dzheen (a small/large/double gin). A minibottle of spirits (eg as served on a plane) is called a *патрончe* pa·*tron*·che.

drinking up

Cheers!
На здраве! · na *zdra*·ve

This is hitting the spot.
Това е върхът. · to·*va* e vuhr·*huht*

I feel fantastic!
Чувствам се страхотно! · *choovs*·tvam se stra·*hot*·no

I think I've had one too many.
Май се понапих. · mai se po·na·*peeh*

I'm feeling drunk.
Пиян/Пияна съм. m/f · pee·*yan*/pee·*ya*·na suhm

I'm pissed.
Аз съм кьоркютук · az suhm kyor·kyoo·*took*
пиян/пияна. m/f · pee·*yan*/pee·*ya*·na

I feel ill.
Не ми е добре. · ne mee e do·*bre*

Where's the toilet?
Къде е тоалетната? · kuh·*de* e to·a·*let*·na·ta

I'm tired, I'd better go home.
Уморен/Уморена съм, · oo·mo·*ren*/oo·mo·*re*·na suhm
по-добре да се · po·do·*bre* da se
прибирам. m/f · pree·*bee*·ram

I don't think you should drive.
Не трябва да карате/ · ne *tryab*·va da *ka*·ra·te/
караш кола. pol/inf · *ka*·rash ko·*la*

---

listen for ...

Какво пиете/пиеш? pol/inf
   kak·*vo* pee·e·te/*pee*·esh — **What are you having?**

Стига толкова.
   stee·ga *tol*·ko·va — **I think you've had enough.**

Последна поръчка.
   po·*sled*·na po·*ruhch*·ka — **Last orders.**

buying food

купуване на храна

What's the local speciality?
Какъв е местният
специалитет?
ka·*kuhv* e *mest*·nee·yuht
spe·tsee·a·lee·*tet*

Is this locally produced?
Това местно
производство ли е?
to·*va mest*·no
pro·eez·*vods*·tvo lee e

What's that?
Какво е това?
kak·*vo* e to·*va*

Can I taste it?
Мога ли да го пробвам?
mo·guh lee da go *prob*·vam

Can I have a bag, please?
Дайте ми един плик, моля.
dai·te mee e·*deen* pleek *mol*·yuh

I don't need a bag, thanks.
Не ми трябва плик,
благодаря.
ne mee *tryab*·va pleek
bla·go·dar·*yuh*

How much is (a kilo of cheese)?
Колко струва (един
килограм кашкавал)?
kol·ko *stroo*·va (e·*deen*
kee·lo·*gram* kash·ka·*val*)

food stuff

cooked	сготвен	*sgot*·ven
cured	пушен	*poo*·shen
dried	сушен	soo·*shen*
fresh	пресен	*pre*·sen
frozen	замразен	za·*mra*·zen
home-made	домашен	do·*ma*·shen
raw	суров	soo·*rov*
smoked	пушен	*poo*·shen
steamed	сварен на пара	sva·*ren* na *pa*·ra

I'd like …	Дайте ми, моля …	*dai*·te mee *mol*·yuh …
(200) grams	(двеста) грама	(*dve*·sta) *gra*·ma
half a dozen	половин дузина	po·lo·*veen* doo·*zee*·na
a dozen	дузина	doo·*zee*·na
half a kilo	половин кило	po·lo·*veen* kee·*lo*
a kilo	едно кило	ed·*no* kee·*lo*
(two) kilos	(две) кила	(dve) kee·*la*
a bottle	една бутилка	ed·*na* boo·*teel*·ka
a jar	един буркан	e·*deen* boor·*kan*
a packet	една опаковка	ed·*na* o·pa·*kov*·ka
a piece	едно парче	ed·*no* par·*che*
(three) pieces	(три) парчета	(tree) par·*che*·ta
a slice	една филия	ed·*na* fee·*lee*·ya
(six) slices	(шест) филии	(shest) fee·*lee*·e
a tin	една кутия	ed·*na* koo·*tee*·ya
(just) a little	(само) малко	(*sa*·mo) *mal*·ko
more	още	*osh*·te
some	няколко	*nya*·kol·ko
that one	онова там	o·no·*va* tam
this one	това тук	to·*va* took

Less.	По-малко.	po·*mal*·ko
Enough.	Достатъчно.	do·*sta*·tuhch·no
More.	Повече.	*po*·ve·che

FOOD

listen for …		
С какво мога да ви помогна?	s kak·*vo* *mo*·guh da vee po·*mog*·nuh	Can I help you?
Какво желаете?	kak·*vo* zhe·*la*·ye·te	What would you like?
Още нещо?	*osh*·te *nesh*·to	Anything else?
Няма.	*nya*·ma	There isn't any.

Where can I find the ... section?	Къде се намира отделът за ...?	kuh·*de* se na·*mee*·ra ot·*de*·luht za ...
dairy	млечни продукти	*mlech*·nee pro·*dook*·tee
fish	риби	*ree*·bee
frozen goods	замразени стоки	za·*mra*·ze·nee *sto*·kee
fruit and vegetable	плодове и зеленчуци	plo·do·*ve* ee ze·len·*choo*·tsee
health-food	здравословни храни	zdra·vo·*slov*·nee hra·*nee*
meat	месо	me·*so*
poultry	домашни птици	do·*mash*·nee *ptee*·tsee

For food items, see the **menu decoder**, page 181, and the **dictionary**.

Do you have …?	Имате ли …?	*ee*·ma·te lee …
anything	нещо	*nesh*·to
cheaper	по-евтино	*po*·ev·tee·no
other kinds	други видове	*droo*·gee *vee*·do·ve

cooking utensils

кухненски съдове и прибори

I need a …	Трябва ми …	*tryab*·va mee …
Could I please	Моля, мога ли	*mol*·yuh *mo*·guh lee
borrow a …?	да взема	da *vze*·muh
	назаем …?	na·*za*·em …
chopping	дъска за	*duhs*·ka za
board	рязане	*rya*·za·ne
frying pan	тиган	tee·*gan*
knife	нож	nozh
saucepan	тенджера	*tend*·zhe·ra

For more cooking implements, see the **dictionary**.

diminutives

Bulgarian is rich in diminutives – these are words (created by the addition of certain endings) that sometimes express the idea of smallness, but more often they indicate famil- iarity or affection (like 'doggy' in English) – for example, *пиле* n *pee*·le (chick) becomes *пиленце* n *pee*·len·tse (sweet- heart). Personal names, nouns, adjectives and even verbs can all be transformed into diminutives in Bulgarian. Here are some more examples of the base word followed by the diminutive form:

Милена f (name) mee·*le*·na	**Миленче** n mee·*len*·che
нож m (knife) nozh	**ножче** n *nozh*·che
ракия f (brandy) ra·*kee*·ya	**ракийка** f ra·*keey*·ka
салата f (salad) sa·*la*·ta	**салатка** f sa·*lat*·ka
спя v (sleep) spyuh	**спинкам** *speen*·kam
хубав a (nice) *hoo*·bav	**хубавички** *hoo*·ba·veech·kee

ordering food

поръчване на храна

Do you have	Имате ли	*ee*·ma·te lee
... food?	... храна?	... hra·*na*
kosher	кашер	ka·*sher*
vegetarian	вегетарианска	ve·ge·ta·ree·*an*·ska
Is it cooked	С ... ли е	s ... lee e
in/with ...?	сготвено?	*sgot*·ve·no
butter	краве масло	*kra*·ve *mas*·lo
eggs	яйца	yai·*tsa*
fish	риба	*ree*·ba
fish stock	рибен бульон	*ree*·ben boo·*lyon*
meat	месо	me·*so*
meat stock	месен бульон	*me*·sen boo·*lyon*
oil	олио	o·lee·o
pork	свинско месо	*sveen*·sko me·*so*
poultry	домашни птици	do·*mash*·nee *ptee*·tsee
red meat	червено месо	cher·*ve*·no me·*so*
Is this ...?	Това ... ли е?	to·*va* ... lee e
decaffeinated	без кофеин	bez ko·fe·*een*
free of animal produce	без животински продукти	bez zhee·vo·*teen*·skee pro·*dook*·tee
genetically modified	генетически модифицирано	ge·ne·*tee*·ches·kee mo·dee·fee·*tsee*·ra·no
gluten-free	без глутен	bez *gloo*·ten
low-fat	ниско на мазнина	*nees*·ko na maz·nee·*na*
low in sugar	с малко захар	s *mal*·ko *za*·har
organic	органично	or·ga·*neech*·no
salt-free	безсолно	bez·*sol*·no

special diets & allergies

I'm on a special diet.
Аз съм на специална
диета.
az suhm na spe·tsee·*al*·na
dee·*e*·ta

I'm a vegan.
Аз съм пълен
вегетарианец. m
az suhm *puh*·len
ve·ge·ta·ree·*a*·nets
Аз съм пълна
вегетарианка. f
az suhm *puhl*·na
ve·ge·ta·ree·*an*·ka

I'm a vegetarian.
Аз съм вегетарианец/
вегетарианка. m/f
az suhm ve·ge·ta·ree·*a*·nets/
ve·ge·ta·ree·*an*·ka

I don't eat …
Аз не ям …
az ne yam …

I'm allergic to …	Аз съм алергичен/ алергична към … m/f	az suhm a·ler·*gee*·chen/ a·ler·*geech*·na kuhm …
dairy produce	млечни продукти	*mlech*·nee pro·*dook*·tee
eggs	яйца	yai·*tsa*
gelatine	желатин	zhe·la·*teen*
gluten	глутен	*gloo*·ten
honey	мед	med
MSG	MSG	em·es·*dzhee*
nuts	ядки	*yad*·kee
peanuts	фъстъци	fuh·*stuh*·tsee
seafood	морски продукти	*mor*·skee pro·*dook*·tee

To explain your dietary restrictions with reference to religious beliefs, see **beliefs & cultural differences**, page 145.

This miniguide to Bulgarian cuisine is designed to help you get the most out of your gastronomic experience by providing you with food terms that you may see on menus. Nouns have their gender indicated by ⓜ (masculine), ⓕ (feminine) or ⓝ (neuter). If it's a plural noun, you'll also see pl. Adjectives are given in the masculine form only. For more information, see the **phrasebuilder**.

> This **menu decoder** has been ordered according to the Cyrillic alphabet, shown below in both roman and italic text:
>
> Аа Бб Вв Гг Дд Ее Жж Зз Ии Йй Кк Лл Мм Нн Оо Пп
> *Аа Бб Вв Гг Дд Ее Жж Зз Ии Йй Кк Лл Мм Нн Оо Пп*
>
> Рр Сс Тт Уу Фф Хх Цц Чч Шш Щщ Ъъ ь Юю Яя
> *Рр Сс Тт Уу Фф Хх Цц Чч Шш Щщ Ъъ ь Юю Яя*

А

агнешка главичка ⓕ
ag·nesh·ka gla·veech·ka lamb's head

агнешка курбан-чорба ⓕ
ag·nesh·ka kur·ban·chor·ba
boiled lamb cut into cubes with chopped onion, paprika, rice, parsley & eggs

агнешка яхния ⓕ *ag·nesh·ka*
yah·nee·ya stewed lamb with onion

агнешко ⓝ *ag·nesh·ko* lamb

агнешко филе с горчица ⓝ
ag·nesh·ko fee·le s gor·chee·tsa
lamb fillet with mustard sauce

агнешко шкембе-чорба ⓕ
ag·nesh·ko shkem·be·chor·ba
seasoned lamb in milk

агнешки кебап ⓜ *ag·nesh·kee ke·bap*
lamb shish kebab

айрян ⓜ *ai·ryan* liquefied yogurt drink

айскафе ⓝ *ais·ka·fe* iced coffee

акула ⓕ *a·koo·la* shark

аланглле *a·lan·gle* rare (of meat)

алкохолни напитки ⓕ pl
al·ko·hol·nee na·peet·kee alcoholic drinks

ананас ⓝ *a·na·nas* pineapple

аперитиви ⓜ pl *a·pe·ree·tee·vee*
apéritifs

артишок ⓜ *ar·tee·shok* artichoke

аспержи ⓜ *as·per·zhe* asparagus

ашуре ⓕ *a·shoo·re*
milk soup with bulgur (cracked wheat)

Б

бадеми ⓜ pl *ba·de·mee* almonds

баклава ⓕ *bak·la·va*
flaky pastry with walnuts or pistachios & cinnamon, honey or sugar syrup

банан ⓜ *ba·nan* banana

баница ⓕ *ba·nee·tsa*
flaky pastry stuffed with white cheese

банички ⓕ pl *ba·neech·kee*
cheese pastries

безалкохолни напитки ⓕ pl
bez·al·ko·hol·nee na·peet·kee
soft drinks

без кофеин bez ko·fe·een decaffeinated

бекон ⓜ *be·kon* bacon

биволско мляко ⓝ *bee·vol·sko mlya·ko*
water buffalo milk

билки ⓕ pl *beel·kee* herbs

билков чай ⓜ *beel·kov chai* herbal tea

бира ⓕ *bee·ra* beer

бисквита ⓕ *beesk·vee·ta* biscuit

бисквити с орехи ⓕ pl
beesk·vee·tee s o·re·hee
biscuits made with crushed walnuts

бифтек m *beef·tek* steak
боб m bob seasoned bean soup
бобово растение n
    bo·bo·vo ras·te·ne·e·e legume
боза f *bo·za*
    millet ale (also made from other grains)
брашно n *brash·no* flour
бульон m *boo·lyon* consommé · stock
бъркан *buhr·kan* scrambled
бъркани яйца с печени чушки n pl
    *buhr·ka·nee yai·tsa s pe·che·nee
    choosh·kee* scrambled eggs with diced
    roasted peppers & grated white cheese
бяло вино n *bya·lo vee·no* white wine

В

варен *va·ren* boiled
варено жито n *va·re·no zhee·to*
    boiled wheat
вечеря f *ve·cher·ya* dinner
виенско кафе n *vee·en·sko ka·fe*
    Viennese coffee
вино n *vee·no* wine
вита баница f *vee·ta ba·nee·tsa*
    thin flaky pastry stuffed with white
    cheese, yogurt & eggs
вишни f pl *veesh·nee* sour cherries
вода f *vo·da* water
водка f *vod·ka* vodka
вретено n *vre·te·no* seasoned pork
    burger filled with melted cheese

Г

газирана минерална вода f
    ga·zee·ra·na mee·ne·ral·na vo·da
    sparkling mineral water
гарнитура f *gar·nee·too·ra*
    garnish · side dish
гевреци m pl *ge·vre·tsee*
    large ring-shaped pretzels
гола праскова f *go·la pras·ko·va*
    nectarine
горчица f *gor·chee·tsa* mustard
градинарска чорба f
    gra·dee·nar·ska chor·ba
    soup of celery, carrots, parsley, cabbage
    & potatoes, with white cheese & milk
грах m *grah* peas

грозде n *groz·de* grapes
гроздова ракия f *groz·do·va ra·kee·ya*
    brandy made from grapes
гъби f pl *guh·bee* mushrooms
гювеч m *gyoo·vech*
    stew – peppers, tomatoes, aubergine,
    onions, potatoes, zucchini, carrots &
    sometimes meat, cooked in the oven
гювеч с овнешко месо m
    gyoo·vech s ov·nesh·ko me·so
    mutton & vegetable stew baked in an
    earthenware dish

Д

десерт m *de·sert* dessert
десертно вино n *de·sert·no vee·no*
    dessert wine
джин m *dzheen* gin
дивеч m *dee·vech* game (meat)
диня f *deen·ya* watermelon
добре изпечен *do·bre eez·pe·chen*
    well-done (of meat)
добуш торта f *do·boosh tor·ta*
    layered chocolate cake
доматен сос m *do·ma·ten sos*
    tomato sauce
домати m pl *do·ma·tee* tomatoes
домашни птици f pl
    do·mash·nee ptee·tsee poultry
домашно вино n *do·mash·no vee·no*
    home-made wine
дреболии f pl *dre·bo·lee·ee* giblets
дроб-сарма f *drob·sar·ma*
    boiled lamb's liver & intestines with
    rice & onions, wrapped in fat & baked
    in the oven
друсан кебап m *droo·san ke·bap* large
    cubes of meat fried in fat, then boiled,
    with spices, onions & parsley
дюли f pl *dyoo·lee* quinces
дюнер кебаб m *dyoo·ner ke·bab*
    doner kebab

Е

едра скарида f *ed·ra ska·ree·da* prawn
език m *e·zeek* tongue
есетра f *e·se·tra* sturgeon
еспресо n *es·pre·so* espresso coffee

З

задушен za·doo·shen *braised • poached*

заешко ⓝ za·esh·ko *rabbit*

закуска ① za·koos·ka *breakfast • snack*

захар ① za·har *sugar*

зеле ⓝ ze·le *cabbage*

зелена чушка ① ze·le·na choosh·ka
  green pepper

зелен лук ⓜ ze·len look *spring onion*

зелен фасул ⓜ ze·len fa·sool
  green beans

зеленчук ⓜ ze·len·chook *vegetable*

зехтин ⓜ zeh·teen *olive oil*

зрял фасул ⓜ zryal fa·sool
  *boiled kidney beans with onions, carrots,
  celery, dried red pepper & mint*

К

каварма ① ka·var·ma
  *meat or vegetable stew (usually pork or
  chicken), served in an earthenware pot*

кадаиф ⓜ ka·da·yeef
  shredded wheat stuffed with nuts in syrup

кайма ① kai·ma *mincemeat*

кайсиева ракия ① kai·see·e·va ra·kee·ya
  brandy made from apricots

кайсия ① kai·see·ya *apricot*

какао ⓝ ka·ka·o *cocoa*

калкан ⓜ kal·kan *turbot (fish)*

калмар ⓜ kal·mar *calamari*

капама ① ka·pa·ma *meat, rice &
  sauerkraut (or other ingredients),
  simmered & served in a clay pot*

капучино ⓝ ka·poo·chee·no
  cappuccino

карантия ① ka·ran·tee·ya *offal*

картофи ⓜ pl kar·to·fee *potatoes*

картофи със сирене ⓜ pl
  kar·to·fee suhs see·re·ne *fried potatoes
  topped with white cheese*

карфиол ⓜ kar·fee·ol *cauliflower*

кафе ⓝ ka·fe *coffee*

кафе без захар ⓝ ka·fe bez za·har
  coffee without sugar

кафе без кофеин ⓝ ka·fe bez ko·fe·een
  decaffeinated coffee

кафе без мляко ⓝ ka·fe bez mlya·ko
  black coffee

кафе с мляко ⓝ ka·fe s mlya·ko
  white coffee

качамак ⓜ ka·cha·mak *polenta*

кашкавал ⓜ kash·ka·val
  hard yellow cheese

кашкавал пане ⓜ kash·ka·val pa·ne
  fried yellow cheese in batter

кашу ⓝ ka·shoo *cashew*

кебабчета ⓝ pl ke·bab·che·ta
  grilled spicy meat sausages

кебап ⓜ ke·bap *kebab*

кебапчета на скара ⓜ pl
  ke·bap·che·ta na ska·ra
  *grilled, sausage-shaped pork meatballs
  mixed with finely chopped onion*

кекс ⓜ keks *loaf cake*

керевиз ⓜ ke·re·veez *celery*

кестени ⓜ pl kes·te·nee *chestnuts*

кисело мляко ⓝ kee·se·lo mlya·ko
  yogurt

кифла с мармалад ①
  keef·la s mar·ma·lad *jam-filled croissant*

козе мляко ⓝ ko·ze mlya·ko *goat's milk*

козунак ⓜ ko·zoo·nak
  plaited sweet bread

козуначена кифла ①
  ko·zoo·na·che·na keef·la
  *small bread roll made from slightly
  sweetened dough & flavoured with
  marmalade*

кокосов орех ⓜ ko·ko·sov o·reh
  coconut

коктейл ⓜ kok·teyl *cocktail*

конфитюр ⓜ kon·fee·tyoor *jam*

коняк ⓜ kon·yak *cognac*

костур ⓜ kos·toor *perch*

котлет на скара ⓜ kot·let na ska·ra
  grilled cutlet

краве масло ⓝ kra·ve mas·lo *butter*

краве мляко ⓝ kra·ve mlya·ko
  cow's milk

краставица ① kras·ta·vee·tsa *cucumber*

крем карамел ⓜ krem ka·ra·mel *custard*

круша ① kroo·sha *pear*

къпана баница ① kuh·pa·na ba·nee·tsa
  *'bathed bread' – ceremonial bread that's
  wrapped in cheesecloth & dropped in a
  large pot of tepid water prior to baking*

къпини ① pl kuh·pee·nee *blackberries*

menu decoder

183

кьопоолу ⓜ *kyo·po·o·loo*
eggplant purée with garlic, salt, vinegar, parsley & slices of tomato

кюфтета ⓜ pl *kyoof·te·ta* round meatballs similar to **кюфте татарско**

кюфте татарско ⓜ *kyoof·te ta·tar·sko* pork burger filled with melted cheese

Л

лайм ⓜ laim *lime*
лед ⓜ led *ice*
лефер ⓜ le·*fer bluefish*
лешници ⓜ pl *lesh·nee·tsee hazelnuts*
леща ⓕ pl *lesh·ta lentils*
лимон ⓜ lee·*mon lemon*
лимонада ⓕ lee·mo·*na·da lemonade*
локум ⓜ lo·*koom Turkish delight*
лук ⓜ look *onion*
луканка ⓕ loo·*kan·ka*
flat sausage, usually made from dried pork, beef & spices

лют lyoot *hot (spicy)*
лютеница ⓕ *lyoo·te·nee·tsa*
piquant sauce of red peppers & herbs • roasted pepper spread

люти чушки ⓕ pl *lyoo·tee choosh·kee*
chilli • hot peppers

М

магданоз ⓜ mag·da·*noz parsley*
майонеза ⓕ ma·yo·*ne·za mayonnaise*
макарони ⓜ ma·ka·ro·*nee pasta*
малини ⓕ pl ma·*lee·na raspberries*
мандарина ⓕ man·da·*ree·na mandarine*
маргарин ⓜ mar·ga·*reen margarine*
маруля ⓕ ma·*roo·lya lettuce*
маслина ⓕ mas·*lee·na olive*
масло ⓝ *mas·lo butter*
мастика ⓕ mas·*tee·ka ouzo*
мед ⓜ med *honey*
меденка ⓕ *me·den·ka*
honeyed round loaf

мента ⓕ *men·ta crème de menthe* • *mint*
ментов чай ⓜ *men·tov chai mint tea*
месен бульон ⓜ *me·sen boo·lyon*
meat stock

месо ⓝ me·*so meat*
мешана салата ⓕ *me·sha·na sa·la·ta*
mixed salad

миди ⓕ pl *mee·dee mussels*
миди цигане ⓕ pl *mee·dee tsee·ga·ne*
mussels sautéed with a spicy cheese & mustard sauce

минерална вода ⓕ *mee·ne·ral·na vo·da*
mineral water

миш-маш ⓜ *meesh·mash*
scrambled eggs with peppers, tomatoes, onions & grated white cheese

млечна баница ⓕ *mlech·na ba·nee·tsa*
sweet pastry made with milk & eggs

млечни продукти ⓜ pl
mlech·nee pro·dook·tee dairy produce

мляко ⓝ *mlya·ko milk*
мляко от соя ⓝ *mlya·ko ot so·ya*
soy milk

мозък ⓜ *mo·zuhk brains*
морков ⓜ *mor·kov carrot*
морски кефал ⓜ *mor·skee ke·fal*
grey mullet

морски костур ⓜ *mor·skee kos·toor*
sea bass

морски продукти ⓜ pl
mor·skee pro·dook·tee seafood

морски рак ⓜ *mor·skee rak crab*
мусака ⓕ moo·sa·*ka moussaka*
мусака от телешко месо ⓕ
moo·sa·*ka ot te·lesh·ko me·so*
minced veal, sliced eggplant & tomatoes, covered with a white sauce & baked

мюсли ⓜ *myoos·lee muesli*

Н

... на гюведже ⓜ *... na gyoo·ved·zhe*
casserole of ...

наденица ⓕ *na·de·nee·tsa sausage*
наливна бира ⓕ *na·leev·na bee·ra*
draught beer

напитки ⓕ pl *na·peet·kee drinks*
на пюре na pyoo·*re mashed*
на скара na ska·*ra grilled*
натурален сок ⓜ na·too·ra·*len sok*
fruit juice not freshly squeezed (unlike фреш от ...)

негазирана минерална вода ⓕ
ne·ga·zee·ra·na mee·ne·ral·na vo·da
still mineral water

нескафе ⓝ nes·ka·*fe instant coffee*

О

обед ⓜ *o·bed* lunch

обезмаслено мляко ⓝ
o·bez·mas·le·no mlya·ko skim milk

овесени ядки ⓝ pl *o·ve·se·nee yad·kee*
oatmeal

овнешко ⓝ *ov·nesh·ko* mutton

овнешко-пилаф ⓜ *ov·nesh·ko·pee·laf*
cubed mutton fried with rice, onions,
seasonings & tomatoes, then cooked

овче мляко ⓝ *ov·che mlya·ko* ewe's milk

олио ⓝ *o·lee·o* oil

омлет ⓜ *om·let* omelette

ордьоври ⓜ pl *or·dyo·vree* entrées

орехи ⓜ pl *o·re·hee* walnuts

ориз ⓜ *o·reez* rice

основни ястия ⓝ pl
os·nov·nee yas·tee·ya main courses

охлюв ⓜ *oh·lyoov* snail

оцет ⓜ *o·tset* vinegar

ошаф ⓜ *o·shaf* stewed dried fruit

П

палачинки ⓕ pl *pa·la·cheen·kee*
pancakes

панирана риба ⓕ *pa·nee·ra·na ree·ba*
deep-fried battered fish

паста ⓕ *pas·ta* pastry

пъстърва ⓕ *pas·tuhr·va* mountain trout

пататник ⓜ *pa·tat·neek* hearty cheese &
potato omelette

патешки сърца ⓝ pl
pa·tesh·kee suhr·tsa ducks' hearts

патица ⓕ *pa·tee·tsa* duck

патладжан ⓜ *pat·lad·zhan*
aubergine • eggplant

пача ⓕ *pa·cha*
jellied leg of pork with onion, carrots,
pepper & pickled cucumbers

печен *pe·chen* baked • broiled • roasted

печени чушки ⓕ pl
pe·che·nee choosh·kee roasted peppers

печени ядки ⓝ pl *pe·che·nee yad·kee*
roasted nuts

печено пиле с домати ⓝ
pe·che·no pee·le s do·ma·tee
chicken with tomatoes roasted in the
oven & served with rice

пилешка дроб-сарма ⓜ
pee·lesh·ka drob·sar·ma
chicken livers with rice & yogurt

пилешка супа (със зеленчуци) ⓕ
pee·leesh·ka soo·pa (suhs
ze·len·choo·tsee)
chicken soup (with vegetables)

пилешко ⓝ *pee·lesh·ko* chicken (meat)

пиле яхния ⓕ *pee·le yah·nee·ya*
chicken & onion stew

пипер ⓜ *pee·per* pepper

пирог ⓜ *pee·rog* pie

питка ⓕ *peet·ka* bread roll

пица ⓕ *pee·tsa* pizza

… плакия ⓕ *… pla·kee·ya*
a way of preparing fish by baking it in
an earthenware pot, usually in a rich
tomato sauce

плод ⓜ *plod* fruit

плодов чай ⓜ *plo·dov chai* fruit tea

понички ⓕ pl *po·neech·kee*
pastries similar in taste to doughnuts
but differently shaped

попарен *po·pa·ren* poached (egg)

портокал ⓜ *por·to·kal* orange

портокалов сок ⓜ *por·to·ka·lov sok*
orange juice

праз ⓜ *praz* leek

праскова ⓕ *pras·ko·va* peach

преварена вода ⓕ *pre·va·re·na vo·da*
boiled water

предястия ⓝ pl *pred·yas·tee·ya*
appetisers • starters

препечен хляб ⓜ *pre·pe·chen hlyab*
toast • toasted sandwich

пресен *pre·sen* fresh

принцеса ⓕ *preen·tse·sa* snack of
mincemeat paste served on toast

пуйка ⓕ *pooy·ka* turkey

пушен *poo·shen* cured • smoked

пушена шунка ⓕ *poo·she·na shoon·ka*
smoked leg of ham

пушено сирене ⓝ *poo·she·no see·re·ne*
smoked cheese

пълнен *puhl·nen* stuffed

пълнена риба на фурна ⓕ
puhl·ne·na ree·ba na foor·na
carp, sea bass or pike stuffed with rice,
hazelnuts, basil & rosemary, then baked

пълнени гъби ① pl
puhl·ne·nee guh·bee stuffed mushrooms
пълнени пиперки с месо ① pl
puhl·ne·nee pee·per·kee s me·so
peppers stuffed with minced veal or
pork, paprika & rice, then cooked
пълнени тиквички ① pl *puhl·ne·nee*
teek·veech·kee zucchini stuffed with
cheese, vegetables and/or meat
пълнени чушки ① pl
puhl·ne·nee choosh·kee stuffed peppers
пълнен патладжан ⓜ
puhl·nen pat·lad·zhan
aubergine stuffed with meat & vegetables
пъпеш ⓜ *puh·pesh* melon
пържен *puhr·zhen*
deep-fried • fried • sautéed
пържени картофи ① pl
puhr·zhe·nee kar·to·fee chips • French fries
пържени картофи по селски ⓜ pl
puhr·zhe·nee kar·to·fee po sel·skee
fried potatoes (country-style)
пържени филийки ① pl
puhr·zhe·nee fee·leey·kee French toast
пържоли ① pl *puhr·zho·lee* chops (meat)
пюре от чушки ⓜ *pyoo·re ot choosh·kee*
red pepper condiment used as a garnish
for broiled or barbecued meat

Р

ракия ① *ra·kee·ya*
brandy (usually made from grapes, but
also from plums or apricots)
репичка ① *re·peech·ka* radish
речен рак ⓜ *re·chen rak* crayfish
риба ① *ree·ba* fish
риба в плик ① *ree·ba v pleek* salted
fish covered with soft dough & cooked
between sheets of greaseproof paper
риба-плакия ① *ree·ba·pla·kee·ya*
baked fish (usually carp) with paprika &
tomato paste
риба тон ① *ree·ba ton* tuna
рогче ⓝ *rog·che* small horn-shaped
bread bun with a cheese filling
розе ① *ro·ze* rosé (wine)
ром ① *rom* rum
рохък *ro·huhk* soft-boiled
ряпа ① *rya·pa* turnip

С

салам ⓜ *sa·lam* salami
салата ① *sa·la·ta* salad
салата от зеле и моркови ①
sa·la·ta ot ze·le ee mor·ko·vee
coleslaw (cabbage & carrot salad)
сандвич ⓜ *sand·veech* sandwich
сардина ① *sar·dee·na* sardine
сарми с лозов лист ① pl
sar·mee s lo·zov leest vine leaves stuffed
with minced lamb or veal & rice, then
cooked in a sauce of tomatoes, served
with sour cream or yogurt
сарми със зелеви листа ① pl
sar·mee suhs ze·le·vee lees·ta
cabbage leaves stuffed with minced
meat & rice (can also be meatless)
сварен на пара *sva·ren na pa·ra* steamed
свински кебап ⓜ *sveen·skee ke·bap*
pork shish kebab
свинско ⓝ *sveen·sko* pork
свинско филе ⓝ *sveen·sko fee·le*
pork fillet
сготвен *sgot·ven* cooked
сини боровинки ① pl
see·nee bo·ro·veen·kee blueberries
сирене ⓝ *see·re·ne* soft white cheese
сирене по шопски ⓜ
see·re·ne po shop·skee white cheese,
eggs & tomatoes baked in a clay pot
скара ① *ska·ra* grill
скарида ① *ska·ree·da* shrimp
скумрия ① *skoom·ree·ya* mackerel
сладолед ⓜ *sla·do·led* ice cream
слива ① *slee·va* plum
сливова ракия ① *slee·vo·va ra·kee·ya*
brandy made from plums
слънчогледови семки ① pl
sluhn·cho·gle·do·vee sem·kee
sunflower seeds
сметана ① *sme·ta·na* cream • sour cream
сметанова торта ① *sme·ta·no·va tor·ta*
cream cake
смокиня ① *smo·kee·nya* fig
снежанка ① *sne·zhan·ka*
salad of pickled cucumbers & plain yogurt
соев сос ⓜ *so·yev sos* soy sauce
сок ⓜ *sok* juice

сол ⑪ sol *salt*

соленка ① so-*len*-ka *cracker*

сом ⑪ som *sheatfish (European catfish)*

сос ⑪ sos *sauce*

спанак ⑪ spa-*nak spinach*

спанак загора ⑪ spa-*nak* za-*go*-ra
*spinach baked with sour cream, walnuts,
parmesan, garlic, onions & spices*

спанак със сирене ⑪
spa-*nak* suhs see-re-ne
spinach purée with white cheese

средно изпечен sred-no eez-pe-chen
medium (of meat)

стафида ① sta-*fee*-da *raisin • sultana*

стрида ① *stree*-da *oyster*

супа ① *soo*-pa *soup*

супа топчета ① *soo*-pa *top*-che-ta
meatball soup

суров *soo*-rov *raw*

сушен *soo*-shen *dried*

сушени плодове ⑪ pl
soo-she-nee plo-do-ve *dried fruit*

сьомга ① *syom*-ga *salmon*

Т

таратор ⑪ ta-ra-*tor*
*chilled soup made with finely chopped
cucumber, yogurt, walnuts & spices*

твърдо сварен tvuhr-do sva-ren
hard-boiled

текила ① te-*kee*-la *tequila*

телешко ⑪ te-*lesh*-ko *beef • veal*

телешко със сини сливи ⑪ te-*lesh*-ko
suhs *see*-nee *slee*-vee *veal with prunes*

телешко филе ⑪ te-*lesh*-ko fee-*le*
veal fillet

тиква ① *teek*-va *pumpkin*

тиквеник ⑪ *teek*-ve-neek *pumpkin pie*

тиквени семки ① pl
teek-ve-nee *sem*-kee *pumpkin seeds*

тиквички ① pl *teek*-veech-kee
courgette • zucchini

тиквички с кисело мляко и чесен ① pl
teek-veech-kee suhs *kee*-se-lo *mlya*-ko
ee *che*-sen *zucchini in yogurt sauce*

топли напитки ① pl *top*-lee na-*peet*-kee
hot drinks

торта ① *tor*-ta *cake*

тофу ⑪ to-*foo tofu*

турско кафе ⑪ *toor*-sko ka-*fe*
Turkish coffee

туршия ① toor-*shee*-ya
pickled vegetables

тюрлюгювеч ⑪ tyoor-lyoo-gyoo-*vech*
*diced mutton stewed with tomatoes,
peppers & potatoes in an
earthenware pot*

У

уиски ⑪ oo-*ees*-kee *whisky*

Ф

фасул ⑪ fa-*sool beans*

филе ⑪ fee-*le fillet*

фреш (от …) ⑪ fresh (ot …)
freshly squeezed juice (of … fruit)

фурма ① foor-*ma date*

фъстъци ⑪ pl fuh-*stuh*-tsee *peanuts*

Х

хайвер ⑪ hai-*ver roe*

халва ① hal-*va dessert of melted butter,
sugar & water, served with crushed
walnuts & cinnamon*

хамбургер ⑪ *ham*-boor-ger *hamburger*

херинга ① he-*reen*-ga *herring*

хлебче ⑪ *hleb*-che *bread roll*

хляб ⑪ hlyab *bread*

хотдог ⑪ *hot*-dog *hot dog*

Ц

царевица ① tsa-re-*vee*-tsa
corn on the cob

Ч

чай ⑪ chai *tea*

чай без захар ⑪ chai bez *za*-har
tea without sugar

чай с лимон ⑪ chai s li-*mon*
tea with lemon

чай с мляко ⑪ chai s *mlya*-ko
tea with milk

червени боровинки ① pl
cher-*ve*-nee bo-ro-*veen*-kee *cranberries*

червено вино ⑪ cher-*ve*-no *vee*-no
red wine

червено месо ⓝ cher·ve·no me·so
  red meat
червен пипер ⓜ cher·ven pee·per
  paprika • red pepper
черен дроб ⓜ che·ren drob liver
черен пипер ⓜ che·ren pee·per pepper
черен чай ⓜ che·ren chai black tea
череши ⓕ pl che·re·shee sweet cherries
черно непресято брашно ⓝ cher·no
  ne·pres·ya·to brash·no wholemeal flour
чесън ⓜ che·suhn garlic
чига ⓕ chee·ga sterlet (fish)
чорба ⓕ chor·ba soup
чорба от зрял фасул ⓕ
  chor·ba ot zryal fa·sool boiled beans
  with tomato purée, paprika & mint
чорба от леща ⓕ chor·ba ot lesh·ta
  lentil stew
чорба от пиле ⓕ chor·ba ot pee·le
  soup made by cooking rice in chicken
  stock, with yogurt, flour & egg yolks
чубрица ⓕ choo·bree·tsa savory (a herb
  with an aromatic flavour similar to thyme)

Ш

шампанско ⓝ sham·pan·sko
  champagne
шам-фъстък ⓜ sham·fuhs·tuhk pistachio
шаран ⓜ sha·ran carp
шаран с орехов пълнеж ⓕ
  sha·ran s o·re·hov puhl·nezh baked
  carp stuffed with rice, onions, tomatoes,
  peppers, walnuts & cinnamon

шардоне ⓝ shar·do·ne Chardonnay
шарена сол ⓕ sha·re·na sol Balkan
  mixed salt – a common condiment that
  includes fenugreek & red pepper
шкембе ⓝ shkem·be tripe
шкембе чорба ⓕ shkem·be chor·ba
  tripe soup
шоколад ⓜ sho·ko·lad chocolate
шоколадова торта ⓕ
  sho·ko·la·do·va tor·ta chocolate cake
шопска салата ⓕ shop·ska sa·la·ta
  salad of fresh tomatoes, cucumbers,
  sweet peppers & grated white cheese
шумящо вино ⓝ shoo·myash·to vee·no
  sparkling wine
шунка ⓕ shoon·ka ham

Щ

щука ⓕ shtoo·ka pike

Я

ябълка ⓝ ya·buhl·ka apple
ягоди ⓕ pl ya·go·dee strawberries
ядки ⓕ pl yad·kee nuts
яйца ⓝ pl yai·tsa eggs
яйца по панагюрски ⓝ pl
  yai·tsa po pa·nag·yoor·skee
  'veiled' eggs – poached eggs served with
  yogurt, melted butter & red pepper

Ю

юфка ⓕ yoof·ka noodles

emergencies

спешни случаи

Help!	Помощ!	*po*·mosht
Stop!	Стоп!	stop
Go away!	Махайте се!	*ma*·hai·te se
Thief!	Крадец!	kra·*dets*
Fire!	Пожар!	po·*zhar*
Watch out!	Внимавайте!	vnee·*ma*·vai·te

signs

Болница	*bol*·nee·tsa	**Hospital**
Полицейски участък	po·lee·*tsey*·skee oo·*chas*·tuhk	**Police Station**
Полиция	po·*lee*·tsee·ya	**Police**
Спешна помощ	*spesh*·na po·mosht	**Emergency Department**

Call ...!	Повикайте ...! **pol**	po·*vee*·kai·te ...
	Повикай ...! **inf**	po·*vee*·kai ...
an ambulance	линейка	lee·*ney*·ka
a doctor	доктор	*dok*·tor
the police	полицията	po·*lee*·tsee·ya·ta

It's an emergency.
Случаят е спешен.   *sloo*·cha·yuht e *spe*·shen

There's been an accident.
Стана катастрофа.   *sta*·na ka·tas·*tro*·fa

Could you please help? pol/inf
Моля ви·те за помощ.   *mo*·lyuh vee/te za po·mosht

Can I use your phone?
Мога ли да използвам телефона?   *mo*·guh lee da eez·*polz*·vam te·le·*fo*·nuh

essentials

189

I'm lost.
Загубих се. za·*goo*·beeh se

Where are the toilets?
Къде са тоалетните? kuh·*de* suh to·a·*let*·nee·te

She's about to have a baby.
Тя всеки момент tya *vse*·kee mo·*ment*
ще роди. shte ro·*dee*

He/She is having Той/Тя има … toy/tya *ee*·ma …
a/an …

allergic reaction	алергична реакция	a·ler·*geech*·na re·*ak*·tsee·ya
asthma attack	астматична криза	ast·ma·*teech*·na *kree*·za
epileptic fit	епилептичен припадък	e·pee·lep·*tee*·chen pree·*pa*·duhk
heart attack	сърдечен удар	suhr·*de*·chen *oo*·dar

police

Where's the police station?
Къде е полицейският kuh·*de* e po·lee·*tsey*·skee·yuht
участък? oo·*chas*·tuhk

I want to report an offence.
Искам да съобщя за *ees*·kam da suh·obsh·*tyuh* za
едно нарушение. ed·*no* na·roo·*she*·nee·e

It was him/her.
Той/Тя беше. toy/tya *be*·she

I have insurance.
Имам застраховка. *ee*·mam za·stra·*hov*·ka

I've been … … ме. … me
He/She has … го/я. … go/ya
been …

assaulted	Нападнаха	na·*pad*·na·ha
raped	Изнасилиха	eez·na·*see*·lee·ha
robbed	Ограбиха	o·*gra*·bee·ha

Вие сте обвинени в ...	vee·e ste ob·vee·ne·nee v ...	You're charged with ...
кражба	krazh·ba	shoplifting/ theft
липсата на виза	leep·sa·ta na vee·za	not having a visa
нападение	na·pa·de·nee·e	assault
нарушаване на реда	na·roo·sha·va·ne na re·duh	disturbing the peace
притежание на незаконни вещества	pree·te·zha·nee·e na ne·za·kon·nee vesh·test·va	possession of illegal substances
Имате глоба за ...	ee·ma·te glo·ba za ...	It's a ... fine.
паркиране	par·kee·ra·ne	parking
превишаване на скоростта	pre·vee·sha·va·ne na sko·rost·ta	speeding

I've lost my ... My ... was/were stolen.	Изгубих си ... Откраднаха ми ...	eez·goo·beeh see ... ot·krad·na·ha mee ...
backpack/ rucksack	раницата	ra·nee·tsa·ta
bags	чантите	chan·tee·te
credit card	кредитната карта	kre·deet·na·ta kar·ta
handbag	дамската чанта	dam·ska·ta chan·ta
jewellery	бижутата	bee·zhoo·ta·ta
money	парите	pa·ree·te
papers	документите	do·koo·men·tee·te
passport	паспорта	pas·por·tuh
travellers cheques	пътническите чекове	puht·nee·ches·kee·tee che·ko·ve
wallet	портмонето	port·mo·ne·to

What am I accused of?

В какво съм обвинен/ v kak·*vo* suhm ob·vee·*nen*/
обвинена? m/f ob·vee·*ne*·na

I didn't realise I was doing anything wrong.

Не знаех, че правя ne *zna*·eh che *prav*·yuh
нещо нередно. *nesh*·to ne·*red*·no

I didn't do it.

Не съм го направил/ ne suhm go na·*pra*·veel/
направила. m/f na·*pra*·vee·la

Can I pay an on-the-spot fine?

Мога ли да платя *mo*·guh lee da plat·*yuh*
глобата веднага? *glo*·ba·ta ved·*na*·ga

I want to contact my embassy.

Искам да се свържа *ees*·kam da se *svuhr*·zhuh
с нашето посолство. s *na*·she·to po·*sols*·tvo

Can I make a phone call?

Мога ли да се обадя *mo*·guh lee da se o·*bad*·yuh
по телефона? po te·le·*fo*·nuh

Can I have a lawyer (who speaks English)?

Моля за адвокат (който *mol*·yuh za ad·vo·*kat* (*koy*·to
говори английски). go·*vo*·ree an·*gleey*·skee)

This drug is for personal use.

Лекарството е за le·*kars*·tvo·to e za
лична употреба. *leech*·na oo·po·*tre*·ba

I have a prescription for this drug.

Имам рецепта за това ee·mam re·*tsep*·ta za to·*va*
лекарство. le·*kars*·tvo

---

lonely letters

The single consonants in the Bulgarian phrases and our coloured pronunciation guides represent some common prepositions. You'll see *в* v for 'at', 'in' or 'to', and *с* s for 'with'. In pronunciation they're usually run together with the following word. They're pronounced twice when the following word starts with a similar sound, and this is reflected in the written form, eg *във влака* vuhv *vla*·kuh (in the train), *със захар* suhs *za*·har (with sugar). For more on prepositions, see the **phrasebuilder**.

doctor

при лекаря

Always address doctors and dentists formally, with the title
доктор dok·tor (Dr) followed by their surname, or using the
vocative *докторе* dok·to·re (the form of the noun used when
addressing someone). For more information on the vocative,
see the box **what's in a name?**, page 135.

Where's the nearest ...?	Къде се намира най-близкият/ най-близката ...? m/f	kuh·de se na·mee·ra nai·bleez·kee·yuht/ nai·bleez·ka·ta ...
dentist	зъболекар m	zuh·bo·le·kar
doctor	лекар m	le·kar
emergency department	спешна помощ f	spesh·na po·mosht
health centre	клиника f	klee·nee·ka
hospital	болница f	bol·nee·tsa
optometrist	очен лекар m	o·chen le·kar
pharmacy	аптека f	ap·te·ka

I need a doctor (who speaks English).

Трябва ми лекар (който говори английски).	tryab·va mee le·kar (koy·to go·vo·ree an·gleey·skee)

Could I see a female doctor?

Може ли да ме прегледа лекарка?	mo·zhe lee da me pre·gle·da le·kar·ka

Could the doctor come here?

Може ли лекарят да ме посети в къщи?	mo·zhe lee le·kar·yuht da me po·se·tee v kuhsh·tee

Is there an after-hours emergency number?

Има ли номер за спешна помощ извън работното време?	ee·ma lee no·mer za spesh·na po·mosht eez·vuhn ra·bot·no·to vre·me

I've run out of my medication.

Свършиха ми се	svuhr·shee·ha mee se
лекарствата.	le·kars·tva·ta

This is my usual medicine.

Аз редовно взимам	az re·dov·no vzee·mam
това лекарство.	to·va le·kars·tvo

My child weighs (20 kilos).

Детето ми тежи	de·te·to mee te·zhee
(двайсет килограма).	(dvai·set kee·lo·gra·ma)

What's the correct dosage?

Каква е дозировката?	kak·va e do·zee·rov·ka·ta

I don't want a blood transfusion.

Не искам да ми	ne ees·kam da mee
преливат кръв.	pre·lee·vat kruhv

Please use a new syringe.

Моля, използвайте	mol·yuh eez·polz·vai·te
нова спринцовка.	no·va spreen·tsov·ka

I have my own syringe.

Нося си спринцовка.	nos·yuh see spreen·tsov·ka

I've been vaccinated against ...	Аз съм ваксиниран/ ваксинирана против ... m/f	az suhm vak·see·nee·ran/ vak·see·nee·ra·na pro·teev ...
encephalitis	енцефалит	en·tse·fa·leet
hepatitis A/B/C	хепатит A/B/C	he·pa·teet a/be/tse
tetanus	тетанус	te·ta·noos
typhoid	тиф	teef

I need new ...	Трябват ми нови ...	tryab·vat mee no·vee ...
contact lenses	контактни лещи	kon·takt·nee lesh·tee
glasses	очила	o·chee·la

My prescription is ...

Рецептата ми е ...	re·tsep·ta·ta mee e ...

How much will it cost?

Колко ще струва?	kol·ko shte stroo·va

Can I have a receipt for my insurance?

Може ли да ми дадете	mo·zhe lee da mee da·de·te
бележка за моята	be·lezh·ka za mo·ya·ta
страхователна компания?	stra·ho·va·tel·na kom·pa·nee·ya

the doctor may say ...

Какво ви боли?
  kak·vo vee bo·lee
Where does it hurt?

Имате ли температура?
  ee·ma·te lee tem·pe·ra·too·ra
Do you have a temperature?

Откога сте така?
  ot·ko·ga ste ta·ka
How long have you been like this?

Случвало ли ви се е преди?
  slooch·va·lo lee vee se e pre·dee
Have you had this before?

Алергичен/Алергична ли сте към нещо? m/f
  a·ler·gee·chen/a·ler·geech·na lee ste kuhm nesh·to
Are you allergic to anything?

Взимате ли лекарства?
  vzee·ma·te lee le·kars·tva
Are you on medication?

Водите ли сексуален живот?
  vo·dee·te lee sek·soo·a·len zhee·vot
Are you sexually active?

Имали ли сте секс без предпазни мерки?
  ee·ma·lee lee ste seks bez pred·paz·nee mer·kee
Have you had unprotected sex?

Пиете ли алкохол?
  pee·e·te lee al·ko·hol
Do you drink?

Пушите ли?
  poo·shee·te lee
Do you smoke?

Взимате ли наркотици?
  vzee·ma·te lee nar·ko·tee·tsee
Do you take drugs?

Колко време още ще сте на път?
  kol·ko vre·me osh·te shte ste na puht
How long are you travelling for?

Трябва да влезете в болница.
tryab·va da *vle*·ze·te
v *bol*·nee·tsa

You need to be admitted to hospital.

Трябва да се прегледате когато се върнете в къщи.
tryab·va da se pre·*gle*·da·te
ko·*ga*·to se *vuhr*·ne·te
v *kuhsh*·tee

You should have it checked when you go home.

Трябва да се приберете в къщи за лечение.
tryab·va da se pree·be·*re*·te
v *kuhsh*·tee za le·*che*·nee·e

You should return home for treatment.

Вие сте хипохондрик.
vee·e ste hee·po·hon·*dreek*

You're a hypochondriac.

symptoms & conditions

симптоми и състояния

I'm sick.
Аз съм болен/болна. m/f   az suhm *bo*·len/*bol*·na

My friend is (very) sick.
Приятелят ми е
(много) болен. m

pree·*ya*·tel·yuht mee e
(*mno*·go) *bo*·len

Приятелката ми е
(много) болна. f

pree·*ya*·tel·ka·ta mee e
(*mno*·go) *bol*·na

My child is (very) sick.
Детето ми е
(много) болно.

de·*te*·to mee e
(*mno*·go) *bol*·no

I've been injured.
Аз съм ранен/ранена. m/f   az suhm *ra*·nen/*ra*·ne·na

He/She has been injured.
Той е ранен. m   toy e *ra*·nen

Тя е ранена. f   tya e *ra*·ne·na

I've been vomiting.
Аз повръщам вече от
известно време.

az po·*vruhsh*·tam *ve*·che ot
eez·*vest*·no *vre*·me

He/She has been vomiting.

| Той/Тя повръща | toy/tya po·*vruhsh*·ta |
| вече от известно време. | ve·che ot eez·*vest*·no *vre*·me |

I feel weak.

| Чувствам слабост. | *choovst*·vam *sla*·bost |

I feel better/worse.

| По-добре/По-лошо ми е. | po·do·bre/po·lo·sho mee e |

I feel …	Чувствам се …	*choovst*·vam se …
anxious	неспокоен **m**	ne·spo·*ko*·yen
	неспокойна **f**	ne·spo·*koy*·na
depressed	потиснат **m**	po·*tees*·nat
	потисната **f**	po·*tees*·na·ta
dizzy	замаян **m**	za·*ma*·yan
	замаяна **f**	za·*ma*·ya·na
strange	странно	*stran*·no

I feel …		
hot and cold	Ту ми е горещо	too mee e go·*resh*·to
	ту ме тресе.	too me tre·*se*
nauseous	Гади ми се.	*ga*·dee mee se
shivery	Тресе ме.	tre·*se* me

---

under pressure

Whether or not they have cause for concern, nearly everyone in Bulgaria is obsessed with, and constantly checking, their *кръвно налягане* kruhv·no na·*lya*·ga·ne (blood pressure). If you share this obsession, the following phrases might come in handy:

What's your blood pressure?

| Колко ви/ти е кръвното | *kol*·ko vee/tee e *kruhv*·no·to |
| налягане? **pol/inf** | na·*lya*·ga·ne |

Can you take my blood pressure?

Можете ли да ми	mo·*zhe*·te lee da mee
измерите кръвното	eez·*me*·ree·te *kruhv*·no·to
налягане? **pol**	na·*lya*·ga·ne
Можеш ли да ми	mo·*zhesh* lee da mee
измериш кръвното	eez·*me*·reesh *kruhv*·no·to
налягане? **inf**	na·*lya*·ga·ne

It hurts here.
Боли ме тук.   bo·*lee* me took

I'm dehydrated.
Аз съм обезводнен/   az suhm o·bez·vod·*nen*/
обезводнена. m/f   o·bez·vod·*ne*·na

I can't sleep.
Не мога да спя.   ne *mo*·guh da spyuh

I think it's the medication I'm on.
Мисля, че е от   *mees*·lyuh che e ot
лекарството,   le·*kars*·tvo·to
което взимам.   ko·*ye*·to *vzee*·mam

I'm on medication for ...
Взимам лекарство за ...   *vzee*·mam le·*kars*·tvo za ...

I have (a/an) ...
Имам ...   *ee*·mam ...

I've recently had (a/an) ...
Скоро имах ...   *sko*·ro *ee*·mah ...

cold n	простуда f	pro·*stoo*·da
constipation	запек m	*za*·pek
cough n	кашлица f	*kash*·lee·tsa
diabetes	диабет m	dee·a·*bet*
diarrhoea	разстройство n	raz·*stroys*·tvo
fever	температура f	tem·pe·ra·*too*·ra
headache	главоболие n	gla·vo·*bo*·lee·e
nausea	гадене n	*ga*·de·ne
pain n	болка f	*bol*·ka
sore throat	възпалено гърло n	vuhz·*pa*·le·no *guhr*·lo

women's health

женски здравни проблеми

I think I'm pregnant.
Мисля, че съм   *mees*·lyuh che suhm
бременна.   *bre*·men·na

I'm pregnant.
Бременна съм.   *bre*·men·na suhm

Използвате ли противозачатъчни средства?
eez·polz·va·te lee
pro·tee·vo·za·cha·tuhch·nee
sreds·tva
Are you using contraception?

Имате ли сега мензис?
ee·ma·te lee se·ga men·zees
Are you menstruating?

Кога беше последният ви мензис?
ko·ga be·she po·sled·nee·yuht
vee men·zees
When did you last have your period?

Бременна ли сте?
bre·men·na lee ste
Are you pregnant?

Бременна сте.
bre·men·na ste
You're pregnant.

I'm on the pill.

Взимам противо-
зачатъчни хапчета.
vzee·mam pro·tee·vo·
za·cha·tuhch·nee hap·che·ta

I haven't had my period for (six) weeks.

(Шест) седмици не съм
имала мензис.
(shest) sed·mee·tsee ne suhm
ee·ma·la men·zees

I've noticed a lump here.

Забелязах една
бучка тук.
za·bel·ya·zah ed·na
booch·ka took

Do you have something for (period pain)?

Имате ли нещо против
(болки при мензис)?
ee·ma·te lee nesh·to pro·teev
(bol·kee pree men·zees)

I need (a/the) ...	Имам нужда от ...	*ee·mam noozh·da* *ot ...*
contraception	противо- зачатъчни средства	*pro·tee·vo·* *za·cha·tuhch·nee* *sreds·tva*
morning-after pill	хапчето, което се взима сутрин след секс	*hap·che·to,* *ko·ye·to se* *vzee·ma soo·treen* *sled seks*
pregnancy test	тест за бременност	*test za* *bre·men·nost*

health

199

I have a ...	Имам ...	*ee*·mam ...
urinary tract infection	инфекция на пикочния канал	een·*fek*·tsee·ya na *pee*·koch·nee·yuh ka·*nal*
yeast infection	гъбички	*guh*·beech·kee

allergies

I have a skin allergy.
    Имам кожна алергия.   *ee*·mam *kozh*·na a·*ler*·gee·ya

I'm allergic to ...	Аз съм алергичен/ алергична към ... **m/f**	az suhm a·ler·*gee*·chen/ a·ler·*geech*·na kuhm ...
antibiotics	анти- биотици	an·tee· bee·*o*·tee·tsee
anti- inflammatories	противовъз- палителни средства	pro·tee·vo·vuhz· pa·*lee*·tel·nee *sreds*·tva
aspirin	аспирин	as·pee·*reen*
bees	пчели	pche·*lee*
codeine	кодеин	ko·de·*een*
penicillin	пеницилин	pe·nee·tsee·*leen*
pollen	полени	po·*le*·nee
sulphur-based drugs	лекарства в които има сяра	le·*kars*·tva v ko·*yee*·to ee·ma *sya*·ra
antihistamines	антихиста- мини **m pl**	an·tee·hees·ta· *mee*·nee
inhaler	инхалатор **m**	een·ha·*la*·tor
injection	инжекция **f**	een·*zhek*·tsee·ya

For food-related allergies, see **special diets & allergies**, page 180.

parts of the body

My ... hurts.
  Боли ме ...   bo·*lee* me ...

I can't move my ...
  Не мога да мръдна ...   ne *mo*·guh da *mruhd*·nuh ...

I have a cramp in my ...
  Имам разтягане на   ee·mam raz·*tya*·ga·ne na
  мускулите на ...   *moos*·koo·lee·te na ...

My ... is swollen.
  ... е подут/подута/   ... e po·*doot*/po·*doo*·ta/
  подуто. **m/f/n**   po·*doo*·to
  ... са подути. **pl**   ... suh po·*doo*·tee

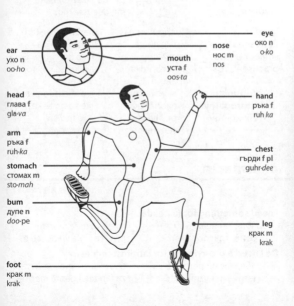

ear
yxo n
oo·*ho*

head
глава f
gla·va

arm
ръка f
ruh·*ka*

stomach
стомах m
sto·*mah*

bum
дупе n
doo·pe

foot
крак m
krak

eye
око n
o·*ko*

nose
нос m
nos

mouth
уста f
oos·*ta*

hand
ръка f
ruh *ka*

chest
гърди f pl
guhr·*dee*

leg
крак m
krak

Bulgarians say *ръка* ruh·*ka* for both 'arm' and 'hand', *крак* krak for 'leg' and 'foot', and *пръст* pruhst for 'finger' and 'toe'. The latter is clarified when necessary by saying *пръст на крака* pruhst na kra·*kuh* (lit: finger on foot).

alternative treatments

алтернативна медицина

I don't use (Western medicine).
Не използвам
(традиционната
медицина).

ne eez·*polz*·vam
(tra·dee·tsee·*on*·na·ta
me·dee·*tsee*·na)

I prefer ...	Предпочитам ...	pred·po·*chee*·tam ...
Can I see	Може ли да	*mo*·zhe lee da
someone who	отида при	o·*tee*·duh pree
practises ...?	някого, който	*nya*·ko·go *koy*·to
	прави ...?	*pra*·vee ...
acupuncture	акупунктура	a·koo·poonk·*too*·ra
naturopathy	екопатека	e·ko·*pa*·te·ka
reflexology	рефлексо-	re·flek·so·
	терапия	te·*ra*·pee·ya

pharmacist

в аптеката

I need something for (a headache).
Трябва ми нещо
против (главоболие).

tryab·va mee *nesh*·to
pro·*teev* (gla·vo·*bo*·lee·e)

Do I need a prescription for (antihistamines)?
Трябва ли ми рецепта
за (антихистамини)?

tryab·va lee mee re·*tsep*·ta
za (an·tee·hees·ta·*mee*·nee)

I have a prescription.
　Имам рецепта.　　　　　*ee*·mam re·*tsep*·ta

How many times a day?
　Колко пъти на ден　　　*kol*·ko *puh*·tee na den
　се взима?　　　　　　　se *vzee*·ma

Will it make me drowsy?
　Ще ме приспи ли?　　　shte me pree·*spee* lee

antiseptic	антисептично n	an·tee·sep·*teech*·no
contraceptives	контрацептиви m pl	kon·tra·tsep·*tee*·vee
painkillers	обезболяващи pl	o·bez·bol·*ya*·vash·tee
rehydration	соли за	*so*·lee za
salts	оводняване f pl	o·vod·*nya*·va·ne
thermometer	термометър m	ter·mo·*me*·tuhr

For more pharmaceutical items, see the **dictionary**.

the pharmacist may say ...

Два/Три пъти на ден.
　dva/tree *puh*·tee na den　　　**Twice/Three times a day.**

Преди/След ядене.
　pre·*dee*/sled *ya*·de·ne　　　**Before/After meals.**

По време на ядене.
　po *vre*·me na *ya*·de·ne　　　**With meals.**

Взимали ли сте го преди?
　vzee·ma·lee lee ste　　　　**Have you taken this**
　go pre·*dee*　　　　　　　**before?**

Трябва да ги вземете всичките.
　tryab·va da gee *vze*·me·te　　**You must complete**
　vseech·kee·te　　　　　　　**the course.**

dentist

I have a ...	Имам ...	*ee*·mam ...
broken tooth	счупен зъб	s·*choo*·pen zuhb
cavity	кариес	ka·*ree*·es

I need ...	Имам нужда от ...	*ee*·mam *noozh*·da ot ...
an anaesthetic	упойка	oo·*poy*·ka
a filling	пломба	*plom*·ba

I have a toothache.
Боли ме зъбът.   bo·*lee* me zuh·*buht*

I've lost a filling.
Падна ми пломбата.   *pad*·na mee *plom*·ba·ta

My dentures are broken.
Протезата ми е счупена. pro·*te*·za·ta mee e s·*choo*·pe·na

My gums hurt.
Болят ми венците.   bol·*yuht* mee ven·*tsee*·te

I don't want it extracted.
Не искам да го вадите.   ne *ees*·kam da go va·dee·te

---

the dentist may say ...

Отворете устата широко. ot·vo·*re*·te oos·*ta*·ta shee·*ro*·ko	**Open wide.**
Няма да ви боли. *nya*·ma da vee bo·*lee*	**This won't hurt a bit.**
Захапете това. za·ha·*pe*·te to·*va*	**Bite down on this.**
Не мърдайте. ne *muhr*·dai·te	**Don't move.**
Изплакнете. eez·plak·*ne*·te	**Rinse.**
Върнете се, още не съм свършил/свършила. m/f vuhr·*ne*·te se *osh*·te ne suhm *svuhr*·sheel/*svuhr*·shee·la	**Come back, I haven't finished.**

DICTIONARY >
english–bulgarian

Bulgarian nouns in the dictionary have their gender indicated by ⓜ (masculine), ⓕ (feminine) or ⓝ (neuter). If it's a plural noun, you'll also see pl. For added clarity, certain words are marked as nouns n, adjectives a, verbs v, adverbs adv, pronouns pron or prepositions prep. The abbreviations sg (singular), pl (plural), inf (informal) and pol (polite) are also used where necessary. Adjectives are given in the masculine singular form only. Verbs are given in their present tense first person singular form. Most verbs are given in two aspects: perfective and imperfective. The two forms are separated by a slash with the perfective form given first. Note that if the verb is followed by the particle ce se – eg *обадя/обаждам се* o-*bad*-yuh/o-*bazh*-dam se (to call) – the particle is used both with the perfective (*обадя се*) and imperfective forms (*обаждам се*). If only one verb form is given, it means that form can be used as both imperfective and perfective. For more information, refer to the **phrasebuilder**.

A

aboard на борда na *bor*-da
abortion аборт ⓜ a-*bort*
about за za
above над nad
abroad в чужбина v choozh-*bee*-na
accident злополука ⓕ zlo-po-*loo*-ka
accommodation жилище ⓝ *zhee*-leesh-te
account (bill) сметка ⓕ *smet*-ka
across през prez
activist n активист/активистка ⓜ/ⓕ ak-tee-*veest*/ak-tee-*veest*-ka
actor актьор/актриса ⓜ/ⓕ ak-*tyor*/ak-*tree*-sa
acupuncture акупунктура ⓕ a-koo-poonk-*too*-ra
adaptor адаптор ⓜ a-*dap*-tor
addiction (drugs) наркомания ⓕ nar-ko-*ma*-nee-ya
address n адрес ⓜ a-*dres*
administration администрация ⓕ ad-mee-nees-*tra*-tsee-ya
admission price входна такса ⓕ *vhod*-na *tak*-sa
admit (let in) пусна/пускам *poos*-nuh/*poos*-kam
adult n възрастен/възрастна ⓜ/ⓕ *vuhz*-ras-ten/*vuhz*-rast-na
advertisement обява ⓕ ob-*ya*-va

advice съвет ⓜ suh-*vet*
Aegean Sea Егейско море ⓝ e-*gey*-sko mo-*re*
Africa Африка ⓕ *a*-free-ka
after след sled
afternoon следобед ⓜ sle-*do*-bed
aftershave афтершейв ⓜ *af*-ter-sheyv
again отново ot-*no*-vo
age n възраст ⓕ *vuhz*-rast
(three days) ago преди (три дена) pre-*dee* (tree *de*-na)
agree съглася/съгласявам се suh-gla-*syuh*/suh-gla-*sya*-vam se
agriculture селско стопанство ⓝ *sel*-sko sto-*panst* vo
ahead напред na-*pred*
AIDS СПИН ⓜ speen
air въздух ⓜ *vuhz*-dooh
air-conditioned с климатик s klee-ma-*teek*
air conditioning климатик ⓜ klee-ma-*teek*
airline самолетна компания ⓕ sa-mo-*let*-na kom-*pa*-nee-ya
airmail въздушна поща ⓕ vuhz-*doosh*-na *posh*-ta
airplane самолет ⓜ sa-mo-*let*
airport летище ⓝ le-*teesht*-te
airport tax летищна такса ⓕ le-*teesht*-na *tak*-sa
aisle (plane, etc) пътека ⓕ puh-*te*-ka

alarm clock будилник ⓜ boo-*deel*-neek

alcohol алкохол ⓜ al-ko-*hol*

all pron всичко *vseech*-ko

allergy алергия ⓕ a-*ler*-gee-ya

almond бадем ⓜ ba-*dem*

almost почти poch-*tee*

alone сам sam

already вече *ve*-che

also също *suhsh*-to

altitude височина ⓕ vee-so-chee-*na*

always винаги *vee*-na-gee

ambassador посланик/посланичка ⓜ/ⓕ
po-*sla*-neek/po-*sla*-neech-ka

ambulance линейка ⓕ lee-*ney*-ka

America Америка ⓕ a-*me*-ree-ka

anaemia анемия ⓕ a-*ne*-mee-ya

anarchist n анархист/анархистка ⓜ/ⓕ
a-nar-*heest*/a-nar-*heest*-ka

ancient древен *dre*-ven

and и ee

angry ядосан ya-*do*-san

animal животно ⓝ zhee-*vot*-no

ankle глезен ⓜ *gle*-zen

another друг droog

answer n отговор ⓜ ot-*go*-vor

answer v отговоря/отговарям
ot-go-*vor*-yuh/ot-go-*var*-yam

ant мравка ⓕ *mrav*-ka

antibiotics антибиотици ⓜ pl
an-tee-bee-o-*tee*-tsee

antinuclear противоядрен
pro-tee-vo-*ya*-dren

antique n антика ⓕ an-*tee*-ka

antiseptic n антисептик ⓜ an-tee-sep-*teek*

any някакъв *nya*-ka-kuhv

apartment апартамент ⓜ a-par-ta-*ment*

appendix (body) апендикс ⓜ a-*pen*-deeks

apple ябълка ⓕ *ya*-buhl-ka

appointment уговорена среща ⓕ
oo-go-*vo*-re-na *sresh*-ta

apricot кайсия ⓕ kai-*see*-ya

archaeological археологичен
ar-he-o-lo-*gee*-chen

architect архитект/архитектка ⓜ/ⓕ
ar-hee-*tekt*/ar-hee-*tekt*-ka

architecture архитектура ⓕ
ar-hee-tek-*too*-ra

argue споря *spo*-ryuh

arm (body) ръка ⓕ ruh-*ka*

aromatherapy ароматерапия ⓕ
a-ro-ma-te-ra-*pee*-ya

arrest v арестувам a-res-*too*-vam

arrivals (airport) пристигане ⓝ
pree-*stee*-ga-ne

arrive пристигна/пристигам
pree-*steeg*-nuh/pree-*stee*-gam

art изкуство ⓝ eez-*koost*-vo

art gallery галерия ⓕ ga-*le*-ree-ya

artist художник/художничка ⓜ/ⓕ
hoo-*dozh*-neek/hoo-*dozh*-neech-ka

ashtray пепелник ⓜ pe-*pel*-neek

Asia Азия ⓕ *a*-zee-ya

ask (a question) питам *pee*-tam

ask (for something) моля *mol*-yuh

asparagus аспержи ⓜ pl as-*per*-zhee

aspirin аспирин ⓜ as-pee-*reen*

asthma астма ⓕ *ast*-ma

at на na

athletics лека атлетика ⓕ
le-ka at-*le*-tee-ka

atmosphere атмосфера ⓕ at-mos-*fe*-ra

aunt леля ⓕ *lel*-ya

ATM банкомат ⓜ ban-ko-*mat*

aubergine патладжан ⓜ pat-*lad*-zhan

Australia Австралия ⓕ av-*stra*-lee-ya

autumn есен ⓜ *e*-sen

avenue улица ⓕ *oo*-lee-tsa

awful ужасен oo-*zha*-sen

B

B&W (film) черно-бял cher-no-*byal*

baby бебе ⓝ *be*-be

baby food бебешка храна ⓕ
be-*besh*-ka hra-*na*

baby powder бебешка пудра ⓕ
be-*besh*-ka *poo*-dra

babysitter бавачка ⓕ ba-*vach*-ka

back (body) гръб ⓜ gruhb

back (position) задна част ⓕ
zad-na chast

backpack раница ⓕ *ra*-nee-tsa

bacon бекон ⓜ be-*kon*

bad лош losh

bag чанта ⓕ *chan*-ta

baggage багаж ⓜ ba-*gazh*

baggage allowance
разрешено количество багаж ⓝ
raz-re-she-no ko-lee-chest-vo ba-gazh
baggage claim получаване на багаж ⓝ
po-loo-cha-va-ne na ba-gazh
bakery хлебарница ⓕ hle-bar-nee-tsa
balance (account) баланс ⓜ ba-lans
balcony балкон ⓜ bal-kon
Balkan Peninsula
Балкански полуостров ⓜ
bal-kan-skee po-loo-os-trov
ball (sport) топка ⓕ top-ka
ballet балет ⓜ ba-let
banana банан ⓜ ba-nan
band (music) оркестър ⓜ or-kes-tuhr
bandage превръзка ⓕ pre-vruhz-ka
Band-Aid лейкопласт ⓜ ley-ko-plast
bank банка ⓕ ban-ka
bank account банкова сметка ⓕ
ban-ko-va smet-ka
banknote банкнота ⓕ bank-no-ta
baptism кръщене ⓝ kruhsh-te-ne
bar (pub) бар ⓜ bar
barber бръснар ⓜ bruhs-nar
bar work работа като барман ⓕ
ra-bo-ta ka-to bar-man
baseball бейзбол ⓜ beyz-bol
basket кошница ⓕ kosh-nee-tsa
basketball баскетбол ⓜ bas-ket-bol
bath баня ⓕ ba-nya
bathing suit бански костюм ⓜ
ban-skee kos-tyoom
bathroom баня ⓕ ba-nya
battery батерия ⓕ ba-te-ree-ya
be бъда buh-duh
beach плаж ⓜ plazh
beach volleyball плажен волейбол ⓜ
pla-zhen vo-ley-bol
beans фасул ⓜ fa-sool
beautiful красив kra-seev
beauty salon козметичен салон ⓜ
koz-me-tee-chen sa-lon
because защото zash-to-to
bed легло ⓝ leg-lo
bedding завивки ⓕ pl za-veev-kee
bedroom спалня ⓕ spal-nya
bee пчела ⓕ pche-la
beef телешко ⓝ te-lesh-ko
beer бира ⓕ bee-ra
before преди pre-dee

beggar просяк/просякиня ⓜ/ⓕ
pros-yak/pros-ya-kee-nya
behind зад zad
Belgium Белгия ⓕ bel-gee-ya
below под pod
berth спално място ⓝ spal-no myas-to
beside до do
best най-добър nai-do-buhr
bet n залог ⓜ za-log
bet v заложа/залагам
za-lo-zhuh/za-la-gam
better по-добър po-do-buhr
between между mezh-doo
Bible Библия ⓕ beeb-lee-ya
bicycle велосипед ⓜ ve-lo-see-ped
bicycle chain верига ⓕ ve-ree-ga
bicycle lock катинар ⓜ ka-tee-nar
bicycle path алея за велосипедисти ⓕ
a-le-ya za ve-lo-see-pe-dees-tee
bicycle shop магазин за велосипеди ⓜ
ma-ga-zeen za ve-lo-see-pe-dee
big голям go-lyam
bigger по-голям po-go-lyam
biggest най-голям nai-go-lyam
bike колело ⓝ ko-le-lo
bill (restaurant, etc) сметка ⓕ smet-ka
binoculars бинокъл ⓜ bee-no-kuhl
bird птица ⓕ ptee-tsa
birth certificate
свидетелство за раждане ⓝ
svee-de-telst-vo za razh-da-ne
birthday рожден ден ⓜ rozh-den den
biscuit бисквита ⓕ bees-kvee-ta
bite (dog) n ухапване от куче ⓝ
oo-hap-va-ne ot koo-che
bite (insect) n ужилване от насекомо ⓝ
oo-zheel-va-ne ot na-se-ko-mo
bitter горчив gor-cheev
black черен che-ren
black market черен пазар ⓜ
che-ren pa-zar
Black Sea Черно море ⓝ cher-no mo-re
bladder пикочен мехур ⓜ
pee-ko-chen me-hoor
blanket одеяло ⓝ o-de-ya-lo
blind a сляп slyap
blister мехур ⓜ me-hoor
blocked задръстен za-druhs-ten
blood кръв ⓕ kruhv

blood group кръвна група ①
kruhv·na *groo*·pa

blood pressure кръвно налягане ⑩
kruhv·no na·*lya*·ga·ne

blood test изследване на кръвта ⑩
eez·*sled*·va·ne na kruhv·*ta*

blue син seen

board (a plane, etc) кача/качвам се
ka·*chuh*/*kach*·vam se

boarding house пансион ⑩ pan·see·*on*

boarding pass бордна карта ①
bord·na *kar*·ta

boat кораб ⑩ *ko*·rab

body тяло ⑪ *tya*·lo

boiled варен va·*ren*

bone кост ① kost

book n книга ① *knee*·ga

book (reserve) v резервирам
re·zer·*vee*·ram

booked out разпродаден raz·pro·*da*·den

book shop книжарница ①
knee·*zhar*·nee·tsa

boots ботуши ⑩ pl bo·*too*·shee

border (country) n граница ① *gra*·nee·tsa

bored отегчен o·*teg*·chen

boring досаден do·*sa*·den

borrow взема/взимам на заем
vze·muh/*vzee*·mam na *za*·em

botanic garden ботаническа градина ①
bo·ta·*nee*·ches·ka gra·*dee*·na

both и двата/двете ⑩/①&⑪
ee *dva*·ta/*dve*·te

bottle бутилка ① boo·*teel*·ka

bottle opener отварачка за бутилки ①
ot·va·*rach*·ka na boo·*teel*·kee

bottle shop
магазин за алкохолни напитки ⑩
ma·ga·*zeen* za al·ko·*hol*·nee na·*peet*·kee

bottom (body) дупе ⑪ *doo*·pe

bottom (position) дъно ⑪ *duh*·no

bowl n купа ① *koo*·pa

box n кутия ① koo·*tee*·ya

boxer shorts боксерки ⑩ pl *bok*·ser·kee

boy момче ⑪ mom·*che*

boyfriend гадже ⑩ *gad*·zhe

bra сутиен ⑩ soo·*tee*·en

brakes спирачки ① pl spee·*rach*·kee

brandy ракия ① ra·*kee*·ya

brave храбър *hra*·buhr

bread хляб ⑩ hlyab

bread roll питка ① *peet*·ka

break v счупя/счупвам
s·*choop*·yuh/s·*choop*·vam

break down разваля/развалям се
raz·val·*yuh*/raz·*val*·yam se

breakfast закуска ① za·*koos*·ka

breasts гърди ① pl guhr·*dee*

breathe дишам *dee*·sham

bribe n подкуп ⑩ *pod*·koop

bridge n мост ⑩ most

briefcase дипломатическо куфарче ⑪
dee·plo·ma·*tee*·ches·ko *koo*·far·che

bring донеса/донасям
do·ne·*suh*/do·*nas*·yam

brochure брошура ① bro·*shoo*·ra

broken повреден po·*vre*·den

broken down развален raz·va·*len*

bronchitis бронхит ⑩ bron·*heet*

brother брат ⑩ brat

brown кафяв kaf·*yav*

bruise n натъртване ⑪ na·*turht*·va·ne

brush (hair) n четка ① *chet*·ka

bucket кофа ① *ko*·fa

budget бюджет ⑩ byood·*zhet*

buffet бюфет ⑩ byoo·*fet*

bug n буболечка ① boo·bo·*lech*·ka

build v построя/строя
po·stro·*yuh*/stro·*yuh*

builder строител ⑩ stroy·*ee*·tel

building сграда ① *sgra*·da

Bulgaria България ① buhl·*ga*·ree·ya

Bulgarian (language) n български ⑩
buhl·gar·skee

Bulgarian (person) n българин/
българка ⑩/① *buhl*·ga·reen/*buhl*·gar·ka

Bulgarian a български *buhl*·gar·skee

burn n изгаряне ⑪ eez·*gar*·ya·ne

burnt изгорен eez·go·*ren*

bus (city) градски автобус ⑩
grad·skee av·to·*boos*

bus (intercity) автобус ⑩ av·to·*boos*

business търговия ① tuhr·*go*·vee·ya

business class бизнес класа ①
beez·nes *kla*·sa

businessperson бизнесмен/бизнесдама
⑩/① beez·nes·*men*/beez·nes·*da*·ma

business trip командировка ①
ko·man·dee·*rov*·ka

bus station автогара ① av·to·*ga*·ra

bus stop автобусна спирка ⓕ
av·to·*boos*·na *speer*·ka
busy зает za·*et*
but но no
butcher касапин ⓜ ka·*sa*·peen
butcher's shop месарница ⓕ
me·*sar*·nee·tsa
butter краве масло ⓝ *kra*·ve *mas*·lo
button n копче ⓝ *kop*·che
buy купя/купувам
koop·yuh/koo·*poo*·vam

C

cabbage зеле ⓝ *ze*·le
cable car кабинков лифт ⓜ
ka·*been*·kov leeft
café кафене ⓝ ka·fe·*ne*
cake торта ⓕ *tor*·ta
cake shop сладкарница ⓕ
slad·*kar*·nee·tsa
calculator калкулатор ⓜ kal·koo·*la*·tor
calendar календар ⓜ ka·len·*dar*
call v обадя/обаждам се
o·*bad*·yuh/o·*bazh*·dam se
camera фотоапарат ⓜ fo·to·a·pa·*rat*
camera shop фотомагазин ⓜ
fo·to·ma·ga·*zeen*
camp v лагерувам la·ge·*roo*·vam
camping ground къмпинг ⓜ *kuhm*·peeng
camping store магазин за
туристически стоки ⓜ ma·ga·*zeen* za
too rees tee ches kee *sto·kee*
camp site място за лагеруване ⓝ
myas·to za la·ge·*roo*·va·ne
can (tin) консервна кутия ⓕ
kon·*serv*·na koo·*tee*·ya
can мога *mo*·guh
Canada Канада ⓕ ka·*na*·da
cancel анулирам a·noo·*lee*·ram
cancer рак ⓜ rak
candle свещ ⓕ svesht
candy бонбон ⓜ bon·*bon*
can opener отварачка за консерви ⓕ
ot·va·*rach*·ka za kon·*ser*·vee
car кола ⓕ ko·*la*
caravan каравана ⓕ ka·ra·*va*·na
cardiac arrest сърдечен удар ⓜ
suhr·*de*·chen oo·*dar*

cards (playing) карти ⓕ pl *kar*·tee
care (for someone) грижа се
gree·zhuh se
car hire наемане на кола ⓝ
na·e·*ma*·ne na ko·*la*
car owner's title акт за собственост на
кола ⓜ akt za *sobst*·ve·nost na ko·*la*
car park паркинг ⓜ *par*·keeng
carpenter дърводелец ⓜ duhr·vo·*de*·lets
car registration регистрационен
талон на автомобил ⓜ
re·gee·stra·tsee·*o*·nen ta·*lon* na
av·to·mo·*beel*
carrot морков ⓜ *mor*·kov
carry нося *nos*·yuh
carton картонена кутия ⓕ
kar·to·*ne*·na koo·*tee*·ya
cash n пари в брой ⓕ pl pa·*ree* v broy
cash (a cheque) v осребря/осребрявам
o·sreb·*ryuh*/o·sreb·*rya*·vam
cashew кашу ⓝ ka·*shoo*
cashier касиер/касиерка ⓜ/ⓕ
ka·see·*er*/ka·see·*er*·ka
cash register каса ⓕ *ka*·sa
casino казино ⓝ ka·*zee*·no
cassette касетка ⓕ ka·*set*·ka
castle замък ⓜ *za*·muhk
casual work временна работа ⓕ
vre·men·na *ra*·bo·ta
cat котка ⓕ *kot*·ka
cathedral катедрала ⓕ ka·te·*dra*·la
cauliflower карфиол ⓜ kar·fee·*ol*
cave пещера ⓕ pesh·te·*ra*
CD сиди ⓝ *see*·dee
celebration тържество ⓝ tuhr·zhest·*vo*
cell phone GSM ⓜ dzhee·es·*em*
cemetery гробище ⓝ *gro*·beesh·te
cent цент ⓜ tsent
centimetre сантиметър ⓜ
san·tee·*me*·tuhr
centre n център ⓜ *tsen*·tuhr
ceramics керамика ⓕ ke·ra·*mee*·ka
cereal (breakfast) овесени ядки ⓕ pl
o·*ve*·se·nee *yad*·kee
certificate удостоверение ⓝ
oo·dos·to·ve·*re*·nee·e
chain n верига ⓕ ve·*ree*·ga
chair n стол ⓜ stol
chairlift (skiing) седалков лифт ⓜ
se·*dal*·kov leeft

champagne шампанско ⓝ sham·*pan*·sko
championships шампионат ⓜ sham·*pee*·o·*nat*
chance n случай ⓜ *sloo*·chai
change n промяна ⓕ pro·*mya*·na
change (coins) n монети ⓕ pl mo·*ne*·tee
change (money) v сменям *smen*·yam
changing room пробна ⓕ *prob*·na
charming прелестен *pre*·les·ten
chat up заговоря/заговарям
za·go·*vor*·yuh/za·go·*var*·yam
cheap евтин *ev*·teen
cheat v излъжа/излъгвам
eez·*luh*·zhuh/eez·*luhg*·vam
check (banking) чек ⓜ chek
check (bill) сметка ⓕ *smet*·ka
check v проверя/проверявам
pro·*ver*·yuh/pro·ver·*ya*·vam
check-in desk рецепция ⓕ re·*tsep*·tsee·ya
checkpoint пропусквателен пункт ⓜ
pro·poosk·*va*·te·len poonkt
cheese (soft, white) сирене ⓝ *see*·re·ne
cheese (hard, yellow) кашкавал ⓜ
kash·ka·*val*
chef (man) главен готвач ⓜ
gla·ven got·*vach*
chef (woman) главна готвачка ⓕ
glav·na got·*vach*·ka
chemist (pharmacist) аптекар/
аптекарка ⓜ/ⓕ ap·te·*kar*/ap·te·*kar*·ka
chemist (pharmacy) аптека ⓕ ap·*te*·ka
cheque (banking) чек ⓜ chek
cherry (sour) вишня ⓕ *veesh*·nya
cherry (sweet) череша ⓕ che·*re*·sha
chess шах ⓜ shah
chessboard шахматна дъска ⓕ
shah·mat·na duhs·*ka*
chest (body) гръден кош ⓜ
gruh·den kosh
chestnut кестен ⓜ *kes*·ten
chewing gum дъвка ⓕ *duhv*·ka
chicken (meat) пилешко ⓝ *pee*·lesh·ko
chicken pox варицела ⓕ va·ree·*tse*·la
child дете ⓝ de·*te*
children деца ⓝ pl de·*tsa*
child seat детска седалка ⓕ
det·ska se·*dal*·ka
chilli люти чушки ⓕ pl
lyoo·tee *choosh*·kee
China Китай ⓜ kee·*tai*

chiropractor мануален терапевт ⓜ
ma·noo·*a*·len te·ra·*pevt*
chocolate шоколад ⓜ sho·ko·*lad*
choose избера/избирам
eez·be·*ruh*/eez·*bee*·ram
chopping board дъска за рязане ⓕ
duhs·*ka* za *rya*·za·ne
chopsticks пръчици за хранене ⓕ pl
pruh·chee·tsee za *hra*·ne·ne
Christmas Коледа ⓕ *ko*·le·da
Christmas Day Коледа ⓕ *ko*·le·da
Christmas Eve Бъдни вечер ⓜ
buhd·nee *ve*·cher
church църква ⓕ *tsuhr*·kva
cigar пура ⓕ *poo*·ra
cigarette цигара ⓕ tsee·*ga*·ra
cigarette lighter запалка ⓕ za·*pal*·ka
cinema кино ⓝ *kee*·no
circus цирк ⓜ tseerk
citizenship гражданство ⓝ
grazh·danst·vo
city град ⓜ grad
city centre центърът на града ⓜ
tsen·tuh·ruht na gra·*da*
civil rights граждански права ⓝ pl
grazh·dan·skee pra·*va*
class (category) класа ⓕ *kla*·sa
classical класически kla·*see*·ches·kee
clean a чист cheest
clean v чистя *cheest*·yuh
cleaning чистене ⓝ *chees*·te·ne
client клиент/клиентка ⓜ/ⓕ
klee·*ent*/klee·*ent*·ka
cliff скала ⓕ ska·*la*
climb v кача/качвам се
ka·*chuh*/*kach*·vam se
cloakroom гардероб ⓜ gar·de·*rob*
clock n часовник ⓜ cha·*sov*·neek
close a близък *blee*·zuhk
close v затворя/затварям
zat·*vor*·yuh/zat·*var*·yam
closed затворен zat·*vo*·ren
clothesline простор pro·*stor*
clothing дрехи ⓕ pl *dre*·hee
clothing store магазин за облекло ⓜ
ma·ga·*zeen* za o·blek·*lo*
cloud n облак ⓜ *o*·blak
cloudy облачен *o*·bla·chen
clutch (car) съединител ⓜ
suh·e·dee·*nee*·tel

coach (bus) n междуградски автобус ⓜ
mezh-doo-*grad*-skee av-to-*boos*
coach (trainer) треньор ⓜ tren-*yor*
coast крайбрежие ⓝ krai-*bre*-zhee-e
coat палто ⓝ pal-*to*
cockroach хлебарка ⓕ hle-*bar*-ka
cocktail коктейл ⓜ kok-*teyl*
cocoa какао ⓝ ka-*ka*-o
coconut кокосов орех ⓜ ko-ko-sov o-reh
coffee кафе ⓝ ka-*fe*
coins монети ⓕ pl mo-*ne*-tee
cold (illness) n простуда ⓕ pro-*stoo*-da
cold a студен stoo-*den*
colleague колега ⓕ ko-*le*-ga
collect call
обаждане за сметка на абоната ⓝ
o-*bazh*-da-ne za *smet*-ka na a-bo-*na*-tuh
college колеж ⓜ ko-*lezh*
colour n цвят ⓜ tsvyat
comb n гребен ⓜ *gre*-ben
come дойда/идвам doy-duh/*eed*-vam
comedy комедия ⓕ ko-*me*-dee-ya
comfortable удобен oo-*do*-ben
commission комисионна ⓕ
ko-mee-see-*on*-na
communion причастие ⓝ pree-*chas*-tee-e
communist n комунист ⓜ ko-moo-*neest*
communist a комунистически
ko-moo-nees-*tee*-ches-kee
companion другар ⓜ droo-*gar*
company компания ⓕ kom-*pa*-nee-ya
compass компас ⓜ kom-*pas*
complain оплача/оплаквам се
o-*pla*-chuh/o-*plak*-vam se
complaint оплакване ⓝ o-*plak*-va-ne
complimentary (free) безплатен
bez-*pla*-ten
computer компютър ⓜ kom-*pyoo*-tuhr
computer game компютърна игра ⓕ
kom-*pyoo*-tuhr-na ee-*gra*
concert концерт ⓜ kon-*tsert*
concussion мозъчно сътресение ⓝ
mo-zuhch-no suh-tre-*se*-nee-e
conditioner (hair) балсам ⓜ bal-*sam*
condom презерватив ⓜ pre-zer-va-*teev*
conference (big) конференция ⓕ
kon-fe-*ren*-tsee-ya
conference (small) събрание ⓝ
suh-*bra*-nee-e

confession (religious) изповед ⓕ
eez-po-ved
confirm (a booking)
потвърдя/потвърждавам
pot-vuhr-*dyuh*/pot-vuhrzh-*da*-vam
congratulate поздравя/поздравявам
poz-drav-*yuh*/poz-drav-*ya*-vam
conjunctivitis конюнктивит ⓜ
kon-yoonk-tee-*veet*
connection (transport) връзка ⓕ
vruhz-ka
conservative a консервативен
kon-ser-va-*tee*-ven
constipation запек ⓜ *za*-pek
consulate консулство ⓝ *kon*-soolst-vo
contact lenses контактни лещи ⓕ pl
kon-*takt*-nee *lesh*-tee
contact lens solution
разтвор за контактни лещи ⓜ
raz-tvor za kon-*takt*-nee *lesh*-tee
contraceptives
противозачатъчни средства ⓝ pl
pro-tee-vo-za-*cha*-tuhch-nee *sreds*-tva
contract n договор ⓜ *do*-go-vor
convenience store денонощен магазин
ⓜ de-no-*nosh*-ten ma-ga-*zeen*
convent женски манастир ⓜ
zhen-skee ma-na-*steer*
cook n готвач/готвачка ⓜ/ⓕ
got-*vach*/got-*vach*-ka
cook v ротвя got-*vyuh*
cookie бисквита ⓕ beesk-*vee*-ta
cooking ротвене ⓝ got-*ve*-ne
cool (groovy) страхотен stra-*ho*-ten
cool (temperature) хладен hla-*den*
corkscrew тирбушон ⓜ teer-boo-*shon*
corn царевица ⓕ *tsa*-re-vee-tsa
corner ъгъл ⓜ *uh*-guhl
cornflakes корнфлейкс ⓜ pl *korn*-fleyks
corrupt a корумпиран ko-room-*pee*-ran
corruption корупция ⓕ ko-*roop*-tsee-ya
cost n цена ⓕ tse-*na*
cost v струвам *stroo*-vam
cotton n памук ⓜ pa-*mook*
cotton balls чист памук ⓜ
cheest pa-*mook*
cotton buds/swabs клечки за уши ⓕ pl
klech-kee za oo-*shee*
cough n кашлица ⓕ *kash*-lee-tsa
cough v кашлям *kash*-lyam

cough medicine сироп за кашлица ⓜ
see-*rop* za *kash*-lee-tsa

count v броя bro-*yuh*

counter (at bar) щанд ⓜ shtand

country държава ⓕ duhr-*zha*-va

countryside провинция ⓕ
pro-*veen*-tsee-ya

coupon купон ⓜ koo-*pon*

courgette тиквичка ⓕ *teek*-veech-ka

court (legal) съдебна зала ⓕ
suh-*deb*-na za-la

court (sport) игрище ⓝ ee-*greesh*-te

cover charge надценка ⓕ nad-*tsen*-ka

cow крава ⓕ *kra*-va

cracker соленка ⓕ so-*len*-ka

crafts занаяти ⓜ pl za-na-*ya*-tee

crash (accident) n катастрофа ⓕ
ka-tas-*tro*-fa

crazy луд lood

cream (lotion) крем ⓜ krem

crèche детска ясла ⓕ *det*-ska yas-la

credit n кредит ⓜ *kre*-deet

credit card кредитна карта ⓕ
kre-deet-na *kar*-ta

cross (religious) кръст ⓜ kruhst

crowded препълнен pre-*puhl*-nen

cucumber краставица ⓕ *kras*-ta-vee-tsa

cup чаша ⓕ *cha*-sha

cupboard шкаф ⓜ shkaf

currency exchange обмяна на валута ⓕ
ob-*mya*-na na va-*loo*-ta

current (electricity) ток ⓜ tok

current affairs текущи събития ⓝ pl
te-*koosh*-tee suh-*bee*-tee-ya

custom обичай ⓜ o-bee-*chai*

customs (immigration) митница ⓕ
meet-nee-tsa

cut n прорез ⓜ *pro*-rez

cut v режа *re*-zhuh

cutlery прибори за хранене ⓜ pl
pree-bo-ree za *hra*-ne-ne

CV автобиография ⓕ
av-to-bee-o-*gra*-fee-ya

cycle v карам велосипед
ka-ram ve-lo-see-*ped*

cycling колоездене ⓝ ko-lo-*ez*-de-ne

cyclist колоездач/колоездачка ⓜ/ⓕ
ko-lo-ez-*dach*/ko-lo-ez-*dach*-ka

cystitis цистит ⓜ tsees-*teet*

D

dad татко ⓜ *tat*-ko

daily adv ежедневно e-zhed-*nev*-no

dance n танц ⓜ tants

dance v танцувам tan-*tsoo*-vam

dancing танцуване ⓝ tan-*tsoo*-va-ne

dangerous опасен o-*pa*-sen

Danube Дунав ⓜ *doo*-nav

dark тъмен *tuh*-men

date (appointment) среща ⓕ *sresh*-ta

date (day) дата ⓕ *da*-ta

date (fruit) фурма ⓕ foor-*ma*

date (go out with) v изляза/излизам с
eez-*lya*-zuh/eez-*lee*-zam s

date of birth дата на раждане ⓕ
da-ta na *razh*-da-ne

daughter дъщеря ⓕ duhsh-ter-*ya*

dawn зора ⓕ zo-*ra*

day ден ⓜ den

dead мъртъв *muhr*-tuhv

deaf глух glooh

deal (cards) v раздам/раздавам
raz-*dam*/raz-*da*-vam

decide реша/решавам re-*shuh*/re-*sha*-vam

deep дълбок duhl-*bok*

degrees (temperature) градуса ⓜ pl
gra-doo-sa

delay n закъснение ⓝ za-kuhs-*ne*-nee-e

delicatessen магазин за деликатеси ⓜ
ma-ga-*zeen* za de-lee-ka-*te*-see

deliver доставя/доставям
do-*stav*-yuh/do-*stav*-yam

democracy демокрация ⓕ
de-mo-*kra*-tsee-ya

demonstration (display) демонстрация
ⓕ de-mon-*stra*-tsee-ya

demonstration (rally) митинг ⓜ
mee-teeng

Denmark Дания ⓕ *da*-nee-ya

dental dam (safe sex) протеза ⓕ
pro-*te*-za

dental floss конец за зъби ⓜ
ko-*nets* za *zuh*-bee

dentist зъболекар/зъболекарка ⓜ/ⓕ
zuh-bo-*le*-kar/zuh-bo-*le*-kar-ka

deodorant дезодорант ⓜ de-zo-do-*rant*

depart замина/заминавам
za-*mee*-nuh/za-mee-*na*-vam

department store универсален магазин ⑩ oo·nee·ver·*sa*·len ma·ga·*zeen*

departure заминаване ⑪ za·mee·*na*·va·ne

departure gate изход ⑩ *eez*·hod

deposit n депозит ⑩ de·*po*·zeet

desert n пустиня ① poos·*tee*·nya

design n дизайн ⑩ dee·*zain*

dessert десерт ⑩ de·*sert*

destination дестинация ① des·tee·*na*·tsee·ya

details подробности ① pl po·*drob*·nos·tee

diabetes диабет ⑩ dee·a·*bet*

dial tone телефонен сигнал ⑩ te·le·*fo*·nen seeg·*nal*

diaper пелена ① pe·le·*na*

diaphragm (contraceptive) спирала ① spee·ra·la

diarrhoea диария ① dee·a·ree·a

diary дневник ⑩ *dnev*·neek

dice n зарове ⑩ pl *za*·ro·ve

dictionary речник ⑩ *rech*·neek

die умра/умирам oom·*ruh*/oo·*mee*·ram

diet n диета ① dee·*e*·ta

different различен raz·*lee*·chen

difficult труден *troo*·den

digital camera цифров фотоапарат ⑩ *tseef*·rov fo·to·a·pa·*rat*

dining car вагон-ресторант ⑩ va·gon·res·to·*rant*

dinner вечеря ① ve·*che*·rya

direct a пряк *pryak*

direction посока ① po·*so*·ka

dirty мръсен *mruhl*·sen

disabled инвалиден een·va·*lee*·den

disco дискотека ① dees·ko·te·ka

discount n намаление ⑪ na·ma·*le*·nee·e

discrimination дискриминация ① dees·kree·mee·*na*·tsee·ya

disease болест ① *bo*·lest

dish ядене ⑪ *ya*·de·ne

disk (CD-ROM) диск ⑩ deesk

disk (floppy) дискета ① dees·*ke*·ta

diving гмуркане ① *gmoor*·ka·ne

diving equipment екипировка за гмуркане ① e·kee·pee·*rov*·ka za *gmoor*·ka·ne

divorced разведен raz·*ve*·den

dizzy замаян za·*ma*·yan

do правя *prav*·yuh

doctor лекар/лекарка ⑩/① *le*·kar/*le*·kar·ka

documentary документален филм ⑩ do·koo·men·*ta*·len feelm

dog куче ⑪ *koo*·che

dole милостиня ① mee·los·*tee*·nya

doll кукла ① *kook*·la

dollar долар ⑩ *do*·lar

door врата ① vra·*ta*

dope (drugs) марихуана ① ma·ree·hoo·*a*·na

double a двоен *dvo*·yen

double bed двойно легло ⑪ *dvoy*·no leg·*lo*

double room стая с две легла ① *sta*·ya s dve leg·*la*

down долу *do*·loo

downhill надолу na·*do*·loo

drama драма ① *dra*·ma

dream n сън ⑩ suhn

dress n рокля ① *rok*·lya

dried сушен soo·*shen*

dried fruit сушени плодове ⑩ pl soo·*she*·nee plo·do·ve

drink n напитка ① na·*peet*·ka

drink v пия *pee*·yuh

drive v карам *ka*·ram

drivers licence шофьорска книжка ① sho·*fyor*·ska *kneesh*·ka

drug (medication) лекарство ① le·*karst*·vo

drug addiction наркомания ① nar·ko·*ma*·nee·ya

drug dealer наркодилър ⑩ nar·ko·*dee*·luhr

drugs (illicit) наркотици ⑩ pl nar·ko·*tee*·tsee

drug trafficking трафик на наркотици ⑩ *tra*·feek na nar·ko·*tee*·tsee

drug user наркоман/наркоманка ⑩/① nar·ko·*man*/nar·ko·*man*·ka

drum (instrument) барабан ⑩ ba·ra·*ban*

drums (kit) барабани ⑩ pl ba·ra·*ba*·nee

drunk пиян pee·*yan*

dry a сух sooh

dry (clothes) v изсуша/изсушавам eez·soo·*shuh*/eez·soo·*sha*·vam

dry (oneself) v избърша/избърсвам се eez·*buhr*·shuh/eez·*buhr*·svam se

duck патица ⓕ *pa*·tee·tsa
dummy (pacifier) биберон ⓜ bee-be-*ron*
duty-free n безмитен магазин ⓜ
　bez-*mee*-ten ma-ga-*zeen*
DVD дивиди ⓝ dee-vee-*dee*

E

each всеки *vse*·kee
ear ухо ⓝ oo·*ho*
early adv рано *ra*·no
earn печеля pe-*chel*·yuh
earplugs тампони ⓜ pl tam·*po*·nee
earrings обици ⓕ pl o·bee·*tsee*
Earth Земя ⓕ zem·*ya*
earthquake земетресение ⓝ
　ze-me-tre·*se*·nee·e
east n изток ⓜ *eez*·tok
Easter Великден ⓜ ve·*leek*·den
easy лесен *le*·sen
eat ям yam
economy class туристическа класа ⓕ
　too·rees·*tee*·ches·ka *kla*·sa
ecstasy (drug) екстази ⓝ *ek*·sta·zee
eczema екзема ⓕ ek·*ze*·ma
education образование ⓝ
　o·bra·zo·*va*·nee·e
egg яйце ⓝ yai·*tse*
eggplant патладжан ⓜ pat·lad·*zhan*
election избори ⓜ pl *eez*·bo·ree
electrical store
　магазин за електроуреди ⓜ
　ma·ga·*zeen* za e·*lek*·tro·oo·re·dee
electrician електротехник ⓜ
　e·lek·tro·teh·*neek*
electricity електричество ⓝ
　e·lek·*tree*·chest·vo
elevator асансьор ⓜ a·san·*syor*
email n и-мейл ⓜ *ee*·meyl
embarrassed притеснен pree·tes·*nen*
embassy посолство ⓝ po·*solst*·vo
emergency спешен случай ⓜ
　spe·shen *sloo*·chai
emotional емоционален
　e·mo·tsee·o·*na*·len
employee служител/служителка ⓜ/ⓕ
　sloo·*zhee*·tel/sloo·*zhee*·tel·ka
employer работодател/работодателка
　ⓜ/ⓕ ra·bo·to·*da*·tel/ra·bo·to·*da*·tel·ka

empty a празен *pra*·zen
end n край ⓜ krai
endangered species застрашен вид ⓜ
　za·stra·*shen* veed
engaged (phone) зает za·*et*
engaged (to be married) сгоден sgo·*den*
engagement (to marry) годеж ⓜ go·*dezh*
engine мотор ⓜ mo·*tor*
engineer инженер ⓜ een·zhe·*ner*
engineering инженерство ⓝ
　een·zhe·*nerst*·vo
England Англия ⓕ *an*·glee·ya
English (language) n английски ⓜ
　an·*gleey*·skee
enjoy (oneself) забавлявам се
　za·bav·*lya*·vam se
enough достатъчен do·*sta*·tuh·chen
enter влиза/влизам *vlya*·zuh/*vlee*·zam
entertainment guide развлекателна
　програма ⓕ raz·vle·*ka*·tel·na pro·*gra*·ma
entry вход ⓜ vhod
envelope плик за писмо ⓜ
　pleek za pees·*mo*
environment околна среда ⓕ
　o·*kol*·na sre·*da*
epilepsy епилепсия ⓕ e·pee·*lep*·see·ya
equality равноправие ⓝ rav·no·*pra*·vee·e
equal opportunity равни възможности
　ⓕ pl *rav*·nee vuhz·*mozh*·nos·tee
equipment оборудване ⓝ
　o·bo·*rood*·va·ne
escalator ескалатор ⓜ es·ka·*la*·tor
estate agency агенция за недвижими
　имоти ⓕ a·*gen*·tsee·ya za
　ned·*vee*·zhee·mee ee·*mo*·tee
euro евро ⓝ *ev*·ro
Europe Европа ⓕ ev·*ro*·pa
European Union Европейският съюз ⓜ
　ev·ro·*pey*·skee·yuht suh·*yooz*
euthanasia евтаназия ⓕ ev·ta·*na*·zee·ya
evening вечер ⓝ *ve*·cher
every всеки *vse*·kee
everyone всеки ⓜ *vse*·kee
everything всичко ⓝ *vseech*·ko
exactly точно *toch*·no
example пример ⓜ *pree*·mer
excellent отличен ot·*lee*·chen
excess baggage свръхбагаж ⓜ
　svuhrh·ba·*gazh*

exchange v разменя/разменям
raz·men·yuh/raz·men·yam

exchange rate
обменен курс на валутата ⓜ
ob·me·nen koors na va·loo·ta·ta

excluded изключен eez·klyoo·chen

exhaust (car) ауспух ⓜ a·oos·pooh

exhibition изложба ⓕ eez·lozh·ba

exit изход ⓜ eez·hod

expensive скъп skuhp

experience n опит ⓜ o·peet

exploitation експлоатация ⓕ
eks·plo·a·ta·tsee·ya

express a експресен eks·pre·sen

express mail бърза поща ⓕ
buhr·za posh·ta

extension (visa) удължаване ⓝ
oo·duhl·zha·va·ne

eye око ⓝ o·ko

eye drops капки за очи ⓕ pl
kap·kee za o·chee

F

fabric плат ⓜ plat

face n лице ⓝ lee·tse

face cloth кърпа за лице ⓕ
kuhr·pa za lee·tse

factory фабрика ⓕ fa·bree·ka

fall (autumn) есен ⓕ e·sen

fall (down) v падна/падам
pad·nuh/pa·dam

family семейство ⓝ se·meyst·vo

family name фамилно име ⓝ
fa·meel·no ee·me

famous известен eez·ves·ten

fan (machine) вентилатор ⓜ
ven·tee·la·tor

fan (supporter) почитател/почитателка
ⓜ/ⓕ po·chee·ta·tel/po·chee·ta·tel·ka

fan belt ремък ⓜ re·muhk

far adv далече da·le·che

farm n ферма ⓕ fer·ma

farmer фермер/фермерка ⓜ/ⓕ
fer·mer/fer·mer·ka

fashion мода ⓕ mo·da

fast a бърз buhrz

fat a тлъст tluhst

father баща ⓜ bash·ta

father-in-law (husband's father) свекър
ⓜ sve·kuhr

father-in-law (wife's father) тъст ⓜ tuhst

faucet кран ⓜ kran

(someone's) fault грешка ⓕ gresh·ka

faulty дефектен de·fek·ten

fax факс ⓜ faks

feed v храня hran·yuh

feel (emotions) чувствам choovst·vam

feel (touch) пипам pee·pam

feeling (physical) чувство ⓝ choovst·vo

feelings чувства ⓝ pl choovst·va

female a женски zhen·skee

fence n ограда ⓕ o·gra·da

ferry n ферибот ⓜ fe·ree·bot

festival фестивал ⓜ fes·tee·val

fever висока температура ⓕ
vee·so·ka tem·pe·ra·too·ra

few малко mal·ko

fiancé годеник ⓜ go·de·neek

fiancée годеница ⓕ go·de·nee·tsa

fiction художествена литература ⓕ
hoo·do·zhest·ve·na lee·te·ra·too·ra

fig смокиня ⓕ smo·kee·nya

fight n бой ⓜ boy

fill v пълня puhl·nyuh

fillet филе ⓝ fee·le

film (cinema/for camera) филм ⓜ feelm

film speed скорост ⓕ sko·rost

filtered филтриран feel·tree·ran

find v намеря/намирам
na·mer·yuh/na·mee·ram

fine a хубав hoo·bav

fine (payment) n глоба ⓕ glo·ba

finger пръст ⓜ pruhst

finish n край ⓜ krai

finish v завърша/завършвам
za·vuhr·shuh/za·vuhr·shvam

Finland Финландия ⓕ feen·lan·dee·ya

fire n огън ⓜ o·guhn

firewood дърва за огън ⓝ pl
duhr·va za o·guhn

first-aid kit аптечка ⓕ ap·tech·ka

first class първа класа ⓕ puhr·va kla·sa

first name собствено име ⓝ
sobst·ve·no ee·me

fish n риба ⓕ ree·ba

fishing риболов ⓜ ree·bo·lov

fish shop рибарски магазин ⓜ
ree·*bar*·skee ma·ga·*zeen*
flag n знаме ⓝ *zna*·me
flannel (face cloth) кърпа ⓕ *kuhr*·pa
flash (camera) светкавица ⓕ
svet·*ka*·vee·tsa
flashlight (torch) фенерче ⓝ fe·*ner*·che
flash memory флаш памет ⓜ flash *pa*·met
flat (apartment) апартамент ⓜ
a·par·ta·*ment*
flat a плосък *plo*·suhk
flea бълха ⓕ buhl·*ha*
fleamarket битпазар ⓜ beet·pa·*zar*
flight полет ⓜ *po*·let
flood n наводнение ⓝ na·vod·*ne*·nee·e
floor под ⓜ pod
floor (storey) етаж ⓜ e·*tazh*
florist (shop) цветарски магазин ⓜ
tsve·*tar*·skee ma·ga·*zeen*
flour брашно ⓝ brash·*no*
flower цвете ⓝ *tsve*·te
flu грип ⓜ greep
fly n муха ⓕ moo·*ha*
fly v летя let·*yuh*
foggy мъглив muhg·*leev*
follow следя/следвам sled·*yuh*/sled·vam
food храна ⓕ hra·*na*
foot (body) крак ⓜ krak
football (soccer) футбол ⓜ *foot*·bol
footpath пътека ⓕ puh·*te*·ka
foreign чуждестранен choozh·de·*stra*·nen
forest гора ⓕ go·*ra*
forever завинаги za·*vee*·na·gee
forget забравя/забравям
za·*brav*·yuh/za·*brav*·yam
forgive простя/прощавам
prost·*yuh*/prosh·*ta*·vam
fork вилица ⓕ *vee*·lee·tsa
fortnight две седмици ⓕ pl
dve *sed*·mee·tsee
fortune teller врачка ⓕ *vrach*·ka
foul (sport) нарушение ⓝ
na·roo·*she*·nee·e
foyer фоайе ⓝ fo·a·*ye*
fragile чуплив choop·*leev*
France Франция ⓕ *fran*·tsee·ya
free (available/not bound) свободен
svo·*bo*·den
free (gratis) безплатен bez·*pla*·ten

freeze v замразя/замразявам
za·mraz·*yuh*/za·mraz·*ya*·vam
fresh пресен *pre*·sen
fridge хладилник ⓜ hla·*deel*·neek
fried пържен *puhr*·zhen
friend приятел/приятелка ⓜ/ⓕ
pree·*ya*·tel/pree·*ya*·tel·ka
from от ot
frost мраз ⓜ mraz
frozen замръзнал za·*mruhz*·nal
fruit плод ⓜ plod
fruit picking бране на плодове ⓝ
bra·*ne* na plo·do·*ve*
fry v пържа *puhr*·zhuh
frying pan тиган ⓜ tee·*gan*
full пълен *puh*·len
full-time на пълен работен ден
na *puh*·len ra·*bo*·ten den
fun a забавен za·*ba*·ven
funeral погребение ⓝ po·gre·*be*·nee·e
funny смешен *sme*·shen
furniture мебели ⓜ pl *me*·be·lee
future n бъдеще ⓝ *buh*·desh·te

G

game (sport) игра ⓕ ee·*gra*
garage гараж ⓜ ga·*razh*
garbage боклук ⓜ bok·*look*
garbage can кофа за боклук ⓕ
ko·fa za bok·*look*
garden n градина ⓕ gra·*dee*·na
gardener градинар/градинарка ⓜ/ⓕ
gra·dee·*nar*/gra·dee·*nar*·ka
gardening градинарство ⓝ
gra·dee·*narst*·vo
garlic чесън ⓜ *che*·suhn
gas (for cooking) газ ⓜ gaz
gas (petrol) бензин ⓜ ben·*zeen*
gas cartridge газова бутилка ⓕ
ga·zo·va boo·*teel*·ka
gastroenteritis гастроентерит ⓜ
gas·tro·en·te·*reet*
gate (airport, etc) изход ⓜ *eez*·hod
gauze марля ⓕ *mar*·lya
gay (homosexual) n&a гей ⓜ&ⓕ gey
gearbox скоростна кутия ⓕ
sko·rost·na koo·*tee*·ya
Germany Германия ⓕ ger·*ma*·nee·ya

get получа/получавам
po-*loo*-chuh/po-*loo*-cha-vam

get off (train, etc) сляза/слизам
slya-zuh/*slee*-zam

gift подарък ⓜ po-*da*-ruhk

gig концерт ⓝ kon-*tsert*

gin джин ⓜ dzheen

girl момиче ⓝ mo-*mee*-che

girlfriend гадже ⓝ *gad*-zhe

give дам/давам dam/*da*-vam

given name собствено име ⓝ
sobst-ve-no *ee*-me

glandular fever възпаление на
лимфните възли ⓝ vuhz-pa-*le*-nee-e
na *leemf*-nee-te *vuhz*-lee

glass (drinking) чаша ⓕ *cha*-sha

glasses (spectacles) очила ⓝ pl o-chee-*la*

gloves (clothing) ръкавици ⓕ pl
ruh-ka-*vee*-tsee

gloves (latex) гумени ръкавици ⓕ pl
goo-me-nee ruh-ka-*vee*-tsee

glue n лепило ⓝ le-*pee*-lo

go отида/отивам o-*tee*-duh/o-*tee*-vam

goal (sport) гол ⓜ gol

goalkeeper вратар ⓜ vra-*tar*

goat коза ⓕ ko-*za*

god (general) бог ⓜ bog

goggles (skiing) скиорски очила ⓝ pl
skee-*or*-skee o-chee-*la*

goggles (swimming) очила за плуване
ⓝ pl o-chee-*la* za *ploo*-va-ne

gold n злато ⓝ *zla*-to

go out (with) изляза/излизам (с)
eez-*lya*-zuh/eez-*lee*-zam (s)

go shopping пазарувам pa-za-*roo*-vam

government правителство ⓝ
pra-*vee*-telst-vo

gram грам ⓜ gram

grandchild внуче ⓝ *vnoo*-che

grandfather дядо ⓜ *dya*-do

grandmother баба ⓕ *ba*-ba

grapes грозде ⓝ *groz*-de

grass трева ⓕ tre-*va*

grateful благодарен bla-go-*da*-ren

grave гроб ⓜ grob

great (fantastic) чудесен choo-*de*-sen

Greece Гърция ⓕ *guhr*-tsee-ya

green зелен ze-*len*

greengrocer
зарзаватчия/зарзаватчийка ⓜ/ⓕ
zar-za-vat-*chee*-ya/ zar-za-vat-*cheey*-ka

grey сив seev

groceries хранителни стоки ⓕ pl
hra-*nee*-tel-nee *sto*-kee

grow раста ras-*tuh*

guarantee n гаранция ⓕ ga-*ran*-tsee-ya

guess v отгатна/отгатвам
ot-*gat*-nuh/ot-*gat*-vam

guesthouse малък хотел ⓜ
ma-luhk ho-*tel*

guide (audio) аудио гид ⓜ
a-oo-dee-o geed

guide (person)
екскурзовод/екскурзоводка ⓜ/ⓕ
eks-koor-zo-*vod*/eks-koor-zo-*vod*-ka

guidebook пътеводител ⓝ
puh-te-vo-*dee*-tel

guide dog куче-водач ⓝ *koo*-che-vo-*dach*

guided tour екскурзия ⓕ eks-*koor*-zee-ya

guilty виновен vee-*no*-ven

guitar китара ⓕ kee-*ta*-ra

gums (mouth) венци ⓜ pl ven-*tsee*

gun оръжие ⓝ o-*ruh*-zhee-e

gym (place) фитнес център ⓜ
feet-nes *tsen*-tuhr

gynaecologist гинеколог/гинеколожка
ⓜ/ⓕ gee-ne-ko-*log*/gee-ne-ko-*lozh*-ka

H

hair коса ⓕ ko-*sa*

hairbrush четка за коса ⓕ *chet*-ka za ko-*sa*

haircut подстригване ⓝ pod-*streeg*-va-ne

hairdresser фризьор/фризьорка ⓜ/ⓕ
freez-*yor*/freez-*yor*-ka

half n половина ⓕ po-lo-*vee*-na

hallucination халюцинация ⓕ
ha-lyoo-tsee-*na*-tsee-ya

ham шунка ⓕ *shoon*-ka

hammer n чук ⓜ chook

hammock хамак ⓜ ha-*mak*

hand ръка ⓕ ruh-*ka*

handbag чанта ⓕ *chan*-ta

handball хандбал ⓜ *hand*-bal

handicraft ръчна изработка ⓕ
ruhch-na eez-ra-*bot*-ka

handkerchief носна кърпичка ⓕ
  nos·na *kuhr*·peech·ka
handlebars кормило ⓝ *kor*·mee·lo
handmade ръчно изработен
  ruhch·no eez·ra·*bo*·ten
handsome красив kra·*seev*
happy щастлив shtast·*leev*
harassment тормоз ⓜ *tor*·moz
harbour n пристанище ⓝ
  pree·*sta*·neesh·te
hard (not soft) твърд tvuhrd
hardware store железария ⓕ
  zhe·le·za·*ree*·ya
hat шапка ⓕ *shap*·ka
have имам *ee*·mam
have a cold настинал/настинала съм
  ⓜ/ⓕ na·*stee*·nal/na·*stee*·na·la suhm
have fun забавлявам се
  za·bav·*lya*·vam se
hay fever сенна хрема ⓕ *sen*·na *hre*·ma
hazelnut лешник ⓜ *lesh*·neek
he той toy
head глава ⓕ gla·*va*
headache главоболие ⓝ gla·vo·*bo*·lee·e
headlight фар ⓜ far
health здраве ⓝ *zdra*·ve
hear чуя/чувам *choo*·yuh/*choo*·vam
hearing aid слухов апарат ⓜ
  sloo·hov a·pa·*rat*
heart сърце ⓝ suhr·*tse*
heart attack инфаркт ⓜ een·*farkt*
heart condition сърдечно заболяване ⓝ
  suhr·*dech*·no za·bo·*lya*·va·ne
heat n горещина ⓕ go·resh·*tee*·na
heated затоплен za·*top*·len
heater радиатор ⓜ ra·dee·*a*·tor
heating отопление ⓝ o·top·*le*·nee·e
heavy тежък *te*·zhuhk
helmet каска ⓕ *kas*·ka
help n помощ ⓕ *po*·mosht
help v помогна/помагам
  po·*mog*·nuh/po·*ma*·gam
hepatitis хепатит ⓜ he·pa·*teet*
her (possessive) неин *ne*·een
herbs билки ⓕ pl *beel*·kee
herbalist билкар/билкарка ⓜ/ⓕ
  beel·*kar*/beel·*kar*·ka
here тука *too*·ka
herring херинга ⓕ *he*·reen·ga
high висок vee·*sok*

highchair детско столче ⓝ
  det·sko *stol*·che
high school гимназия ⓕ geem·*na*·zee·ya
highway магистрала ⓕ ma·gees·*tra*·la
hike v отида/отивам на поход
  o·*tee*·duh/o·*tee*·vam na po·*hod*
hiking пешеходство ⓝ pe·she·*hod*·stvo
hiking boots туристически обувки ⓕ pl
  too·rees·*tee*·ches·kee o·*boov*·kee
hill хълм ⓜ huhlm
hire v наема/наемам na·e·muh/na·e·mam
his негов *ne*·gov
historical исторически ees·to·*ree*·ches·kee
history история ⓕ ees·*to*·ree·ya
hitchhike пътувам на автостоп
  puh·*too*·vam na *av*·to·stop
HIV вирус на СПИН ⓜ *vee*·roos na speen
holiday n празник ⓜ *praz*·neek
holidays ваканция ⓕ va·*kan*·tsee·ya
home дом ⓜ dom
homeless бездомен bez·*do*·men
homemaker домакиня ⓕ do·ma·*kee*·nya
homesick обзет от носталгия
  ob·*zet* ot nos·*tal*·gee·ya
homosexual a гей gey
honey мед ⓜ med
honeymoon меден месец ⓜ
  me·den *me*·sets
horse кон ⓜ kon
horse racing надбягване с коне ⓝ
  nad·*byag*·va·ne na ko·*ne*
horse riding конна езда ⓕ *kon*·na ez·*da*
hospital болница ⓕ *bol*·nee·tsa
hospitality гостоприемство ⓝ
  gos·to·pree·*emst*·vo
hot (temperature) горещ go·*resht*
hotel хотел ⓜ ho·*tel*
hot water топла вода ⓕ *top*·la vo·*da*
hot water bottle грейка ⓕ *grey*·ka
hour час ⓜ chas
house къща ⓕ *kuhsh*·ta
housework домакинска работа ⓕ
  do·ma·*keen*·ska ra·*bo*·ta
how как kak
how much колко *kol*·ko
hug v прегърна/прегръщам
  pre·*guhr*·nuh/pre·*gruhsh*·tam
huge огромен o·*gro*·men
human rights човешки права ⓝ pl
  cho·*vesh*·kee pra·*va*

hungry гладен *gla*·den
hurt v боли bo·*lee*
husband мъж ⓜ muhzh

I аз az
ice лед ⓜ led
ice cream сладолед ⓜ sla·do·*led*
ice hockey хокей на лед ⓜ *ho*·key na led
identification лична карта ⓕ
leech·na *kar*·ta
idiot идиот ⓜ ee·de·*ot*
if ако a·*ko*
ill болен *bo*·len
immigration имиграция ⓕ
ee·mee·*gra*·tsee·ya
important важен *va*·zhen
impossible невъзможен ne·vuhz·*mo*·zhen
in в v
in a hurry набързо na·*buhr*·zo
included включен *vklyoo*·chen
income tax данък общ доход ⓜ
da·nuhk obsht *do*·hod
India Индия ⓕ *een*·dee·ya
indicator показател ⓜ po·ka·*za*·tel
indigestion лошо храносмилане ⓜ
lo·sho hra·no·*smee*·la·ne
indoor на закрито na za·*kree*·to
industry промишленост ⓕ
pro·*meesh*·le·nost
infection инфекция ⓕ een·*tek*·tsee·ya
inflammation възпаление ⓜ
vuhz·pa·*le*·nee·e
influenza грип ⓜ greep
information информация ⓕ
een·for·*ma*·tsee·ya
in front of пред pred
ingredient съставка ⓕ suh·*stav*·ka
inject инжектирам een·zhek·*tee*·ram
injection инжекция ⓕ een·*zhek*·tsee·ya
injured ранен ra·*nen*
injury контузия ⓕ kon·*too*·zee·ya
innocent невинен ne·*vee*·nen
insect насекомо ⓝ na·se·*ko*·mo
insect repellent репелент ⓜ re·pe·*lent*
inside adv вътре *vuh*·tre
instructor инструктор/инструкторка
ⓜ/ⓕ een·*strook*·tor/een·*strook*·tor·ka

insurance застраховка ⓕ za·stra·*hov*·ka
interesting интересен een·te·*re*·sen
intermission пауза ⓕ *pa*·oo·za
international международен
mezh·doo·na·*ro*·den
internet Интернет ⓜ *een*·ter·net
internet café Интернет кафе ⓝ
een·ter·net ka·*fe*
interpreter преводач/преводачка ⓜ/ⓕ
pre·vo·*dach*/pre·vo·*dach*·ka
interview n интервю ⓜ een·ter·*vyoo*
invite v каня *kan*·yuh
iron (for clothes) ютия ⓕ yoo·*tee*·ya
Ireland Ирландия ⓕ eer·*lan*·dee·ya
island остров ⓜ *os*·trov
Israel Израел ⓕ eez·ra·*el*
it то to
IT информационни технологии ⓕ pl
een·for·ma·tsee·o·nee teh·no·*lo*·gee·ee
Italy Италия ⓕ ee·*ta*·lee·ya
itch n сърбеж ⓜ suhr·*bezh*
itemised описан точка по точка
o·*pee*·san *toch*·ka po *toch*·ka
itinerary маршрут ⓜ marsh·*root*
IUD вътрематочен контрацептив ⓜ
vuh·tre·*ma*·to·chen kon·tra·tsep·*teev*

J

jacket яке ⓝ *ya*·ke
jail n затвор ⓜ *zat*·vor
jam конфитюр ⓜ kon·fee·*tyoor*
Japan Япония ⓕ ya·*po*·nee·ya
jar буркан ⓜ boor·*kan*
jaw челюст ⓕ *chel*·yoost
jealous ревнив rev·*neev*
jewellery бижута ⓕ bee·*zhoo*·ta
job работа ⓕ *ra*·bo·ta
jogging джогинг ⓝ *dzho*·geeng
joke n шега ⓕ she·*ga*
journalist журналист/журналистка ⓜ/ⓕ
zhoor·na·*leest*/zhoor·na·*leest*·ka
journey n пътуване ⓝ puh·*too*·va·ne
judge n съдия/съдийка ⓜ/ⓕ
suh·dee·*ya*/suh·*deey*·ka
juice сок ⓜ sok
jump v скоча/скачам *sko*·chuh/*ska*·cham
jumper (sweater) пуловер ⓜ poo·*lo*·ver

english–bulgarian

K

ketchup кетчуп ⓝ *ket*-choop
key n ключ ⓜ klyooch
keyboard клавиатура ① kla-vee-a-*too*-ra
kick v ритна/ритам *reet*-nuh/*ree*-tam
kidney бъбрек ⓜ *buh*-brek
kill v убия/убивам oo-*bee*-yuh/oo-*bee*-vam
kilogram килограм ⓜ kee-lo-*gram*
kilometre километър ⓜ kee-lo-*me*-tuhr
kind (nice) любезен lyoo-*be*-zen
kindergarten детска градина ①
det-ska gra-*dee*-na
king крал ⓜ kral
kiosk будка ① *bood*-ka
kiss n целувка ① tse-*loov*-ka
kiss v целуна/целувам
tse-*loo*-nuh/tse-*loo*-vam
kitchen кухня ① *kooh*-nya
knee коляно ⓝ ko-*lya*-no
knife нож ⓜ nozh
know зная *zna*-yuh
kosher кашер *ka*-sher

L

labourer работник/работничка ⓜ/①
ra-*bot*-neek/ra-*bot*-neech-ka
lace n дантела ① dan-*te*-la
lake n езеро ① *e*-ze-ro
lamb (meat) агнешко ⓝ *ag*-nesh-ko
land n земя ① zem-*ya*
landlady хазайка ① ha-*zai*-ka
landlord хазаин ⓜ ha-*za*-een
landslide свличане ⓝ *svlee*-cha-ne
language език ⓜ e-*zeek*
laptop лаптоп ⓜ *lap*-top
large голям go-*lyam*
last (final) последен po-*sle*-den
last (previous) минал *mee*-nal
late adv късно *kuhs*-no
later adv по-късно po-*kuhs*-no
laugh v смея се *sme*-yuh se
laundrette обществена перална на
самообслужване ① obsh-*test*-ve-na
pe-*ral*-nya na sa-mo-ob-*sloozh*-va-ne
laundry (clothes) пране ⓝ *pra*-ne
laundry (room) перална ① pe-*ral*-nya
law (rule) закон ⓜ *za*-kon

law (study/profession) право ⓝ *pra*-vo
lawyer адвокат ⓜ ad-vo-*kat*
laxative n очистително ⓝ
o-chees-*tee*-tel-no
lazy мързелив muhr-ze-*leev*
leaf листо ① lees-*to*
learn уча *oo*-chuh
leather n кожа ① *ko*-zha
ledge полица ① po-*lee*-tsa
left (direction) ляв lyav
left-luggage office гардероб ⓜ
gar-de-*rob*
left-wing ляв lyav
leg (body) крак ⓜ krak
legal законен za-*ko*-nen
legislation законодателство ⓝ
za-ko-no-*da*-telst-vo
legume бобово растение ⓝ
bo-bo-vo ras-*te*-nee-e
lemon лимон ⓜ lee-*mon*
lemonade лимонада ① lee-mo-*na*-da
lens (camera) обектив ⓜ o-bek-*teev*
lentils леща ① pl *lesh*-ta
lesbian a гей gey
less по-малко po-*mal*-ko
letter (mail) писмо ⓝ pees-*mo*
lettuce маруля ① ma-*roo*-lya
liar лъжец/лъжкиня ⓜ/①
luh-*zhets*/luhzh-*kee*-nya
librarian
библиотекар/библиотекарка ⓜ/①
bee-blee-o-te-*kar*/bee-blee-o-te-*kar*-ka
library библиотека ① bee-blee-o-*te*-ka
lice въшки ① pl *vuhsh*-kee
licence n разрешение ⓝ raz-re-*she*-nee-e
license plate number номер на кола ⓜ
no-mer na ko-*la*
lie (down) v легна/лягам *leg*-nuh/*lya*-gam
lie (to someone) v лъжа luh-*zhuh*
life живот ⓜ zhee-*vot*
life jacket спасителна жилетка ①
spa-*see*-tel-na zhee-*let*-ka
lift (elevator) асансьор ⓜ a-san-*syor*
light n светлина ① svet-lee-*na*
light (colour) a светъл *sve*-tuhl
light (weight) a лек lek
light bulb електрическа крушка ①
e-lek-*tree*-ches-ka *kroosh*-ka
lighter (cigarette) запалка ① za-*pal*-ka
light meter светломер ⓜ svet-lo-*mer*

ke v харесам/харесвам
ha-*re*-sam/ha-*res*-vam

me лайм ⓜ laim

nen (fabric) лен ⓜ len

nen (sheets) спално бельо ⓝ
spal-no bel-*yo*

ip balm гланц за устни ⓜ
glants za *oost*-nee

ips устни ⓕ pl *oost*-nee

liquor store магазин за алкохолни напитки ⓜ
ma-ga-*zeen* za al-ko-*hol*-nee na-*peet*-kee

isten слушам sloo-sham

ittle (quantity) малко *mal*-ko

ittle (size) малък ma-*luhk*

ive живея zhee-*ve*-yuh

iver черен дроб ⓜ *che*-ren drob

ocal a местен *mes*-ten

ock n ключалка ⓕ klyoo-*chal*-ka

ock v заключа/заключвам
za-*klyoo*-chuh/za-*klyooch*-vam

ocked заключен za-*klyoo*-chen

ollies бонбони ⓜ pl bon-*bo*-nee

ong дълъг *duh*-luhg

ook v гледам *gle*-dam

ook after грижа се за *gree*-zhuh se za

ook for търся *tuhr*-syuh

ookout наблюдателен пост ⓜ
nab-lyoo-*da*-te-len post

oose (clothing) широк shee-*rok*

ose губя *goob*-yuh

ost изгубен eez-*goo*-ben

ost-property office бюро за изгубени вещи ⓝ
byoo-*ro* za eez-*goo*-be-nee *vesh*-tee

a) lot много *mno*-go

oud шумен *shoo*-men

ove n обич ⓕ *o*-beech

ove v обичам o-*bee*-cham

over любовник/любовница ⓜ/ⓕ
lyoo-*bov*-neek/lyoo-*bov*-nee-tsa

ow нисък *nee*-suhk

ubricant смазочно масло ⓝ
sma-zoch-no *mas*-lo

uck късмет ⓜ kuhs-*met*

ucky късметлия kuhs-met-*lee*-ya

uggage багаж ⓜ ba-*gazh*

uggage locker гардероб ⓜ gar-de-*rob*

uggage tag етикет за багаж ⓜ
e-tee-*ket* za ba-*gazh*

lump буца ⓕ *boo*-tsa

lunch обед ⓜ *o*-bed

lung бял дроб ⓜ byal drob

luxury разкош ⓜ ras-*kosh*

M

Macedonia Македония ⓕ
ma-ke-*do*-nee-ya

machine машина ⓕ ma-*shee*-na

magazine списание ⓝ spee-*sa*-nee-e

mail (letters/postal system) n поща ⓕ
posh-ta

mail v пратя/пращам по пощата
prat-yuh/*prash*-tam po *posh*-ta-ta

mailbox пощенска кутия ⓕ
posh-ten-ska koo-*tee*-ya

main главен *gla*-ven

main road главен път ⓜ *gla*-ven puht

make направя/правя
na-*prav*-yuh/*prav*-yuh

make-up n грим ⓜ greem

mammogram мамограма ⓕ
ma-mo-*gra*-ma

man човек ⓜ cho-*vek*

manager (business) директор/директорка ⓜ/ⓕ
dee-*rek*-tor/dee-*rek*-tor-ka

manager (sport) мениджър/мениджърка ⓜ/ⓕ
me need zhuhr/*me* need zhuhr-ka

mandarin мандарина ⓕ man-da-*ree*-na

manual worker работник ⓜ ra-*bot*-neek

many много *mno*-go

map (of country) карта ⓕ *kar*-ta

map (of town) план ⓜ plan

margarine маргарин ⓜ mar-ga-*reen*

marijuana марихуана ⓕ ma-ree-hoo-*a*-na

marital status семейно положение ⓝ
se-*mey*-no po-lo-*zhe*-nee-e

market n пазар ⓜ pa-*zar*

marriage брак ⓜ brak

married женен/омъжена ⓜ/ⓕ
zhe-nen/o-*muh*-zhe-na

marry (by man/woman) v оженя/
омъжа се o-*zhen*-yuh/o-*muh*-zhuh se

martial arts бойни изкуства ⓝ pl
boy-nee eez-*koost*-va

mass (Catholic) католическа литургия ⓕ
ka-to-lee-ches-ka lee-toor-ge-ya

massage n масаж ⓜ ma-sazh

masseur масажист ⓜ ma-sa-zheest

masseuse масажистка ⓕ ma-sa-zheest-ka

mat подложка ⓕ pod-lozh-ka

match (sports) мач ⓜ mach

matches (for lighting) кибрит ⓜ kee-breet

mattress матрак ⓜ mat-rak

maybe може би mo-zhe bee

mayonnaise майонеза ⓕ ma-yo-ne-za

mayor кмет ⓜ kmet

me мене me-ne

meal ядене ⓝ ya-de-ne

measles шарка ⓕ shar-ka

meat месо ⓝ me-so

mechanic механик ⓜ me-ha-neek

media медии ⓕ pl me-dee-ee

medicine (medication) лекарство ⓝ
le-karst-vo

medicine (study/profession) медицина ⓕ
me-dee-tsee-na

meditation медитация ⓕ
me-dee-ta-tsee-ya

meet (first time)
запозная/запознавам se
za-poz-na-yuh/za-poz-na-vam se

meet (get together) срещна/срещам
sresht-nuh/sresh-tam

melon пъпеш ⓜ puh-pesh

member член ⓜ chlen

memory card/stick флаш памет ⓜ
flash pa-met

menstruation менструация ⓕ
mens-troo-a-tsee-ya

menu меню ⓝ men-yoo

message съобщение ⓝ
suh-ob-shte-nee-e

metal n метал ⓜ me-tal

metre метър ⓜ me-tuhr

microwave oven микровълнова печка ⓕ
mee-kro-vuhl-no-va pech-ka

midday обяд ⓝ ob-yad

midnight полунощ ⓕ po-loo-nosht

migraine мигрена ⓕ mee-gre-na

military n военните ⓝ pl vo-en-nee-te

military service военна служба ⓕ
vo-en-na sloozh-ba

milk мляко ⓝ mlya-ko

millimetre милиметър ⓜ mee-lee-me-tuhr

mincemeat кайма ⓕ kai-ma

mineral water минерална вода ⓕ
mee-ne-ral-na vo-da

minute минута ⓕ mee-noo-ta

mirror n огледало ⓝ o-gle-da-lo

miscarriage спонтанен аборт ⓜ
spon-ta-nen a-bort

miss (feel absence of ...) ... ми липсва
... mee leep-sva

miss (train, etc) изпусна/изпускам
ees-poos-nuh/ees-poos-kam

mistake n грешка ⓕ gresh-ka

mix v смеся/смесвам smes-yuh/smes-var

mobile phone GSM ⓜ dzhee-es-em

modem модем ⓜ mo-dem

modern съвременен suh-vre-me-nen

moisturiser овлажнител ⓜ o-vlazh-nee-te

monastery манастир ⓜ ma-nas-teer

money пари ⓕ pl pa-ree

monk монах ⓜ mo-nah

month месец ⓜ me-sets

monument паметник ⓜ pa-met-neek

moon луна ⓕ loo-na

more повече po-ve-che

morning утро ⓝ oo-tro

mosque джамия ⓕ dzha-mee-ya

mosquito комар ⓜ ko-mar

mosquito net комарник ⓜ ko-mar-neek

motel мотел ⓜ mo-tel

mother майка ⓕ mai-ka

mother-in-law (husband's mother)
свекърва ⓕ sve-kuhr-va

mother-in-law (wife's mother)
тъща ⓕ tuhsh-ta

motorbike мотоциклет ⓜ mo-to-tsee-kle

motorboat моторница ⓕ mo-tor-nee-ts

motorway магистрала ⓕ ma-gees-tra-la

mountain планина ⓕ pla-nee-na

mountain bike планински велосипед ⓜ
pla-neen-skee ve-lo-see-ped

mountaineering планинарство ⓝ
pla-nee-narst-vo

mountain path пътека по планините
puh-te-ka po pla-nee-nee-te

mountain range планинска верига ⓕ
pla-neen-ska ve-ree-ga

mouse (animal/computer) мишка ⓕ
meesh-ka

mouth уста ⓕ oos-ta

movie кино ⓝ kee-no

ud кал ① kal
uesli мюсли ⑩ myoos·lee
um мама ① ma·ma
umps заушки ⑩ pl za·oosh·kee
urder n убийство ⑪ oo·beeys·tvo
urder v убия/убивам
  oo·bee·yuh/oo·bee·vam
uscle мускул ⑩ moos·kool
useum музей ⑩ moo·zey
ushroom гъба ① guh·ba
usic музика ① moo·zee·ka
usician музикант/музикантка ⑩/①
  moo·zee·kant/moo·zee·kant·ka
usic shop музикален магазин ⑩
  moo·zee·ka·len ma·ga·zeen
ussel мида ① mee·da
ustard горчица ① gor·chee·tsa
ute ням nyam
y мой moy

N

ail clippers ноктерезачка ①
  nok·to·re·zach·ka
ame n име ⑪ ee·me
apkin салфетка ① sal·fet·ka
appy пелена ① pe·le·na
appy rash подсичане ⑪ pod·see·cha·ne
ationality националност ①
  na·tsee·o·nal·nost
ational park национален парк ⑩
  na·tsee·o·na·len park
ature природа ① pree·ro·da
aturopath екопатевт ⑪ e·ko·pa·tevt
ausea гадене ⑪ ga·de·ne
ear prep близо до blee·zo do
earby adv наблизо na·blee·zo
earest най-близкият nai·bleez·kee·yuht
ecessary необходим ne·ob·ho·deem
eck шия ① shee·ya
ecklace огърлица ① o·guhr·lee·tsa
ectarine гола праскова ①
  go·la pras·ko·va
eed v нуждая се от noozh·da·yuh se ot
eedle (sewing) игла ① eeg·la
eedle (syringe) спринцовка ①
  spreen·tsov·ka
egative a отрицателен ot·ree·tsa·te·len
egatives (photos) негатив ⑩ ne·ga·teev

neither adv нито … нито nee·to … nee·to
net мрежа ① mre·zha
Netherlands Холандия ① ho·lan·dee·ya
network (phone) мрежа ① mre·zha
never никога nee·ko·ga
new нов nov
news новина ① no·vee·na
newsagency информационна агенция ①
  een·for·ma·tsee·on·na a·gen·tsee·ya
newspaper вестник ⑩ vest·neek
newsstand вестникарска будка ①
  vest·nee·kar·ska bood·ka
New Year's Day Нова година ①
  no·va go·dee·na
New Year's Eve Новогодишна нощ ①
  no·vo·go·deesh·na nosht
New Zealand Нова Зеландия ①
  no·va ze·lan·dee·ya
next (following) следващ sled·vasht
next to до do
nice приятен pree·ya·ten
nickname прякор ⑩ prya·kor
night нощ ① nosht
nightclub нощен клуб ⑩ nosh·ten kloob
night out нощ на открито ①
  nosht na ot·kree·to
no не ne
noisy шумен shoo·men
none никакъв nee·ka·kuhv
nonsmoking за непушачи
  za ne·poo·sha·chee
noodles юфка ① yoof·ka
noon обяд ⑩ ob·yad
north n север ⑩ se·ver
Norway Норвегия ① nor·ve·gee·ya
nose нос ⑩ nos
not не ne
notebook тетрадка ① tet·rad·ka
nothing нищо neesh·to
now сега se·ga
nuclear energy атомна енергия ①
  a·tom·na e·ner·gee·ya
nuclear testing ядрени опити ⑩ pl
  ya·dre·nee o·pee·tee
nuclear waste
  радиоактивни отпадъци ⑩ pl
  ra·dee·o·ak·teev·nee ot·pa·duh·tsee
number n число ⑪ chees·lo
numberplate номер на кола ⑩
  no·mer na ko·la

nun монахиня ① mo·na·*hee*·nya
nurse n медицинска сестра ①
me·dee·*tseen*·ska ses·*tra*
nut ядка ① *yad*·ka

O

oatmeal овесени ядки ① pl
o·ve·se·nee *yad*·kee
ocean океан ① o·ke·*an*
off (power) изключен eesk·*lyoo*·chen
off (spoiled) развален raz·va·*len*
office офис ⓜ *o*·fees
office worker служител/служителка ⓜ/①
sloo·*zhee*·tel/sloo·*zhee*·tel·ka
often често *ches*·to
oil (cooking) олио ① o·lee·o
oil (petrol) нефт ⓜ neft
old стар star
olive маслина ① mas·*lee*·na
olive oil зехтин ⓜ zeh·*teen*
omelette омлет ⓜ om·*let*
on на na
on (power) включен vklyoo·chen
once веднъж ved·*nuhzh*
one-way ticket еднопосочен билет ⓜ
ed·no·po·*so*·chen bee·*let*
onion лук ⓜ look
only само *sa*·mo
on time навреме na·*vre*·me
open (business) a отворен ot·*vo*·ren
open v отворя/отварям
ot·*vor*·yuh/ot·*var*·yam
opening hours работно време ⓝ
ra·*bot*·no *vre*·me
opera опера ① *o*·pe·ra
opera house опера ① *o*·pe·ra
operation (medical) операция ①
o·pe·*ra*·tsee·ya
operator (telephone)
телефонист/телефонистка ⓜ/①
te·le·fo·*neest*/te·le·fo·*neest*·ka
opinion мнение ⓝ *mne*·nee·e
opposite prep срещу sresh·*too*
optometrist оптик ⓜ op·*teek*
or или ee·*lee*
orange (colour) оранжев o·*ran*·zhev
orange (fruit) портокал ⓜ por·to·*kal*

orange juice портокалов сок ⓜ
por·to·*ka*·lov sok
orchestra оркестър ⓜ or·*kes*·tuhr
order n ред ⓜ red
order v поръчвам/поръчам
po·*ruh*·cham/po·*ruhch*·vam
ordinary обикновен o·beek·no·*ven*
orgasm оргазъм ⓜ or·*ga*·zuhm
original a първоначален
puhr·vo·na·*cha*·len
other друг droog
our наш nash
out of order повреден po·*vre*·den
outside adv навън na·*vuhn*
ovarian cyst киста на яйчниците ①
kees·ta na yaich·nee·tsee·te
ovary яйчник ⓜ *yaich*·neek
oven фурна ① *foor*·na
overcoat палто ⓝ pal·to
overdose n свръхдоза ① *svruh*·do·za
overnight adv за една нощ za ed·*na* nosh
overseas adv в чужбина v choozh·*bee*·na
owe дължа duhl·*zhuh*
owner собственик/собственичка ⓜ/①
sobst·ve·neek/*sobst*·ve·neech·ka
oxygen кислород ⓜ kees·lo·*rod*
oyster стрида ① *stree*·da
ozone layer озонов слой ⓜ o·*zo*·nov sloy

P

pacemaker пейсмейкър ⓜ *peys*·mey·kuhr
pacifier (dummy) биберон ⓜ bee·be·*ron*
package пакет ⓜ pa·*ket*
packet пакет ⓜ pa·*ket*
padlock катинар ⓜ ka·tee·*nar*
page страница ① *stra*·nee·tsa
pain болка ① *bol*·ka
painful болезнен bo·*lez*·nen
painkillers
болкоуспокоителни лекарства ⓝ pl
bol·ko·oos·po·ko·ee·tel·nee le·*karst*·va
painter (artist)
художник/художничка ⓜ/①
hoo·*dozh*·neek/hoo·*dozh*·neech·ka
painter (tradesperson) бояджия ⓜ
bo·yad·*zhee*·ya
painting (a work) картина ① kar·*tee*·na

painting (the art) изобразително изкуство ⓝ
ee·zo·bra·*zee*·tel·no eez·*koost*·vo

pair (couple) двойка ⓕ *dvoy*·ka

palace дворец ⓜ dvo·*rets*

pan тенджера ⓕ *tend*·zhe·ra

pants (trousers) панталони ⓜ pl
pan·ta·*lo*·nee

pantyhose чорапогащник ⓜ
cho·ra·po·*gasht*·neek

panty liners дамски превръзки ⓕ pl
dam·skee pre·*vruhz*·kee

paper n хартия ⓕ har·*tee*·ya

paperwork попълване на документи ⓝ
po·*puhl*·va·ne na do·koo·*men*·tee

paraplegic a параплегичен
pa·ra·ple·*gee*·chen

parcel колет ⓜ ko·*let*

parents родители ⓜ pl ro·*dee*·te·lee

park n парк ⓜ park

park (a car) v паркирам par·*kee*·ram

parliament парламент ⓜ par·la·*ment*

part (component) част ⓕ chast

part-time на непълен работен ден
na ne·*puh*·len ra·*bo*·ten den

party (entertainment) купон ⓜ koo·*pon*

party (politics) партия ⓕ *par*·tee·ya

pass (go by) мина/минавам
mee·nuh/mee·*na*·vam

pass (in sport) v подам/подавам
po·*dam*/po·*da*·vam

passenger пътник/пътничка ⓜ/ⓕ
puht·neek/*puht*·neech·ka

passport паспорт ⓜ pas·*port*

passport number номер на паспорта ⓜ
no·mer na pas·*por*·ta

past n минало ⓝ *mee*·na·lo

pasta макарони ⓜ pl ma·ka·*ro*·nee

pastry паста ⓕ *pas*·ta

path пътека ⓕ puh·*te*·ka

pay v платя/плащам plat·*yuh*/*plash*·tam

payment плащане ⓝ *plash*·ta·ne

peace мир ⓜ meer

peach праскова ⓕ *pras*·ko·va

peak (mountain) връх ⓜ vruhh

peanut фъстък ⓜ fuhs·*tuhk*

pear круша ⓕ *kroo*·sha

peas грах ⓜ grah

pedal n педал ⓜ pe·*dal*

pedestrian n пешеходец/пешеходка
ⓜ/ⓕ pe·she·*ho*·dets/pe·she·*hod*·ka

pen писалка ⓕ pee·*sal*·ka

pencil молив ⓜ *mo*·leev

penis пенис ⓜ *pe*·nees

penknife джобно ножче ⓝ
dzhob·no *nozh*·che

pensioner пенсионер/пенсионерка
ⓜ/ⓕ pen·see·o·*ner*/pen·see·o·*ner*·ka

people хора pl *ho*·ra

pepper пипер ⓜ pee·*per*

per (day, etc) на na

per cent процент pro·*tsent*

perfect a съвършен suh·vuhr·*shen*

performance представление ⓝ
pred·stav·*le*·nee·e

perfume парфюм ⓜ par·*fyoom*

period pain менструална болка ⓕ
mens·troo·*al*·na *bol*·ka

permission позволение ⓝ poz·vo·*le*·nee·e

permit n разрешително ⓝ
raz·re·*shee*·tel·no

person човек ⓜ cho·*vek*

petition молба ⓕ mol·*ba*

petrol бензин ⓜ ben·*zeen*

petrol station бензиностанция ⓕ
ben·zee·no·*stan*·tsee·ya

pharmacist аптекар/аптекарка ⓜ/ⓕ
ap·te·*kar*/ap·te·*kar*·ka

pharmacy аптека ⓕ ap·*te*·ka

phone book телефонен указател ⓜ
te·le·*fo*·nen oo·ka·*za*·tel

phone box телефонна кабина ⓕ
te·le·*fon*·na ka·*bee*·na

phonecard фонокарта ⓕ fo·no·*kar*·ta

photo снимка ⓕ *sneem*·ka

photograph v снимам *snee*·mam

photographer фотограф ⓜ fo·to·*graf*

photography фотография ⓕ
fo·to·*gra*·fee·ya

phrasebook разговорник ⓜ
raz·go·*vor*·neek

piano пиано ⓝ pee·*a*·no

pickles туршия ⓕ toor·*shee*·ya

picnic пикник ⓜ *peek*·neek

pie пирог ⓜ pee·*rog*

piece парче ⓝ par·*che*

pig свиня ⓕ svee·*nya*

pill таблетка ⓕ tab·*let*·ka

(the) pill противозачатъчно ⓝ
pro·tee·vo·za·cha·tuhch·no

pillow възглавница ① vuhz·glav·nee·tsa

pillowcase калъфка за възглавница ①
ka·luhf·ka za vuhz·glav·nee·tsa

pineapple ананас ⓝ a·na·nas

pink розов ro·zov

pistachio шам-фъстък ⓜ sham·fuhs·tuhk

place n място ⓝ myas·to

place of birth място на раждане ⓝ
myas·to na razh·da·ne

plane самолет ⓜ sa·mo·let

planet планета ① pla·ne·ta

plant n растение ⓝ ras·te·nee·e

plastic a пластмасов plast·ma·sov

plate чиния ① chee·nee·ya

plateau плато ⓝ pla·to

platform трибуна ① tree·boo·na

play (game) v играя ee·gra·yuh

play (instrument) v свиря sveer·yuh

play (theatre) n пиеса ① pee·e·sa

plug (bath) запушалка ① za·poo·shal·ka

plug (electricity) щепсел ⓜ shtep·sel

plum слива ① slee·va

plumber водопроводчик ⓜ
vo·do·pro·vod·cheek

poached (egg) попарен po·pa·ren

pocket n джоб ⓜ dzhob

pocket knife джобно ножче ⓝ
dzhob·no nozh·che

poetry поезия ① po·e·zee·ya

point v соча so·chuh

poisonous отровен o·tro·ven

police полиция ① po·lee·tsee·ya

police officer полицай/полицайка ⓜ/①
po·lee·tsai/po·lee·tsai·ka

police station полицейски участък ⓜ
po·lee·tsey·skee oo·chas·tuhk

policy политика ① po·lee·tee·ka

politician политик ⓜ po·lee·teek

politics политика ① po·lee·tee·ka

pollen цветен прашец ⓜ
tsve·ten pra·shets

pollution замърсяване ⓝ
za·muhr·sya·va·ne

pool (game) билярд ⓜ beel·yard

pool (swimming) плувен басейн ⓜ
ploo·ven ba·seyn

poor (wealth) беден be·den

popular популярен po·poo·lya·ren

pork свинско ⓝ sveen·sko

port (river/sea) пристанище ⓝ
pree·sta·neesh·te

positive положителен po·lo·zhee·te·len

possible възможен vuhz·mo·zhen

post n поща ① posh·ta

post v изпратя/изпращам по пощата
eez·prat·yuh/eez·prash·tam po posh·ta·ta

postage пощенски разноски ① pl
posh·ten·skee raz·nos·kee

postcard пощенска картичка ①
posh·ten·ska kar·teech·ka

postcode пощенски код ⓜ
posh·ten·skee kod

poster плакат ⓜ pla·kat

post office поща ① posh·ta

pot (ceramics) гърне ⓝ guhr·ne

pot (cooking) тенджера ① tend·zhe·ra

potato картоф ⓜ kar·tof

pottery керамика ① ke·ra·mee·ka

pound (money) лира ① lee·ra

pound (weight) фунт ⓜ foont

poverty бедност ① bed·nost

powder n пудра ① pood·ra

power (political) n власт ① vlast

prawn едра скарида ① ed·ra ska·ree·da

prayer молитва ① mo·leet·va

prayer book молитвеник ⓜ
mo·leet·ve·neek

prefer предпочета/предпочитам
pred·po·che·tuh/pred·po·chee·tam

pregnancy test kit тест за бременност ⓜ
test za bre·men·nost

pregnant бременна bre·men·na

premenstrual syndrome
предменструален синдром
pred·mens·troo·a·len seen·drom

prepare подготвя/подготвям
pod·got·vyuh/pod·got·vyam

prescription рецепта ① re·tsep·ta

present (gift) подарък ⓜ po·da·ruhk

present (time) настоящ момент ⓜ
na·sto·yasht mo·ment

president председател/председателка
ⓜ/① pred·se·da·tel/pred·se·da·tel·ka

pressure (tyre) налягане ⓝ na·lya·ga·ne

pretty хубав hoo·bav

price n цена ① tse·na

priest свещеник ⓜ svesh·te·neek

printer (computer) принтър ⓜ preen·tuhr

prison затвор ⓜ *zat-vor*

prisoner затворник/затворничка ⓜ/ⓕ *zat-vor-neek/zat-vor-neech-ka*

private a частен *chas-ten*

produce v произведа/произвеждам *pro-eez-ve-duh/pro-eez-vezh-dam*

profit n печалба ⓕ *pe-chal-ba*

programme n програма ⓕ *pro-gra-ma*

projector прожекционен апарат ⓜ *pro-zhek-tsee-o-nen a-pa-rat*

promise v обещая/обещавам *o-besh-ta-ya/o-besh-ta-vam*

prostitute n проститутка ⓕ *pros-tee-toot-ka*

protect защитя/защитавам *zash-tee-tyuh/zash-tee-ta-vam*

protected (species, etc) защитен *zash-tee-ten*

protest n протест ⓜ *pro-test*

protest v протестирам *pro-tes-tee-ram*

pub (bar) кръчма ⓕ *kruch-ma*

public gardens парк ⓜ *park*

public phone уличен телефон ⓜ *oo-lee-chen te-le-fon*

public relations
връзки с обществеността ⓕ pl *vruzh-kee s obsh-test-ve-nost-ta*

public toilet обществена тоалетна ⓕ *obsh-test-ve-na to-a-let-na*

pull дърпам *duhr-pam*

pump n помпа ⓕ *pom-pa*

pumpkin тиква ⓕ *teek-va*

puncture спукана гума ⓕ *spoo-ka-na goo-ma*

pure чист *cheest*

purple лилав цвят *lee-lav tsvyat*

purse дамска чанта ⓕ *dam-ska chan-ta*

push v бутам *boo-tam*

put сложа/слагам *slo-zhuh/sla-gam*

Q

quadriplegic a парализиран на всички крайници *pa-ra-lee-zee-ran na vseech-kee krai-nee-tsee*

qualifications умения ⓝ pl *oo-me-nee-ya*

quality n качество ⓝ *ka-chest-vo*

quarantine карантина ⓕ *ka-ran-tee-na*

quarter n четвърт ⓕ *chet-vuhrt*

queen кралица ⓕ *kra-lee-tsa*

question n въпрос ⓜ *vuh-pros*

queue n опашка ⓕ *o-pash-ka*

quick бърз *buhrz*

quiet тих *teeh*

quit откажа/отказвам се *ot-ka-zhuh/ot-kaz-vam se*

R

rabbit (meat) заешко ⓝ *za-esh-ko*

race (sport) n състезание ⓝ *suhs-te-za-nee-e*

racetrack писта ⓕ *pees-ta*

racing bike състезателен велосипед ⓜ *suhs-te-za-te-len ve-lo-see-ped*

racism расизъм ⓜ *ra-see-zuhm*

radish репичка ⓕ *re-peech-ka*

racquet ракета ⓕ *ra-ke-ta*

radiator (car) радиатор ⓜ *ra-dee-a-tor*

radio радио ⓝ *ra-dee-o*

railway station гара ⓕ *ga-ra*

rain n дъжд ⓜ *duhzhd*

raincoat дъждобран ⓜ *duhzh-do-bran*

raisin стафида ⓕ *sta-fee-da*

rally (protest) n митинг ⓜ *mee-teeng*

rape n изнасилване ⓝ *eez-na-seel-va-ne*

rape v изнасиля/изнасилвам *eez-na-seel-yuh/eez-na-seel-vam*

rare (uncommon) рядък *rya-duhk*

rash обрив ⓜ *ob-reev*

raspberry малина ⓕ *ma-lee-na*

rat плъх ⓜ *pluhh*

rave party рейв парти ⓜ *reyv par-tee*

raw суров *soo-rov*

razor самобръсначка ⓕ *sa-mo-bruhs-nach-ka*

razor blade ножче за бръснене ⓝ *nozh-che za bruhs-ne-ne*

read v чета *che-tuh*

reading четене ⓝ *che-te-ne*

ready готов *go-tov*

real estate agent
агент за недвижими имоти ⓜ *a-gent za ned-vee-zhee-mee ee-mo-tee*

realistic реалистичен *re-a-lees-tee-chen*

rear (location) n задна част ⓕ *zad-na chast*

reason n причина ⓕ *pree-chee-na*

receipt разписка ① *raz*-pees-ka
recently неотдавна ne-ot-*dav*-na
recommend
препоръчам/препоръчвам
pre-po-*ruh*-cham/pre-po-*ruhch*-vam
record v запиша/записвам
za-*pee*-shuh/za-*pees*-vam
recording запис ⑩ *za*-pees
recyclable годен за рециклиране
go-den za re-tsee-*klee*-ra-ne
recycle рециклирам re-tsee-*klee*-ram
red червен cher-*ven*
red wine червено вино ⑩
cher-*ve*-no *vee*-no
referee n съдия ① suh-dee-*ya*
reference n справка ① *sprav*-ka
refrigerator хладилник ⑩ hla-*deel*-neek
refugee бежанец/бежанка ⑩/①
be-zha-*nets*/be-*zhan*-ka
refund n връщане на парите ⑩
vruhsh-ta-ne na pa-*ree*-te
refuse v откажа/отказвам
ot-*ka*-zhuh/ot-*kaz*-vam
regional регионален re-ge-o-*na*-len
registered mail препоръчана поща ①
pre-po-*ruh*-cha-na *posh*-ta
rehydration salts соли за оводняване
① pl *so*-lee za o-vod-*nya*-va-ne
relationship връзка ① *vruhz*-ka
relax v отпусна/отпускам се
ot-*poos*-nuh/ot-*poos*-kam se
relic останка ① o-*stan*-ka
religion религия ① re-*lee*-gee-ya
religious религиозен re-lee-gee-o-*zen*
remote далечен da-*le*-chen
remote control
дистанционно управление ⑩
dees-tan-tsee-*o*-no oo-prav-*le*-nee-e
rent n наем ⑩ *na*-em
rent v взема/взимам под наем
vze-muh/*vzee*-mam pod *na*-em
repair v поправя/поправям
po-*prav*-yuh/po-*prav*-yam
republic република ① re-*poob*-lee-ka
reservation (booking) резервация ①
re-zer-*va*-tsee-ya
rest n почивка ① po-*cheev*-ka
restaurant ресторант ⑩ res-to-*rant*
résumé (CV) автобиография ①
av-to-bee-o-*gra*-fee-ya

retired пенсиониран pen-see-o-*nee*-ran
return v върна/връщам се
vuhr-na/*vruhsh*-tam se
return ticket двупосочен билет ⑩
dvoo-po-*so*-chen bee-*let*
review n преглед ⑩ *pre*-gled
rhythm ритъм ⑩ *ree*-tuhm
rib (body) ребро ⑩ reb-*ro*
rice ориз ⑩ o-*reez*
rich (wealthy) богат bo-*gat*
ride n езда ① ez-*da*
ride (bike) v карам колело *ka*-ram ko-le-*lo*
ride (horse) v яздя кон yaz-*dyuh* kon
right (correct) правилен *pra*-vee-len
right (direction) десен de-sen
right-wing десен de-*sen*
ring (jewellery) пръстен ⑩ *pruhs*-ten
ring (phone) v звъня *zvuh*-nya
rip-off n измама ① eez-*ma*-ma
risk v рискувам rees-*koo*-vam
river река ① re-*ka*
road път ⑩ puht
road map пътна карта ① *puht*-na *kar*-ta
rob (steal) v обера/обирам o-be-*ruh*/o-*bee*-ram
rock n скала ① ska-*la*
rock (music) рок ⑩ rok
rock climbing скалнокатерене ⑩
skal-no-ka-*te*-re-ne
rock group рокгрупа ① rok-*groo*-pa
roll (bread) хлебче ⑩ *hleb*-che
rollerblading каране на ролкови кънки
⑩ *ka*-ra-ne na *rol*-ko-vee *kuhn*-kee
Romania Румъния ① roo-*muh*-nee-ya
romantic a романтичен ro-man-*tee*-chen
room стая ① *sta*-ya
room number номер на стаята ⑩
no-mer na *sta*-ya-ta
rope въже ⑩ *vuh*-zhe
round (drinks) n по едно питие за всеки
⑩ po ed-*no* pee-tee-e za *vse*-kee
round a кръгъл *kruh*-guhl
route n маршрут ⑩ marsh-*root*
rowing гребане ⑩ *gre*-ba-ne
rubbish боклук ⑩ *bok*-look
rubella рубеола ① roo-be-o-la
rug килим ⑩ *kee*-leem
rugby ръгби ⑩ *ruhg*-bee
ruins останки ⑩ pl o-*stan*-kee
rule n правило ⑩ *pra*-vee-lo
rum ром ① rom

run v тичам *tee*-cham

running бягане ⑩ *bya*-ga-ne

runny nose хрема ① *hre*-ma

Russia Русия ① roo-*see*-ya

S

sad тъжен *tuh*-zhen

safe n сейф ⑩ seyf

safe a безопасен bez-o-*pa*-sen

safe sex безопасен секс ⑩
bez-o-*pa*-sen seks

sailboarding каране на уинд ⑩
ka-ra-ne na oo-*eend*

saint n светец/светица ⑩/①
sve-*tets*/sve-*tee*-tsa

salad салата ① sa-*la*-ta

salami салам ⑩ sa-*lam*

salary заплата ① za-*pla*-ta

sale n разпродажба ① raz-pro-*dazh*-ba

sales assistant продавач/продавачка
⑩/① pro-da-*vach*/pro-da-*vach*-ka

sales tax данък добавена стойност ⑩
da-nuhk do-*ba*-ve-na *stoy*-nost

salmon сьомга ① *syom*-ga

salt n сол ① sol

same същият *suhsh*-tee-yuht

sand пясък ⑩ *pya*-suhk

sandals сандали ⑩ pl san-*da*-lee

sanitary napkin дамска превръзка ①
dam-ska pre-*vruhz*-ka

sardine сардина ① sar-*dee*-na

sauce сос ⑩ sos

saucepan тенджера ① *tend*-zhe-ra

sauna сауна ① sa-oo-na

sausage наденица ① na-*de*-nee-tsa

say кажа/казвам *ka*-zhuh/*kaz*-vam

scalp скалп ⑩ skalp

scarf шал ⑩ shal

school училище ⑩ oo-*chee*-leesh-te

science наука ① na-oo-ka

scientist учен ⑩ *oo*-chen

scissors ножица ① *no*-zhee-tsa

score v отбележа/отбелязвам
ot-be-*le*-zhuh/ot-be-*lyaz*-vam

scoreboard табло за резултатите ⑩
tab-lo za re-*zool*-*ta*-tee-te

Scotland Шотландия ① shot-*lan*-dee-ya

scrambled бъркан *buhr*-kan

sculpture скулптура ① skoolp-*too*-ra

sea море ⑩ *mo*-re

seasick болен от морска болест
bo-len ot *mor*-ska *bo*-lest

seaside n морски бряг ⑩ *mor*-skee bryag

season n сезон ⑩ se-*zon*

seat (chair, etc) седалка ① se-*dal*-ka

seatbelt предпазен колан ⑩
pred-*pa*-zen ko-*lan*

second (time unit) n секунда ①
se-*koon*-da

second a втори *vto*-ree

second class втора класа ① *vto*-ra *kla*-sa

secondhand от втора употреба
ot *vto*-ra oo-*po*-tre-ba

secondhand shop магазин за стоки
втора употреба ⑩ ma-ga-*zeen* za
sto-kee *vto*-ra oo-*po*-tre-ba

secretary секретар/секретарка ⑩/①
se-kre-*tar*/se-kre-*tar*-ka

see видя/виждам *veed*-yuh/*veezh*-dam

self-employed на свободна практика
na svo-*bod*-na *prak*-tee-ka

selfish егоистичен e-go-ees-*tee*-chen

self-service на самообслужване
na sa-mo-ob-*sloozh*-va-ne

sell продам/продавам
pro-*dam*/pro-*da*-vam

send изпратя/изпращам
eez-*prat*-yuh/eez-*prash*-tam

sensible разумен ra-*zoo*-men

sensual чувствен *choovs*-tven

separate a отделен ot-*de*-len

Serbia Сърбия *suhr*-bee-ya

serious сериозен se-ree-*o*-zen

service n обслужване ⑩ ob-*sloozh*-va-ne

service charge процент за обслужване ⑩
pro-*tsent* za ob-*sloozh*-va-ne

serviette салфетка ① sal-*fet*-ka

several няколко *nya*-kol-ko

sew шия *shee*-yuh

sex (gender) пол ⑩ pol

sex (intercourse) секс ⑩ seks

sexism сексизъм ⑩ sek-*see*-zuhm

sexually transmitted infection
венерическа болест ①
ve-ne-*ree*-ches-ka *bo*-lest

sexy сексапилен sek-sa-*pee*-len

shade n сянка ① *syan*-ka

shadow n сянка ① *syan*-ka

shampoo шампоан ⓜ sham·po·*an*
shape n форма ① *for*·ma
share (a room, etc) v споделя/споделям
 spo·*del*·yuh/spo·*del*·yam
shave v бръсна се *bruhs*·nuh se
shaving cream крем за бръснене ⓜ
 krem za *bruhs*·ne·ne
she тя tya
sheep овца ① ov·*tsa*
sheet (bed) чаршаф ⓜ char·*shaf*
shelf полица ① *po*·lee·tsa
shiatsu шиатсу ⓜ shee·*at*·soo
shingles (illness) херпес ⓜ *her*·pes
ship n кораб ⓜ *ko*·rab
shirt риза ① *ree*·za
shoes обувки ① pl o·*boov*·kee
shoelace връзка за обувки ①
 vruhz·ka za o·*boov*·kee
shoe shop магазин за обувки ⓜ
 ma·ga·*zeen* za o·*boov*·kee
shoot v стрелям *strel*·yam
shop n магазин ⓜ ma·ga·*zeen*
shop v пазарувам pa·za·*roo*·vam
shopping пазаруване ⓝ pa·za·*roo*·va·ne
shopping centre търговски център ⓜ
 tuhr·*gov*·skee *tsen*·tuhr
short (height) нисък *nee*·suhk
short (length) къс kuhs
shortage недостиг ⓜ ne·*dos*·teeg
shorts шорти ① pl *shor*·tee
shoulder рамо ⓝ *ra*·mo
shout v викам *vee*·kam
show n представление ⓝ
 pred·*stav*·le·nee·e
show v покажа/показвам
 po·*ka*·zhuh/po·*kaz*·vam
shower n душ ⓜ doosh
shrine светилище ① sve·*tee*·leesh·te
shut a затворен zat·*vo*·ren
shut v затворя/затварям
 zat·*vor*·yuh/zat·*var*·yam
shy срамежлив sra·*mezh*·leev
sick болен *bo*·len
side n страна ① *stra*·na
sign n знак ⓜ znak
sign v подпиша/подписвам
 pod·*pee*·shuh/pod·*pees*·vam
signature подпис ⓜ *pod*·pees
silk n коприна ① ko·*pree*·na
silver n сребро ⓝ *sreb*·ro

SIM card сим-карта ① *seem*·kar·ta
similar подобен po·*do*·ben
simple прост prost
since (time) от ot
sing пея *pe*·yuh
singer певец/певица ⓜ/①
 pe·*vets*/pe·*vee*·tsa
single (person) a неженен/неомъжена
 ⓜ/① ne·*zhe*·nen/ne·o·*muh*·zhe·na
single room единична стая ①
 e·dee·*neech*·na *sta*·ya
singlet потник ⓜ *pot*·neek
sister сестра ① ses·*tra*
sit седна/сядам *sed*·nuh/*sya*·dam
size номер ⓜ *no*·mer
skate v пързалям се на кънки
 puhr·*zal*·yam se na *kuhn*·kee
skateboarding каране на скейтборд ⓜ
 ka·ra·ne na *skeyt*·bord
ski v карам ски *ka*·ram skee
skiing каране на ски ⓝ *ka*·ra·ne na skee
skim milk обезмаслено мляко ⓝ
 o·bez·*mas*·le·no *mlya*·ko
skin кожа ① *ko*·zha
skirt пола ① po·*la*
skull череп ⓜ *che*·rep
sky небе ⓝ ne·*be*
sleep n сън ⓜ suhn
sleep v спя spyuh
sleeping bag спален чувал ⓜ
 spa·len choo·*val*
sleeping berth легло ⓝ leg·*lo*
sleeping car спален вагон ⓜ
 spa·len va·*gon*
sleeping pills приспивателно ⓝ
 pree·spee·*va*·tel·no
sleepy сънлив suhn·*leev*
slice n филия ① fee·*lee*·ya
slide film диапозитивен филм ⓜ
 dee·a·po·zee·*tee*·ven feelm
slow бавен *ba*·ven
slowly бавно *bav*·no
small малък *ma*·luhk
smaller по-малък po·*ma*·luhk
smallest най-малкият nai·*mal*·kee·yuht
smell n миризма ① mee·*reez*·ma
smile v усмихна/усмихвам се
 oo·*smeeh*·nuh/oo·*smeeh*·vam se
smoke v пуша *poo*·shuh
snack n закуска ① za·*koos*·ka

snail охлюв ⓜ oh-*lyoov*

snake змия ⓕ zmee-*ya*

snorkelling плуване със шнорхел ⓝ *ploo*-va-ne suhs *shnor*-hel

snow n сняг ⓜ snyag

snowboarding
пързаляне със сноуборд ⓝ puhr-*za*-lya-ne suhs *sno*-oo-bord

soap сапун ⓜ sa-*poon*

soap opera сапунена опера ⓕ sa-*poo*-ne-na *o*-pe-ra

soccer футбол ⓜ *foot*-bol

socialist n социалист ⓜ so-tsee-a-*leest*

socialist a социалистически so-tsee-a-lees-*tee*-ches-kee

social welfare социално подпомагане ⓝ so-tsee-*al*-no pod-po-*ma*-ga-ne

socks чорапи ⓜ pl cho-*ra*-pee

Sofia София ⓕ so-*fee*-ya

soft drink безалкохолна напитка ⓕ bez-al-ko-*hol*-na na-*peet*-ka

soldier войник ⓜ voy-*neek*

some някакъв *nya*-ka-kuhv

someone някой *nya*-koy

something нещо *nesh*-to

sometimes понякога po-*nya*-ko-ga

son син ⓜ seen

song песен ⓕ *pe*-sen

soon скоро *sko*-ro

sore a болезнен bo-*lez*-nen

soup супа ⓕ *soo*-pa

south n юг ⓜ yoog

souvenir сувенир ⓜ soo-ve-*neer*

souvenir shop магазин за сувенири ⓜ ma-ga-*zeen* za soo-ve-*nee*-ree

soy milk мляко от соя ⓝ *mlya*-ko ot *so*-ya

soy sauce соев сос ⓜ *so*-yev sos

space (area) място ⓝ *myas*-to

Spain Испания ⓕ ees-*pa*-nee-ya

sparkling wine шумящо вино ⓝ shoom-*yash*-to *vee*-no

speak говоря go-*vor*-yuh

special a особен o-*so*-ben

specialist n специалист/специалистка ⓜ/ⓕ spe-tsee-a-*leest*/spe-tsee-a-*leest*-ka

speed (drug) амфетамин ⓜ am-fe-ta-*meen*

speed (travel) n скорост ⓕ *sko*-rost

speed limit
максимална позволена скорост ⓕ mak-see-*mal*-na poz-vo-*le*-na *sko*-rost

speedometer скоростомер ⓜ sko-ros-to-*mer*

spider паяк ⓜ *pa*-yak

spinach спанак ⓜ spa-*nak*

spoilt (food) развален raz-va-*len*

spoke спица ⓕ *spee*-tsa

spoon лъжица ⓕ luh-*zhee*-tsa

sport спорт ⓜ sport

sportsperson спортист/спортистка ⓜ/ⓕ spor-*teest*/spor-*teest*-ka

sports store спортен магазин ⓜ *spor*-ten ma-ga-*zeen*

sprain n навяхване ⓝ nav-*yah*-va-ne

spring (coil) пружинка ⓕ proo-*zheen*-ka

spring (season) пролет ⓜ *pro*-let

square (town) площад ⓜ plosh-*tad*

stadium стадион ⓜ sta-dee-*on*

stairway стълбище ⓝ *stuhl*-beesh-te

stale стар star

stamp (postage) n марка ⓕ *mar*-ka

star n звезда ⓕ zvez-*da*

(four-)star с (четири) звезди s (*che*-tee-ree) zvez-*dee*

start n начало ⓝ na-*cha*-lo

start v започна/започвам za-*poch*-nuh/za-*poch*-vam

station гара ⓕ *ga*-ra

statue статуя ⓕ *sta*-too-a

stay (at a hotel) отседна/отсядам ot-*sed*-nuh/ot-*sya*-dam

stay (in one place) остана/оставам o-*sta*-nuh/o-*sta*-vam

steak бифтек ⓜ beef-*tek*

steal v открадна/открадвам ot-*krad*-nuh/ot-*krad*-vam

steep стръмен struh-*men*

step n стъпка ⓕ *stuhp*-ka

stereo n стерео ⓝ *ste*-re-o

stockings чорапи ⓜ pl cho-*ra*-pee

stolen откраднат ot-*krad*-nat

stomach стомах ⓜ sto-*muh*

stomachache болки в стомаха ⓕ pl *bol*-kee v sto-*ma*-huh

stone n камък ⓜ *ka*-muhk

stoned (drugged) дрогиран dro-*gee*-ran

stop (bus, tram) n спирка ⓕ *speer*-ka

stop (cease) спра/спирам
spruh/*spee*-ram

stop (prevent) попреча/попречвам
po-*pre*-chuh/po-*prech*-vam

storm n буря ① *boor*-ya

story разказ ⑩ *raz*-kaz

stove печка ① *pech*-ka

straight прав prav

strange странен *stra*-nen

stranger непознат човек ⑩
ne-*poz*-nat cho-*vek*

strawberry ягода ① *ya*-go-da

stream n поток ⑩ po-*tok*

street улица ① *oo*-lee-tsa

street market уличен пазар ⑩
oo-lee-chen pa-*zar*

strike n стачка ① *stach*-ka

string n връв ⑩ vruhv

stroke (health) удар ⑩ *oo*-dar

stroller (pram) бебешка количка ①
be-*besh*-ka ko-*leech*-ka

strong силен *see*-len

stubborn упорит oo-*po*-reet

student студент/студентка ⑩/①
stoo-*dent*/stoo-*dent*-ka

studio ателие ⑩ a-te-*lee*-e

stupid глупав *gloo*-pav

style n стил ⑩ steel

subtitles субтитри ⑩ pl soob-*teet*-ree

suburb предградие ⑩ pred-*gra*-dee-e

subway (train) метро ⑩ *met*-ro

sugar захар ① *za*-har

suitcase куфар ⑩ *koo*-far

sultana стафида ① sta-*fee*-da

summer лято ⑩ *lya*-to

sun слънце ⑩ *sluhn*-tse

sunblock слънцезащитен крем ⑩
sluhn-tse-zash-*tee*-ten krem

sunburn слънчево изгаряне ⑩
sluhn-che-vo eez-*gar*-ya-ne

sunglasses слънчеви очила ⑩ pl
sluhn-che-vee o-chee-*la*

sunny слънчев *sluhn*-chev

sunrise изгрев слънце ⑩
eez-grev *sluhn*-tse

sunset залез слънце ⑩ *za*-lez *sluhn*-tse

sunstroke слънчев удар ⑩
sluhn-chev oo-*dar*

supermarket супермаркет ⑩
soo-per-*mar*-ket

superstition суеверие ⑩ soo-e-*ve*-ree-e

supporter (politics)
поддръжник/поддръжница ⑩/①
pod-*druzh*-neek/pod-*druzh*-nee-tsa

supporter (sport) запалянко ⑩
za-pa-*lyan*-ko

surf v сърфирам suhr-*fee*-ram

surface mail (land/sea) обикновена поща
① o-beek-no-ve-na *posh*-ta

surfboard сърф ⑩ suhrf

surfing сърфиране ⑩ suhr-*fee*-ra-ne

surname фамилно име ⑩
fa-*meel*-no ee-me

surprise n изненада ① eez-ne-*na*-da

sweater пуловер ⑩ poo-*lo*-ver

Sweden Швеция ① *shve*-tsee-ya

sweet сладък *sla*-duhk

sweets сладкиши ⑩ pl slad-*kee*-shee

swelling подутина ① po doo tee-*na*

swim v плувам *ploo*-vam

swimming плуване ⑩ *ploo*-va-ne

swimming pool плувен басейн ⑩
ploo-ven ba-*seyn*

swimsuit бански костюм ⑩
ban-skee kos-*tyoom*

Switzerland Швейцария ①
shvey-*tsa*-ree-ya

synagogue синагога ① see-na-*go*-ga

synthetic a синтетичен seen-te-*tee*-chen

syringe спринцовка ① spreen-*tsov*-ka

T

table маса ① *ma*-sa

tablecloth покривка ① po-*kreev*-ka

table tennis тенис на маса ⑩
te-nees na *ma*-sa

tail n опашка ① o-*pash*-ka

tailor n шивач/шивачка ⑩/①
shee-*vach*/shee-*vach*-ka

take v взема/взимам vze-muh/*vzee*-mam

take a photo снимам *snee*-mam

talk v говоря go-*vor*-yuh

tall висок vee-*sok*

tampon тампон ⑩ *tam*-pon

tanning lotion плажно масло ⑩
plazh-no *mas*-lo

tap n кран ⑩ kran

tap water течаща вода ①
te-*chash*-ta vo-*da*

tasty вкусен vkoo-sen

tax n данък ⓜ *da*-nuhk

taxi такси ⓝ tak-*see*

taxi stand/rank таксиметрова стоянка ①
tak-see-*me*-tro-va sto-*yan*-ka

tea чай ⓜ chai

teacher учител/учителка ⓜ/①
oo-*chee*-tel/oo-*chee*-tel-ka

team отбор ⓜ ot-*bor*

teaspoon чаена лъжичка ①
cha-e-na luh-*zheech*-ka

technique техника ① teh-*nee*-ka

teeth зъби ⓜ pl *zuh*-bee

telegram телеграма ① te-le-*gra*-ma

telephone n телефон ⓜ te-le-*fon*

telephone v обадя/обаждам се
o-*bad*-yuh/o-*bazh*-dam se

telephone centre телефонна централа ①
te-le-*fon*-na tsen-*tra*-la

telescope телескоп ⓜ te-le-*skop*

television телевизия ① te-le-*vee*-zee-ya

tell кажа/казвам *ka*-zhuh/*kaz*-vam

temperature (fever/weather)
температура ① tem-pe-ra-*too*-ra

tennis тенис ⓜ *te*-nees

tennis court тенискорт ⓜ te-nees-*kort*

tent палатка ① pa-*lat*-ka

tent peg копче на опъване на палатка ⓝ
kop-che za o-*puh*-va-ne na pa-*lat*-ka

terrible ужасен oo-*zha*-sen

terrorism тероризъм ⓜ te-ro-*ree*-zuhm

terrorist терорист/терористка ⓜ/①
te-ro-*reest*/te-ro-*reest*-ka

test n изпит ⓜ *eez*-peet

thank благодаря bla-go-dar-*yuh*

that а този *to*-zee

that (one) pron онзи *on*-zee

theatre театър ⓜ te-*a*-tuhr

their техен *te*-hen

there там tam

they те te

thick гъст guhst

thief крадец/крадка ⓜ/①
kra-dets/*krad*-ka

thin тънък *tuh*-nuhk

think мисля *mees*-lyuh

thirsty жаден *zha*-den

this а този *to*-zee

this (one) pron този *to*-zee

thread n конец ⓜ ko-*nets*

throat гърло ⓝ *guhr*-lo

thrush (illness) стоматомикоза ①
sto-ma-to-mee-*ko*-za

thunder гръмотевица ①
gruh-mo-*te*-vee-tsa

ticket билет ⓜ bee-*let*

ticket collector кондуктор ⓜ kon-*dook*-tor

ticket machine
автомат за продаване на билети ⓜ
av-to-*mat* za pro-*da*-va-ne na bee-*le*-tee

ticket office билетен център ⓜ
bee-*le*-ten *tsen*-tuhr

(high/low) tide прилив/отлив ⓜ
pree-leev/*ot*-leev

tight тесен *te*-sen

time n време ⓝ *vre*-me

time difference часова разлика ①
cha-so-va *raz*-lee-ka

timetable разписание ⓝ raz-pee-*sa*-nee-e

tin (can) консервна кутия ①
kon-*serv*-na koo-*tee*-ya

tin opener отварачка за консерви ①
ot-va-*rach*-ka za kon-*ser*-vee

tiny мъничък *muh*-nee-chuhk

tip (gratuity) n бакшиш ⓜ bak-*sheesh*

tire (car) гума ① *goo*-ma

tired уморен oo-mo-*ren*

tissues хартиени кърпички ① pl
har-*tee*-e-nee kuhr-*peech*-kee

to за za

toast препечен хляб ⓜ pre-*pe*-chen hlyab

toaster тостер ⓜ *tos*-ter

tobacco тютюн ⓜ tyoo-*tyoon*

tobacconist продавач на цигари ⓜ
pro-da-*vach* za tsee-*ga*-ree

tobogganing спускане с тобоган ⓝ
spoos-ka-ne s to-bo-*gan*

today днес dnes

toe пръст на крака ⓜ pruhst na kra-*kuh*

tofu тофу ⓝ *to*-foo

together заедно za-ed-no

toilet тоалетна ① to-a-*let*-na

toilet paper тоалетна хартия ①
to-a-*let*-na har-*tee*-ya

tomato домат ⓜ do-*mat*

tomorrow утре oo-*tre*

tonight довечера do-*ve*-che-ra

too (also) също *suhsh*-to

too (much) прекалено pre·ka·*le*·no
tooth зъб ⓜ zuhb
toothache зъбобол ⓜ zuh·bo·*bol*
toothbrush четка за зъби ⓕ
  chet·ka za zuh·bee
toothpaste паста за зъби ⓕ
  pas·ta za zuh·bee
toothpick клечка за зъби ⓕ
  klech·ka za zuh·bee
torch (flashlight) фенерче ⓝ fe·*ner*·che
touch v пипам pee·pam
tour n обиколка ⓕ o·bee·*kol*·ka
tourist n турист/туристка ⓜ/ⓕ
  too·*reest*/too·*reest*·ka
tourist office туристическо бюро ⓝ
  too·rees·*tee*·ches·ko byoo·*ro*
towards към kuhm
towel кърпа ⓕ *kuhr*·pa
tower кула ⓕ *koo*·la
toxic waste токсични отпадъци ⓜ pl
  tok·*seech*·nee ot·*pa*·duh·tsee
toy shop магазин за играчки ⓜ
  ma·ga·*zeen* za ee·*grach*·kee
track (path) пътека ⓕ puh·*te*·ka
track (sport) писта ⓕ *pees*·ta
trade n търговия ⓕ tuhr·go·*vee*·ya
tradesperson търговец/търговка ⓜ/ⓕ
  tuhr·go·vets/tuhr·*gov*·ka
traffic n движение ⓝ dvee·*zhe*·nee·e
traffic light светофар ⓜ sve·to·*far*
trail n пътека ⓕ puh·*te*·ka
train n влак ⓜ vlak
train station гара ⓕ *ga*·ra
tram трамвай ⓜ tram·*vai*
transit lounge
  зала за транзитни пътници ⓕ
  za·la za tran·*zeet*·nee puht·*nee*·tsee
translate преведа/превеждам
  pre·ve·*duh*/pre·*vezh*·dam
translator преводач/преводачка ⓜ/ⓕ
  pre·vo·*dach*/pre·vo·*dach*·ka
transport n транспорт ⓜ trans·*port*
trash (garbage) боклук ⓜ bok·*look*
travel n пътуване ⓝ puh·*too*·va·ne
travel agency пътническа агенция ⓕ
  puht·*nee*·ches·ka a·*gen*·tsee·ya
travellers cheque пътнически чек ⓜ
  puht·*nee*·ches·kee chek

travel sickness прилошаване по време
  на пътуване ⓝ pree·lo·*sha*·va·ne po
  vre·me na puh·*too*·va·ne
tree дърво ⓝ duhr·*vo*
trip (journey) пътуване ⓝ puh·*too*·va·ne
trolley тролейбус ⓜ tro·ley·*boos*
trousers панталони ⓜ pl pan·ta·*lo*·nee
truck камион ⓜ ka·mee·*on*
trust v доверя/доверявам се
  do·ver·*yuh*/do·ver·*ya*·vam se
try (attempt) опитам/опитвам се
  o·*pee*·tam/o·*peet*·vam se
try (taste) опитам/опитвам
  o·*pee*·tam/o·*peet*·vam
T-shirt тениска ⓕ te·*nees*·ka
tube (tyre) вътрешна гума ⓕ
  vuh·tresh·na *goo*·ma
tumour тумор ⓜ *too*·mor
tuna риба тон ⓕ *ree*·ba ton
tune n мелодия ⓕ me·lo·*dee*·ya
turkey пуйка ⓕ *pooy*·ka
Turkey Турция ⓕ *toor*·tsee·ya
turn v завия/завивам
  za·*vee*·yuh/za·*vee*·vam
TV (set) телевизор ⓜ te·le·*vee*·zor
tweezers пинцета ⓕ peen·*tse*·ta
twice два пъти dva *puh*·tee
twin beds две единични легла ⓝ pl
  dve e·dee·*neech*·nee leg·*la*
twins близнаци ⓜ pl bleez·*na*·tsee
type n вид ⓜ veed
typical типичен tee·*pee*·chen
tyre гума ⓕ *goo*·ma

U

ultrasound ултразвук ⓜ *ool*·tra·zvook
umbrella чадър ⓜ cha·*duhr*
uncomfortable неудобен ne·oo·*do*·ben
understand разбера/разбирам
  raz·be·*ruh*/raz·*bee*·ram
underwear бельо ⓝ bel·*yo*
unemployed безработен bez·ra·*bo*·ten
unfair несправедлив ne·spra·ved·*leev*
uniform n униформа ⓕ oo·nee·*for*·ma
universe вселена ⓕ vse·*le*·na
university университет ⓜ
  oo·nee·ver·see·*tet*

unleaded petrol безоловен бензин ⓜ bez·o·*lo*·ven ben·*zeen*
unsafe несигурен ne·o·see·goo·*ren*
until до do
unusual необикновен ne·o·beek·no·*ven*
up rope *go*·re
uphill нагоре na·*go*·re
urgent спешен *spe*·shen
urinary tract infection инфекция на пикочните канали ⓕ een·*fek*·tsee·ya na *pee*·koch·nee·te ka·*na*·lee
USA САЩ sasht
useful полезен po·*le*·zen

V

vacancy свободни стаи ⓕ pl svo·*bod*·nee *sta*·yee
vacant свободен svo·*bo*·den
vacation ваканция ⓕ va·*kan*·tsee·ya
vaccination ваксинация ⓕ vak·see·*na*·tsee·ya
vagina влагалище ⓝ vla·*ga*·leesh·te
validate потвърдя/потвърждавам pot·vuhr·*dyuh*/pot·vuhrzh·*da*·vam
valley долина ⓕ do·lee·*na*
valuable скъпоценен skuh·po·*tse*·nen
value (price) стойност ⓕ *stoy*·nost
van микробус ⓜ mee·kro·*boos*
veal телешко ⓝ *te*·lesh·ko
vegetable n зеленчук ⓜ ze·len·*chook*
vegetarian n вегетарианец/вегетарианка ⓜ/ⓕ ve·ge·ta·ree·*a*·nets/ve·ge·ta·ree·*an*·ka
vegetarian a вегетариански ve·ge·ta·ree·*an*·skee
vein вена ⓕ *ve*·na
venue място ⓝ *myas*·to
very много *mno*·go
video camera видеокамера ⓕ vee·de·o·*ka*·me·ra
video recorder видеомагнетофон ⓜ vee·de·o·mag·ne·to·*fon*
video tape видеокасета ⓕ vee·de·o·ka·*se*·ta
view n гледка ⓕ *gled*·ka
village село ⓝ *se*·lo
vine лоза ⓕ lo·*za*
vinegar оцет ⓜ *o*·tset
vineyard лозе ⓝ *lo*·ze
violin цигулка ⓕ tsee·*gool*·ka

virus вирус ⓜ *vee*·roos
visa виза ⓕ *vee*·za
visit v посетя/посещавам po·*set*·yuh/po·sesh·*ta*·vam
visually impaired с увредено зрение s oo·*vre*·de·no zre·nee·e
vitamin витамин ⓜ vee·ta·*meen*
vodka водка ⓕ *vod*·ka
voice n глас ⓜ glas
volleyball (sport) волейбол ⓜ *vo*·ley·bol
volume обем ⓜ o·*bem*
vote v гласувам gla·*soo*·vam

W

wage n заплата ⓕ za·*pla*·ta
wait чакам *cha*·kam
waiter сервитьор/сервитьорка ⓜ/ⓕ ser·veet·*yor*/ser·veet·*yor*·ka
waiting room чакалня ⓕ cha·*kal*·nya
wake (someone) up събудя/събуждам suh·*bood*·yuh/suh·*boozh*·dam
Wales Уелс ⓜ oo·*els*
walk v вървя vuhr·*vyuh*
wall (inner) зид ⓜ zeed
wall (outer) стена ⓕ ste·*na*
want искам *ees*·kam
war n война ⓕ *voy*·na
wardrobe гардероб ⓜ gar·de·*rob*
warm a топъл *to*·puhl
warn предупредя/предупреждавам pre·doo·pre·*dyuh*/pre·doo·prezh·*da*·vam
wash (oneself) мия се *mee*·yuh se
wash (something) мия *mee*·yuh
washcloth (flannel) парцал за миене ⓜ par·*tsal* za mee·e·ne
washing machine перална машина ⓕ pe·*ral*·na ma·*shee*·na
wasp оса ⓕ o·*sa*
watch n часовник ⓜ cha·*sov*·neek
watch v гледам *gle*·dam
water n вода ⓕ vo·*da*
water bottle бутилка за вода ⓕ boo·*teel*·ka za vo·*da*
waterfall водопад ⓜ vo·do·*pad*
watermelon диня ⓕ *deen*·ya
waterproof водонепромокаем vo·do·ne·pro·mo·*ka*·em
water-skiing каране на водни ски ⓜ *ka*·ra·ne na *vod*·nee skee
wave (ocean) вълна ⓕ vuhl·*na*

english–bulgarian

235

way (road) път ⓜ puht
way (manner) начин ⓜ na·cheen
we ние nee·e
weak слаб slab
wealthy богат bo·gat
wear v нося nos·yuh
weather n време ⓝ vre·me
wedding сватба ① svat·ba
week седмица ① sed·mee·tsa
weekend уикенд ⓜ oo·ee·kend
weigh тежа te·zhuh
weight тежест ① te·zhest
weights (gym) тежести ① pl te·zhes·tee
welcome v посрещна/посрещам
    po·sresht·nuh/po·sresh·tam
welfare n благосъстояние ⓝ
    bla·go·suhs·to·ya·nee·e
well adv добре do·bre
west запад ⓜ za·pad
wet a мокър mo·kuhr
what какво kak·vo
wheel колело ⓝ ko·le·lo
wheelchair инвалидна количка ①
    een·va·leed·na ko·leech·ka
when кога ko·ga
where къде kuh·de
which кой koy
whisky уиски ⓜ oo·ees·kee
white бял byal
white wine бяло вино ⓝ bya·lo vee·no
who кой koy
why защо zash·to
wide широк shee·rok
wife жена ① zhe·na
win v печеля pe·chel·yuh
wind n вятър vya·tuhr
window прозорец ⓜ pro·zo·rets
windscreen предно стъкло ⓝ
    pred·no stuhk·lo
wine вино ⓝ vee·no
wings крила ⓝ pl kree·la
winner победител/победителка ⓜ/①
    po·be·dee·tel/po·be·dee·tel·ka
winter зима ① zee·ma
wire n жица ① zhee·tsa
wish v желая zhe·la·yuh
with c s
within (time) в рамките на v ram·kee·te na
without без bez
woman жена ① zhe·na
wonderful чудесен choo·de·sen

wood дървен материал ⓜ
    duhr·ven ma·te·ree·al
wool вълна ① vuhl·na
word дума ① doo·ma
work n работа ① ra·bo·ta
work v работя ra·bot·yuh
work experience професионален опит ⓜ
    pro·fe·see·o·na·len o·peet
work out v тренирам tre·nee·ram
work permit разрешително за работа ⓝ
    raz·re·shee·tel·no za ra·bo·ta
workshop семинар ⓜ se·mee·nar
world n свят ⓜ svyat
worms (intestinal) глисти ① pl glees·tee
worried притеснен pree·tes·nen
worship v практикувам религия
    prak·tee·koo·vam re·lee·gee·ya
wrist китка ① keet·ka
write пиша pee·shuh
writer писател/писателка ⓜ/①
    pee·sa·tel/pee·sa·tel·ka
wrong a погрешен po·gre·shen

Y

year година ① go·dee·na
yellow жълт zhuhlt
yes да da
yesterday вчера vche·ra
(not) yet още (не) osh·te (ne)
yoga йога ① yo·ga
yogurt кисело мляко ⓝ kee·se·lo mlya·ko
you inf sg ти tee
you pol sg вие vee·e
you pl вие vee·e
young млад mlad
your inf sg твой tvoy
your pol sg ваш vash
your pl ваш vash
youth hostel хостел ⓜ hos·tel

Z

zip/zipper цип ⓜ tseep
zodiac зодиак ⓜ zo·dee·ak
zoo зоопарк ⓜ zo·o·park
zoom lens вариообектив ⓜ
    va·ree·o·ob·ek·teev
zucchini тиквички ① pl teek·veech·kee

bulgarian–english

Bulgarian nouns in the dictionary have their gender indicated by ⓜ (masculine), ⓕ (feminine) or ⓝ (neuter). If it's a plural noun, you'll also see pl. For added clarity, certain words are marked as nouns n, adjectives a, verbs v, adverbs adv, pronouns pron or prepositions prep. The abbreviations sg (singular), pl (plural), inf (informal) and pol (polite) are also used where necessary. Adjectives are given in the masculine singular form only. Verbs are given in their present tense first person singular form. Most verbs are given in two aspects: perfective and imperfective. The two forms are separated by a slash with the perfective form given first. Note that if the verb is followed by the particle **ce** se – eg *обадя/обаждам се* o·*bad*·yuh/o·*bazh*·dam se (to call) – the particle is used both with the perfective (*обадя се*) and imperfective form (*обаждам се*). If only one verb form is given, it means that form can be used as both imperfective and perfective. For more information, refer to the phrasebuilder.

> The **bulgarian–english dictionary** has been ordered according to the Cyrillic alphabet, shown below in both roman and italic text:
>
> Аа Бб Вв Гг Дд Ее Жж Зз Ии Йй Кк Лл Мм Нн Оо Пп
> *Аа Бб Вв Гг Дд Ее Жж Зз Ии Йй Кк Лл Мм Нн Оо Пп*
>
> Рр Сс Тт Уу Фф Хх Цц Чч Шш Щщ Ъъ ь Юю Яя
> *Рр Сс Тт Уу Фф Хх Цц Чч Шш Щщ Ъъ ь Юю Яя*

А

Австралия ⓕ av·*stra*·lee·ya *Australia*
автобус ⓜ av·to·*boos* bus
автобусна спирка ⓕ
av·to·*boos*·na *speer*·ka bus stop
автогара ⓕ av·to·*ga*·ra bus station
агенция за недвижими имоти ⓕ
a·*gen*·tsee·ya za ned·*vee*·zhee·mee
ee·*mo*·tee estate agency
адаптор ⓜ a·*dap*·tor adaptor
адвокат ⓜ ad·vo·*kat* lawyer
адрес ⓜ a·*dres* address n
аз az I
Азия ⓕ a·zee·ya Asia
актьор/актриса ⓜ/ⓕ
ak·*tyor*/ak·*tree*·sa actor
алергия ⓕ a·*ler*·gee·ya allergy
алкохол ⓜ al·ko·*hol* alcohol
Америка ⓕ a·*me*·ree·ka America
английски ⓜ an·*glee*y·skee
English (language) n
Англия ⓕ an·*glee*·ya England

антибиотици ⓜ pl an·tee·bee·o·*tee*·tsee
antibiotics
антика ⓕ an·*tee*·ka antique n
антисептик ⓜ an·tee·sep·*teek*
antiseptic n
анулирам a·noo·*lee*·ram cancel
апартамент ⓜ a·par·ta·*ment* apartment
аптека ⓕ ap·*te*·ka chemist • pharmacy
аптекар/аптекарка ⓜ/ⓕ ap·te·*kar*/
ap·te·*kar*·ka chemist • pharmacist
аптечка ⓕ ap·*tech*·ka first-aid kit
архитект/архитектка ⓜ/ⓕ
ar·hee·*tekt*/ar·hee·*tekt*·ka architect
архитектура ⓕ ar·hee·tek·*too*·ra
architecture
асансьор ⓜ a·san·*syor* elevator • lift
аспирин ⓜ as·pee·*reen* aspirin
Африка ⓕ a·*free*·ka Africa
афтершейв ⓜ af·ter·*sheyv* aftershave

Б

баба ⓕ *ba*·ba grandmother
бавачка ⓕ ba·*vach*·ka babysitter

бавно *bav*-no slowly
багаж ⓜ ba-*gazh* baggage · luggage
бакшиш ⓜ bak-*sheesh* tip (gratuity)
Балкански полуостров ⓜ bal-*kan*-skee po-loo-*os*-trov Balkan Peninsula
балсам ⓜ bal-*sam* hair conditioner
банка ⓕ *ban*-ka bank
банкнота ⓕ bank-*no*-ta banknote
банкова сметка ⓕ *ban*-ko-va *smet*-ka bank account
банкомат ⓜ ban-ko-*mat* ATM
бански костюм ⓜ *ban*-skee kos-*tyoom* swimsuit
баня ⓕ *ba*-nya bath · bathroom
бар ⓜ bar bar
батерия ⓕ ba-*te*-ree-ya battery
баща ⓜ bash-*ta* father
бебе ⓝ *be*-be baby
бебешка количка ⓕ *be*-besh-ka ko-*leech*-ka pram · stroller
бебешка храна ⓕ *be*-besh-ka hra-*na* baby food
без bez without
безмитен магазин ⓜ bez-*mee*-ten ma-ga-*zeen* duty-free shop
безопасен секс ⓜ bez-*o*-pa-sen seks safe sex
безплатен bez-*pla*-ten complimentary (free)
бельо ⓝ bel-*yo* underwear
бензин ⓜ ben-*zeen* gas · petrol
бензиностанция ⓕ ben-zee-no-*stan*-tsee-ya petrol station
биберон ⓜ bee-be-*ron* dummy · pacifier
библиотека ⓕ bee-blee-o-*te*-ka library
бижута ⓕ bee-*zhoo*-ta jewellery
бизнес класа ⓕ *beez*-nes *kla*-sa business class
билет ⓜ bee-*let* ticket
билетен център ⓜ bee-*le*-ten *tsen*-tuhr ticket office
битпазар ⓜ beet-pa-*zar* fleamarket
благодарен bla-go-*da*-ren grateful
близо до *blee*-zo do near prep
близък *blee*-zuhk close a
болезнен bo-*lez*-nen painful
болен *bo*-len sick
болка ⓕ *bol*-ka pain
болки в стомаха ⓕ pl *bol*-kee v sto-ma-*huh* stomach ache

болкоуспокоителни лекарства ⓝ pl bol-ko-oos-po-ko-ee-tel-nee le-*karst*-va painkillers
болница ⓕ *bol*-nee-tsa hospital
бордна карта ⓕ *bord*-na *kar*-ta boarding pass
брат ⓜ brat brother
бременна *bre*-men-na pregnant
брошура ⓕ bro-*shoo*-ra brochure
бръсна се *bruhs*-nuh se shave v
будилник ⓜ boo-*deel*-neek alarm clock
будка ⓕ *bood*-ka kiosk
бутилка ⓕ boo-*teel*-ka bottle
българин/българка ⓜ/ⓕ *buhl*-ga-reen/ *buhl*-gar-ka Bulgarian (person) n
България ⓕ buhl-*ga*-ree-ya Bulgaria
български ⓜ *buhl*-gar-skee Bulgarian (language) n
български *buhl*-gar-skee Bulgarian a
бърз buhrz fast a
бърза поща ⓕ *buhr*-za *posh*-ta express mail
бюджет ⓜ byood-*zhet* budget n
бюфет ⓜ byoo-*fet* buffet
бял byal white

В

вагон-ресторант ⓜ va-gon-res-to-*rant* dining car
важен *va*-zhen important
ваканция ⓕ va-*kan*-tsee-ya vacation
ваксинация ⓕ vak-see-*na*-tsee-ya vaccination
ваш vash your sg pol&pl
вегетарианец/вегетарианка ⓜ/ⓕ ve-ge-ta-ree-*a*-nets/ve-ge-ta-ree-*an*-ka vegetarian n
вегетариански ve-ge-ta-ree-*an*-skee vegetarian a
Великден ⓜ ve-*leek*-den Easter
велосипед ⓜ ve-lo-see-*ped* bicycle
вентилатор ⓜ ven-tee-*la*-tor fan (machine)
вестник ⓜ *vest*-neek newspaper
вечер ⓕ *ve*-cher evening
вечеря ⓕ ve-*che*-rya dinner
взема/взимам под наем *vze*-muh/*vzee*-mam pod *na*-em rent v

видеокамера ① vee·de·o·*ka*·me·ra
video camera

видеокасета ① vee·de·o·ka·*se*·ta
video tape

видеомагнетофон ⓜ
vee·de·o·mag·ne·to·*fon* video recorder

вие vee·e you sg pol&pl

виза ① *vee*·za visa

вилица ① *vee*·lee·tsa fork

висока температура ①
vee·*so*·ka tem·pe·ra·*too*·ra fever

вкусен vkoo·sen tasty

влак ⓜ vlak train n

вляза/влизам *vlya*·zuh/*vlee*·zam enter

внуче ⓝ *vnoo*·che grandchild

вода ① vo·*da* water n

връщане на парите ⓝ
vrush·ta·ne na pa·*ree*·te refund n

всеки *vse*·kee each • every • everyone

всичко *vseech*·ko all pron • everything

втора класа ① *vto*·ra *kla*·sa second class

вход ⓜ vhod entry

входна такса ① *vhod*·na *tak*·sa
admission price

вчера *vche*·ra yesterday

в чужбина v choozh·*bee*·na overseas

възглавница ① vuhz·*glav*·nee·tsa pillow

въздушна поща ①
vuhz·*doosh*·na *posh*·ta airmail

вълна ① *vuhl*·na wool

вървя vuhr·*vyuh* walk v

върна/връщам се
vuhr·na/*vruhsh*·tam se return v

вътрешна гума ① *vuh*·tresh·na *goo*·ma
tyre

Г

гадене ⓝ *ga*·de·ne nausea

гадже ⓜ *gad*·zhe boyfriend • girlfriend

газ ⓜ gaz gas (for cooking)

галерия ① ga·*le*·ree·ya art gallery

гара ① *ga*·ra railway station

гаранция ① ga·*ran*·tsee·ya guarantee n

гардероб ⓜ gar·de·*rob* cloakroom •
left-luggage office • luggage locker

гастроентерит ⓜ gas·tro·en·te·*reet*
gastroenteritis

гей ⓜ&① gey gay (homosexual) n&a

глава ① gla·*va* head

главен готвач ⓜ *gla*·ven got·*vach*
chef (man)

главна готвачка ① *glav*·na got·*vach*·ka
chef (woman)

главоболие ⓝ gla·vo·bo·*lee*·e headache

гладен *gla*·den hungry

гледам *gle*·dam look v • watch v

гледка ① *gled*·ka view n

глезен *gle*·zen ankle

глоба ① *glo*·ba fine (payment) n

говоря go·*vor*·yuh speak

годеж ⓜ go·*dezh* engagement (to marry)

годеник ⓜ go·de·*neek* fiancé

годеница ① go·de·*nee*·tsa fiancée

година ① go·*dee*·na year

голям go·*lyam* big

гора ① go·*ra* forest

горе go·re up

горещ go·*resht* hot (temperature)

горещина ① go·resh·tee·*na* heat n

горчив gor·*cheev* bitter

готвач/готвачка ⓜ/①
got·*vach*/got·*vach*·ka cook n

готвя got·*vyuh* cook v

град ⓜ grad city

градина ① gra·*dee*·na garden n

градски автобус ⓜ
grad·skee av·to·*boos* city bus

грам ⓜ gram gram

граница ① *gra*·nee·tsa border (country)

гребен ⓜ *gre*·ben comb n

грейка ① *grey*·ka hot water bottle

грим ⓜ greem make-up

грип ⓜ greep flu

гробище ⓝ *gro*·beesh·te cemetery

гръб ⓜ gruhb back (body)

гръден кош ⓜ *gruh*·den kosh chest (body)

гума ① *goo*·ma tyre

гърло ⓝ *guhr*·lo throat

Гърция ① *guhr*·tsee·ya Greece

Д

да da yes

далече da·*le*·che far adv

дамска превръзка ①
dam·ska pre·*vruhz*·ka
panty liner • sanitary napkin

дамска чанта ⓕ *dam*·ska *chan*·ta *purse*

дата ⓕ *da*·ta *date (day)*

дата на раждане ⓕ *da*·ta na *razh*·da·ne *date of birth*

две седмици ⓕ pl dve *sed*·mee·tsee *fortnight*

двойно легло ⓝ *dvoy*·no *leg*·lo *double bed*

дворец ⓜ dvo·*rets* *palace*

двупосочен билет ⓜ dvoo·po·*so*·chen bee·*let* *return ticket*

дезодорант ⓜ de·zo·do·*rant* *deodorant*

ден ⓜ den *day*

денонощен магазин ⓜ de·no·*nosh*·ten ma·ga·*zeen* *convenience store*

депозит ⓜ de·po·*zeet* *deposit* n

десен de·*sen* *right (direction)* a

дестинация ⓕ des·tee·*na*·tsee·ya *destination*

дете ⓝ de·*te* *child*

детска седалка ⓕ *det*·ska se·*dal*·ka *child seat (car)*

дефектен de·*fek*·ten *faulty*

деца ⓝ pl de·*tsa* *children*

джобно ножче ⓝ *dzhob*·no *nozh*·che *penknife*

диабет ⓜ dee·a·*bet* *diabetes*

диапозитивен филм ⓜ dee·a·po·zee·*tee*·ven feelm *slide film*

диария ⓕ dee·a·*ree*·a *diarrhoea*

дипломатическо куфарче ⓝ dee·plo·ma·*tee*·ches·ko koo·*far*·che *briefcase*

директор/директорка ⓜ/ⓕ dee·*rek*·tor/dee·*rek*·tor·ka *manager (business)*

диск ⓜ deesk *disk (CD-ROM)*

дискета ⓕ dees·*ke*·ta *floppy disk*

дистанционно управление ⓝ dees·tan·tsee·o·no oo·prav·*le*·nee·e *remote control*

дневник ⓜ *dnev*·neek *diary*

днес dnes *today*

до do *beside • until*

добър do·*buhr* *good*

довечера do·*ve*·che·ra *tonight*

долар ⓜ *do*·lar *dollar*

долу *do*·loo *down*

дом ⓜ dom *home*

досаден do·*sa*·den *boring*

доставя/доставям do·*stav*·yuh/do·*stav*·yam *deliver*

достатъчен do·*sta*·tuh·chen *enough*

дрехи ⓕ pl *dre*·hee *clothing*

друг droog *another • other*

другар ⓜ droo·*gar* *companion*

Дунав ⓜ *doo*·nav *Danube*

душ ⓜ doosh *shower* n

дъжд ⓜ duhzhd *rain* n

дъждобран ⓜ duhzh·do·*bran* *raincoat*

дълъг *duh*·luhg *long*

дъщеря ⓕ duhsh·ter·*ya* *daughter*

дядо ⓜ *dya*·do *grandfather*

E

евро ⓝ *ev*·ro *euro*

Европа ⓕ ev·*ro*·pa *Europe*

Европейският съюз ⓜ ev·ro·*pey*·skee·yuht suh·*yooz* *European Union*

евтин *ev*·teen *cheap*

Егейско море ⓝ e·*gey*·sko mo·*re* *Aegean Sea*

единична стая ⓕ e·dee·*neech*·na *sta*·ya *single room*

еднопосочен билет ⓜ ed·no·po·*so*·chen bee·*let* *one-way ticket*

ежедневно e·zhed·*nev*·no *daily* adv

езеро ⓝ *e*·ze·ro *lake*

език ⓜ e·*zeek* *language*

екскурзия ⓕ eks·koor·*zee*·ya *guided tour*

екскурзовод/екскурзоводка ⓜ/ⓕ eks·koor·zo·*vod*/eks·koor·zo·*vod*·ka *guide (person)*

електричество ⓝ e·lek·*tree*·chest·vo *electricity*

ескалатор ⓜ es·ka·*la*·tor *escalator*

етаж ⓜ e·*tazh* *floor (storey)*

Ж

жаден *zha*·den *thirsty*

жена ⓕ zhe·*na* *wife • woman*

женен ⓜ *zhe*·nen *married (man)*

женски *zhen*·skee *female* a

жилище ⓝ *zhee*·leesh·te *accommodation*

журналист/журналистка ⑩/①
zhoor·na·*leest*/zhoor·na·*leest*·ka
journalist
жълт zhuhlt *yellow*

З

за za *about* • *to*
зад zad *behind*
задръстен za·*druhs*·ten *blocked*
за една нощ za ed·*na* nosht
overnight adv
заедно za·ed·no *together*
заключен za·*klyoo*·chen *locked*
закуска ① za·*koos*·ka *breakfast* • *snack*
закъснение ⑩ za·kuhs·*ne*·nee·e *delay* n
залез слънце ⑩ za·lez sluhn·tse *sunset*
замина/заминавам
za·*mee*·nuh/za·mee·*na*·vam *depart*
заминаване ⑩ za·mee·*na*·va·ne
departure
замръзнал za·*mruhz*·nal *frozen*
замък ⑩ *za*·muhk *castle*
занаяти ⑩ pl za·na·*ya*·tee *crafts*
за непушачи za ne·poo·*sha*·chee
nonsmoking
запад ⑩ *za*·pad *west*
запалка ① za·*pal*·ka *cigarette lighter*
запек ⑩ *za*·pek *constipation*
запушалка ① za·*poo*·shal·ka
plug (bath)
застраховка ① za·stra·*hov*·ka *insurance*
затворен zat·*vo*·ren *closed* • *shut*
затваря/затварям
zat·*vor*·yuh/zat·*var*·yam *close* v • *shut* v
затоплен za·*top*·len *heated*
защо zash·*to* *why*
зелен ze·*len* *green*
зеленчук ⑩ ze·len·*chook* *vegetable* n
зима ① *zee*·ma *winter*
злато ⑩ *zla*·to *gold* n
злополука ① zlo·po·*loo*·ka *accident*
зоопарк ⑩ zo·o·*park* *zoo*
зора ① zo·*ra* *dawn*
зъбобол ⑩ zuh·bo·*bol* *toothache*
зъболекар/зъболекарка ⑩/①
zuh·bo·le·*kar*/zuh·bo·le·*kar*·ka *dentist*

И

и ee *and*
игла ① eeg·*la* *needle (sewing)*
игрище ⑩ ee·*greesh*·te *sports court*
и двата/двете ⑩/①&⑩
ee *dva*·ta/*dve*·te *both*
изгаряне ⑩ eez·*gar*·ya·ne *burn* n
изгрев слънце ⑩ *eez*·grev sluhn·tse
sunrise
изгубен eez·*goo*·ben *lost*
изкуство ⑩ eez·*koost*·vo *art*
изложба ① eez·*lozh*·ba *exhibition*
изляза/излизам (с)
eez·*lya*·zuh/eez·*lee*·zam (s) *go out (with)*
изпусна/изпускам ees·*poos*·nuh/
ees·*poos*·kam *miss (train, etc)* v
изсуша/изсушавам eez·soo·*shuh*/
eez·soo·*sha*·vam *dry (clothes)* v
изток ⑩ *eez*·tok *east* n
изход ⑩ *eez*·hod *exit*
имам ee·*mam* *have*
име ⑩ *ee*·me *name* n
и-мейл ⑩ *ee*·meyl *email* n
инвалиден een·va·*lee*·den *disabled*
инвалидна количка ①
een·va·*leed*·na ko·*leech*·ka *wheelchair*
инжекция ① een·*zhek*·tsee·ya *injection*
инженер ⑩ een·zhe·*ner* *engineer*
инженерство ⑩ een·zhe·*nerst*·vo
engineering
Интернет ⑩ *een*·ter·net *internet*
Интернет кафе ⑩ *een*·ter·net ka·*fe*
internet café
инфекция ① een·*fek*·tsee·ya *infection*
информационна агенция ①
een·for·ma·tsee·*on*·na a·*gen*·tsee·ya
newsagency
информационни технологии ① pl
een·for·ma·tsee·o·nee teh·no·*lo*·gee·ee
IT (information technology)
информация ① een·for·*ma*·tsee·ya
information

К

калкулатор ⑩ kal·koo·*la*·tor *calculator*
калъфка за възглавница ① ka·*luhf*·ka
za vuhz·*glav*·nee·tsa *pillowcase*

Канада ⓕ *ka·na·*da Canada
карам *ka·*ram drive v
каране на ски *ka·ra·*ne na skee skiing
карта ⓕ *kar·*ta map (of country)
каса ⓕ *ka·*sa cash register
касетка ⓕ *ka·set·*ka cassette
касиер/касиерка ⓜ/ⓕ
  *ka·see·er/ka·see·er·*ka cashier
катедрала ⓕ *ka·te·dra·*la cathedral
катинар ⓜ *ka·tee·*nar padlock
кафене ⓝ *ka·fe·*ne café
кафяв *kaf·*yav brown
кача/качвам се *ka·chuh/kach·*vam se
  board (a plane, etc)
кашлям *kash·*lyam cough v
кибрит ⓜ *kee·*breet
  matches (for lighting)
килограм ⓜ *kee·lo·*gram kilogram
километър ⓜ *kee·lo·me·*tuhr kilometre
кино ⓝ *kee·*no cinema • movie
класически *kla·see·ches·*kee classical
клиент/клиентка ⓜ/ⓕ
  *klee·ent/klee·ent·*ka client
ключ ⓜ *klyooch* key n
ключалка ⓕ *klyoo·chal·*ka lock n
книга ⓕ *knee·*ga book n
книжарница ⓕ *knee·zhar·nee·*tsa
  book shop
кога *ko·*ga when
кожа ⓕ *ko·*zha leather n
козметичен салон ⓜ
  *koz·me·tee·chen sa·*lon beauty salon
кой *koy* which • who
кола ⓕ *ko·*la car
колега ⓕ *ko·le·*ga colleague
колет ⓜ *ko·*let parcel
коляно ⓝ *ko·lya·*no knee
командировка ⓕ *ko·man·dee·rov·*ka
  business trip
комисионна ⓕ *ko·mee·see·on·*na
  commission
компания ⓕ *kom·pa·nee·*ya company
компютър ⓜ *kom·pyoo·*tuhr computer
комунистически
  *ko·moo·nees·tee·ches·*kee communist a
конец за зъби ⓜ *ko·*nets za *zuh·*bee
  dental floss
конна езда ⓕ *kon·*na ez·*da horse riding
консервна кутия ⓕ
  *kon·serv·*na koo·*tee·*ya can • tin

консулство ⓝ *kon·*soolst·vo consulate
контактни лещи ⓕ pl
  *kon·takt·*nee *lesh·*tee contact lenses
контузия ⓕ *kon·too·zee·*ya injury
конференция ⓕ *kon·fe·ren·*tsee·ya
  big conference
концерт ⓜ *kon·*tsert concert • gig
коприна ⓕ *ko·pree·*na silk n
копче ⓝ *kop·*che button n
кораб ⓜ *ko·*rab boat
кофа за боклук ⓕ *ko·*fa za bok·*look
  garbage can
край ⓜ *krai* end n
крак ⓜ *krak* foot (body) • leg (body)
кран ⓜ *kran* faucet • tap
красив *kra·seev* beautiful • handsome
кредит ⓜ *kre·*deet credit n
кредитна карта ⓕ *kre·deet·*na *kar·*ta
  credit card
крем за бръснене ⓜ
  krem za *bruhs·ne·*ne shaving cream
кръв ⓕ *kruhv* blood
кръвна група ⓕ *kruhv·*na *groo·*pa
  blood group
кръчма ⓕ *kruhch·*ma bar • pub
купа ⓕ *koo·*pa bowl n
купон ⓜ *koo·*pon party (entertainment)
купя/купувам *koop·yuh/koo·poo·*vam
  buy
кутия ⓕ *koo·tee·*ya box n
куфар ⓜ *koo·*far suitcase
кухня ⓕ *kooh·*nya kitchen
куче ⓝ *koo·*che dog
къде *kuh·*de where
къмпинг ⓜ *kuhm·*peeng
  camping ground
кърпа ⓕ *kuhr·*pa towel
кърпа за лице ⓕ *kuhr·*pa za lee·*tse
  face cloth
късно *kuhs·*no late adv

Л

лаптоп ⓜ *lap·*top laptop
лед ⓜ *led* ice
лейкопласт ⓜ *ley·ko·*plast Band-Aid
лек *lek* light (weight) a
лекар/лекарка ⓜ/ⓕ *le·kar/le·kar·*ka
  doctor

лекарство ⑩ le-*karst*-vo drug (medication)

леля ⑥ *lel*-ya aunt

лен ⑩ len linen (fabric)

летище ⑩ le-*teesh*-te airport

летищна такса ⑥ le-*teesht*-na *tak*-sa airport tax

лилав цвят lee-*lav* tsvyat purple

линейка ⑥ lee-*ney*-ka ambulance

лице ⑩ lee-*tse* face n

лична карта ⑥ *leech*-na *kar*-ta identification

лош losh bad

лошо храносмилане ⑩ *lo*-sho hra-no-*smee*-la-ne indigestion

лъжица ⑥ luh-*zhee*-tsa spoon

любезен lyoo-*be*-zen kind (nice)

ляв lyav left (direction)

лято ⑩ *lya*-to summer

M

магазин ⑩ ma-ga-*zeen* shop n

магазин за деликатеси ⑩ ma-ga-*zeen* za de-lee-ka-*te*-see delicatessen

магазин за електроуреди ⑩ ma-ga-*zeen* za e-lek-tro-oo-*re*-dee electrical store

магазин за облекло ⑩ ma-ga-*zeen* za o-blek-*lo* clothing store

магазин за обувки ⑩ ma-ga-*zeen* za o-*boov*-kee shoe shop

магазин за сувенири ⑩ ma-ga-*zeen* za soo-ve-*nee*-ree souvenir shop

магистрала ⑥ ma-gees-*tra*-la highway • motorway

майка ⑥ *mai*-ka mother

Македония ⑥ ma-ke-*do*-nee-ya Macedonia

малък *ma*-luhk small

малък хотел ⑩ *ma*-luhk ho-*tel* guesthouse

мама ⑥ *ma*-ma mum

марка ⑥ *mar*-ka postage stamp

маршрут ⑩ marsh-*root* itinerary

масаж ⑩ ma-*sazh* massage n

масажист ⑩ ma-sa-*zheest* masseur

масажистка ⑥ ma-sa-*zheest*-ka masseuse

матрак ⑩ mat-*rak* mattress

мач ⑩ mach sports match

мебели pl *me*-be-lee furniture

меден месец ⑩ *me*-den *me*-sets honeymoon

медицина ⑥ me-dee-*tsee*-na medicine (study/profession)

медицинска сестра ⑥ me-dee-*tseen*-ska ses-*tra* nurse n

междуградски автобус ⑩ mezh-doo-*grad*-skee av-to-*boos* coach (bus)

мене *me*-ne me

меню ⑩ men-*yoo* menu

месарница ⑥ me-*sar*-nee-tsa butcher's shop

месец ⑩ *me*-sets month

месо ⑩ *me*-so meat

местен *mes*-ten local a

метър ⑩ *me*-tuhr metre

мехур ⑩ me-*hoor* blister

микровълнова печка ⑥ mee-kro-*vuhl*-no-va *pech*-ka microwave oven

милиметър ⑩ mee-lee-*me*-tuhr millimetre

минал *mee*-nal last (previous)

минута ⑥ mee-*noo*-ta minute

миризма ⑥ mee-*reez*-ma smell n

митница ⑥ *meet*-nee-tsa customs (immigration)

мия *mee*-yuh wash (something)

мляко ⑩ *mlya*-ko milk

мода ⑥ *mo*-da fashion

модем ⑩ mo-*dem* modem

мозъчно сътресение ⑩ mo-*zuhch*-no suh-tre-*se*-nee-e concussion

мой moy my

молив ⑩ *mo*-leev pencil

момиче ⑩ mo-*mee*-che girl

момче ⑩ mom-*che* boy

монети ⑥ pl mo-ne-*tee* change (coins) n

море ⑩ mo-*re* sea

мост ⑩ most bridge n

мотел ⑩ mo-*tel* motel

мотор ⑩ mo-*tor* engine

мръсен mruh-sen dirty

музей ⑩ moo-*zey* museum

музика ⑥ *moo*-zee-ka music

музикален магазин ⑩ moo-zee-*ka*-len ma-ga-*zeen* music shop

муха ① moo·ha fly n
мъж ⓜ muhzh husband

Н

на na at • on • per (day, etc)
наблизо na·blee·zo nearby adv
на борда na bor·da aboard
набързо na·buhr·zo in a hurry
навреме na·vre·me on time
навън na·vuhn outside adv
навяхване ⓝ nav·yah·va·ne sprain n
надценка ① nad·tsen·ka cover charge
наем ⓜ na·em rent n
наема/наемам na·e·muh/na·e·mam hire v
наемане на кола ⓝ na·e·ma·ne na ko·la
    car hire
най-близкият nai·bleez·kee·yuht nearest
най-голям nai·go·lyam biggest
най-добър nai·do·buhr best
най-малкият nai·mal·kee·yuht smallest
намаление ⓝ na·ma·le·nee·e discount n
напитка ① na·peet·ka drink n
наркотик ⓜ nar·ko·teek dope (drugs)
наркотици ⓟ pl nar·ko·tee·tsee
    illicit drugs
на самообслужване
    na sa·mo·ob·sloozh·va·ne self-service
наука ① na·oo·ka science
наш nash our
не ne no
негов ne·gov his
неженен ⓜ ne·zhe·nen single (man) a
неин ne·een her (possessive)
неомъжена ① ne·o·muh·zhe·na
    single (woman) a
неудобен ne·oo·do·ben uncomfortable
нефт ⓜ neft oil (petrol)
нисък nee·suhk short (height)
нищо neesh·to nothing
нов nov new
Нова година ① no·va go·dee·na
    New Year's Day
Нова Зеландия ① no·va ze·lan·dee·ya
    New Zealand
новина ① no·vee·na news
Новогодишна нощ ①
    no·vo·go·deesh·na nosht New Year's Eve
нож ⓜ nozh knife

ножица ① no·zhee·tsa scissors
ножче за бръснене ⓝ
    nozh·che za bruhs·ne·ne razor blade
нокторезачка ① nok·to·re·zach·ka
    nail clippers
номер ⓜ no·mer size
номер на паспорта ⓜ
    no·mer na pas·por·ta passport number
номер на стаята ⓝ no·mer na sta·ya·ta
    room number
нос ⓜ nos nose
носна кърпичка ①
    nos·na kuhr·peech·ka handkerchief
нощ ① nosht night
нощен клуб ⓜ nosh·ten kloob nightclub
нощ на открито ① nosht na ot·kree·to
    night out

О

обадя/обаждам се o·bad·yuh/
    o·bazh·dam se v • telephone v
обед ⓜ o·bed lunch
обектив ⓜ o·bek·teev lens (camera)
обикновена поща ① o·beek·no·ve·na
    posh·ta surface mail (land/sea)
обиколка ① o·bee·kol·ka tour n
обици ⓟ pl o·bee·tsee earrings
обич ① o·beech love n
обичай o·bee·chai custom
обичам o·bee·cham love v
обменен курс на валутата ⓜ
    ob·me·nen koors na va·loo·ta·ta
    exchange rate
обмяна на валута ① ob·mya·na na
    va·loo·ta currency exchange
обслужване ⓝ ob·sloozh·va·ne service n
обувки ⓟ pl o·boov·kee shoes
обществена тоалетна ①
    obsh·test·ve·na to·a·let·na public toilet
обяд ⓜ ob·yad midday
огледало ⓝ o·gle·da·lo mirror n
огърлица ① o·guhr·lee·tsa necklace
одеяло ⓝ o·de·ya·lo blanket
око ⓝ o·ko eye
олио ⓝ o·lee·o oil (cooking)
омъжена ① o·muh·zhe·na
    married (woman)
онзи on·zee that a • that one pron

опасен o-*pa*-sen *dangerous*
опитам/опитвам o-*pee*-tam/o-*peet*-vam
  try (taste)
опитам/опитвам се
  o-*pee*-tam/o-*peet*-vam se *try (attempt)*
оплакване ⓝ o-*plak*-va-ne *complaint*
оранжев o-*ran*-zhev *orange (colour)*
осребря/осребрявам o-sreb-*ryuh*/
  o-sreb-*rya*-vam *cash (a cheque)* v
останки pl o-*stan*-kee *ruins*
остров ⓜ *os*-trov *island*
от ot *from*
отварачка за бутилки ⓕ ot-va-*rach*-ka
  na boo-*teel*-kee *bottle opener*
отварачка за консерви ⓕ ot-va-*rach*-ka
  za kon-*ser*-vee *can opener • tin opener*
отида/отивам o-*tee*-duh/o-*tee*-vam *go*
отида/отивам на поход
  o-*tee*-duh/o-*tee*-vam na po-*hod* *hike* v
откраднат ot-*krad*-nat *stolen*
отново ot-*no*-vo *again*
очила ⓝ pl o-chee-*la* *glasses (spectacles)*
очистително ⓝ o-chees-*tee*-tel-no
  laxative n

П

пазар ⓜ pa-*zar* *market* n
пазарувам pa-za-*roo*-vam *shop* v
пакет ⓜ pa-*ket* *package • packet*
палто ⓝ pal-*to* *coat*
памук ⓜ pa-*mook* *cotton* n
пансион ⓜ pan-see-*on* *boarding house*
панталони ⓜ pl pan-ta-*lo*-nee
  pants • trousers
пари ⓝ pl pa-*ree* *money*
пари в брой ⓝ pl pa-*ree* v broy *cash* n
паркирам par-*kee*-ram *park (a car)* v
парфюм ⓜ par-*fyoom* *perfume*
паспорт ⓜ pas-*port* *passport*
паста за зъби ⓕ *pas*-ta za *zuh*-bee
  toothpaste
пауза ⓕ *pa*-oo-za *intermission*
пелена ⓕ pe-le-*na* *diaper • nappy*
пенсионер/пенсионерка ⓜ/ⓕ
  pen-see-o-*ner*/pen-see-o-*ner*-ka
  pensioner
пепелник ⓜ pe-*pel*-neek *ashtray*

перална машина ⓕ
  pe-*ral*-na ma-*shee*-na *washing machine*
пешеходство ⓝ pe-she-*hod*-stvo *hiking*
пиеса ⓕ pee-*e*-sa *play (theatre)* n
пикник ⓜ *peek*-neek *picnic* n
пинцета ⓕ peen-*tse*-ta *tweezers*
писалка ⓕ pee-*sal*-ka *pen*
писмо ⓝ pees-*mo* *letter (mail)*
пиша *pee*-shuh *write*
пия pee-*yuh* *drink* v
пиян pee-*yan* *drunk*
плаж ⓜ plazh *beach*
плажно масло ⓝ *plazh*-no *mas*-lo
  tanning lotion
план ⓜ plan *map (of town)*
планина ⓕ pla-nee-*na* *mountain*
плащане ⓝ *plash*-ta-ne *payment*
плик за писмо ⓜ pleek za pees-*mo*
  envelope
плод ⓜ plod *fruit*
плосък *plo*-suhk *flat* a
площад ⓜ plosh-*tad* *town square*
плувам *ploo*-vam *swim* v
плувен басейн ⓜ *ploo*-ven ba-*seyn*
  swimming pool
повече po-*ve*-che *more*
повреден po-vre-*den* *broken • out of order*
по-голям po-go-*lyam* *bigger*
подарък ⓜ po-*da*-ruhk *gift*
по-добър po-*do*-buhr *better*
подстригване ⓝ pod-*streeg*-va-ne
  haircut
поздравя/поздравявам poz-drav-*yuh*/
  poz-drav-*ya*-vam *congratulate*
покажа/показвам
  po-ka-*zhuh*/po-*kaz*-vam *show* v
по-късно po-*kuhs*-no *later* adv
пол ⓜ pol *sex (gender)*
пола ⓕ po-*la* *skirt*
полет ⓜ *po*-let *flight*
полицай/полицайка ⓜ/ⓕ
  po-lee-*tsai*/po-lee-*tsai*-ka *police officer*
полицейски участък ⓜ po-lee-*tsey*-skee
  oo-*chas*-tuhk *police station*
полиция ⓕ po-*lee*-tsee-ya *police*
половина ⓕ po-lo-*vee*-na *half* n
полунощ ⓕ po-loo-*nosht* *midnight*
получаване на багаж ⓝ
  po-loo-*cha*-va-ne na ba-*gazh*
  baggage claim

по-малко po·mal·ko *less*
по-малък po·ma·luhk *smaller*
помогна/помагам
po·mog·nuh/po·ma·gam *help* v
помощ ① po·mosht *help* n
поправя/поправям
po·prav·yuh/po·prav·yam *repair* v
последен po·sle·den *last (final)*
посока ① po·so·ka *direction*
посолство ⑩ po·solst·vo *embassy*
потвърдя/потвърждавам
pot·vuhr·dyuh/pot·vuhrzh·da·vam
confirm (a booking) • *validate*
почивка ① po·cheev·ka *rest* n
поща ① posh·ta *mail* • *post office*
пощенска картичка ①
posh·ten·ska kar·teech·ka *postcard*
пощенска кутия ①
posh·ten·ska koo·tee·ya *mailbox*
пощенски код ⑩ posh·ten·skee kod
postcode
право ⑩ pra·vo *law (study/profession)*
празен pra·zen *empty* a
празник ⑩ praz·neek *holiday*
пране ⑩ pra·ne *laundry (clothes)*
превода/превеждам
pre·ve·duh/pre·vezh·dam *translate*
превръзка ① pre·vruhz·ka *bandage*
преди pre·dee *before*
предпазен колан ⑩ pred·pa·zen ko·lan
seatbelt
представление ⑩ pred·stav·le·nee·e
show n
презерватив ⑩ pre·zer·va·teev *condom*
препоръчам/препоръчвам
pre·po·ruh·cham/pre·po·ruhch·vam
recommend
препоръчана поща ①
pre·po·ruh·cha·na posh·ta
registered mail
прибори за хранене ⑩ pl
pree·bo·ree za hra·ne·ne *cutlery*
принтър ⑩ preen·tuhr
printer (computer)
пристигане ⑩ pree·stee·ga·ne
arrivals (airport)
приятел/приятелка ⑩/①
pree·ya·tel/pree·ya·tel·ka *friend*
пробна ① prob·na *changing room*

провинция ①
pro·veen·tsee·ya
countryside
прозорец ⑩ pro·zo·rets *window*
пролет ① pro·let *spring (season)*
промяна ① pro·mya·na *change* n
проститутка ① pros·tee·toot·ka
prostitute n
процент за обслужване ⑩ pro·tsent za
ob·sloozh·va·ne *service charge*
пръст ⑩ pruhst *finger*
пръстен ⑩ pruhs·ten *ring (jewellery)*
пряк pryak *direct* a
пуловер ⑩ poo·lo·ver *jumper* • *sweater*
пура ① poo·ra *cigar*
пуша poo·shuh *smoke* v
пълен puh·len *full*
първа класа ① puhr·va kla·sa *first class*
път ⑩ puht *road* • *way*
пътеводител ⑩ puh·te·vo·dee·tel
guidebook
пътека ① puh·te·ka
aisle (plane, etc) • *footpath* • *path*
пътник/пътничка ⑩/①
puht·neek/puht·neech·ka *passenger*
пътническа агенция ①
puht·nee·ches·ka a·gen·tsee·ya
travel agency
пътнически чек ⑩ puht·nee·ches·kee
chek *travellers cheque*
пътувам на автостоп
puh·too·vam na av·to·stop *hitchhike*
пътуване ⑩ puh·too·va·ne *journey* n

Р

работа ① ra·bo·ta *job*
работно време ⑩ ra·bot·no vre·me
opening hours
радио ⑩ ra·dee·o *radio*
развален raz·va·len *broken down*
разведен raz·ve·den *divorced*
развлекателна програма ①
raz·vle·ka·tel·na pro·gra·ma
entertainment guide
разговорник ⑩ raz·go·vor·neek
phrasebook
разкош ⑩ ras·kosh *luxury*
различен raz·lee·chen *different*

разменя/разменям
raz·men·yuh/raz·men·yam *exchange* v

разписание ⓝ raz·pee·*sa*·nee·e
timetable

разписка ⓕ *raz*·pees·ka *receipt*

рамо ⓝ *ra*·mo *shoulder*

ранен ra·*nen* *injured*

раница ⓕ *ra*·nee·tsa *backpack*

рано ra·no *early* adv

режа re·zhuh *cut* v

резервация ⓕ re·zer·va·tsee·ya
booking • reservation

резервирам re·zer·*vee*·ram
book v • *reserve*

рейв парти ⓜ reyv *par*·tee *rave party*

река ⓕ re·*ka* *river*

ресторант ⓜ res·to·*rant* *restaurant*

рецепта ⓕ re·*tsep*·ta *prescription*

рецепция ⓕ re·*tsep*·tsee·ya
check-in desk

речник ⓜ *rech*·neek *dictionary*

рибарски магазин ⓜ
ree·*bar*·skee ma·ga·*zeen* *fish shop*

риболов ⓜ ree·bo·*lov* *fishing*

риза ⓕ *ree*·za *shirt*

родители ⓜ pl ro·dee·te·*lee* *parents*

рожден ден ⓜ rozh·*den* den *birthday*

розов *ro*·zov *pink*

рок ⓜ rok *rock music*

рокля ⓕ *rok*·lya *dress* n

романтичен ro·man·*tee*·chen *romantic* a

Румъния ⓕ roo·*muh*·nee·ya *Romania*

ръка ⓕ ruh·*ka* *arm (body)* • *hand*

ръкавици ⓕ pl ruh·ka·*vee*·tse
gloves (clothing)

ръчна изработка ⓕ
ruhch·na eez·ra·*bot*·ka *handicraft*

ръчно изработен
ruhch·no eez·ra·*bo*·ten *handmade*

рядък *rya*·duhk *rare* • *uncommon*

С

салфетка ⓕ sal·*fet*·ka *napkin*

сам/сама ⓜ/ⓕ sam/sa·*ma* *alone*

самобръсначка ⓕ sa·mo·bruhs·*nach*·ka
razor

самолет ⓜ sa·mo·*let* *airplane*

самолетна компания ⓕ
sa·mo·*let*·na kom·*pa*·nee·ya *airline*

сантиметър ⓜ san·tee·*me*·tuhr *centimetre*

сапун ⓜ sa·*poon* *soap*

САЩ sasht *USA*

свекър ⓜ *sve*·kuhr
father-in-law (husband's father)

свекърва ⓕ sve·*kuhr*·va
mother-in-law (husband's mother)

светлина ⓕ svet·lee·*na* *light* n

светломер ⓜ svet·lo·*mer* *light meter*

светъл *sve*·tuhl *light (colour)* a

свободен svo·*bo*·den
free (available) • *vacant*

свободни стаи ⓕ pl
svo·*bod*·nee *sta*·yee *vacancy*

свръхбагаж ⓜ svuhrh·ba·*gazh*
excess baggage

сгоден sgo·*den* *engaged (to be married)*

сграда ⓕ *sgra*·da *building*

север ⓜ *se*·ver *north* n

сега se·*ga* *now*

седалка ⓕ se·*dal*·ka *seat (chair, etc)*

седалков лифт ⓜ se·*dal*·kov leeft
chairlift (skiing)

седмица ⓕ *sed*·mee·tsa *week*

сезон ⓜ se·*zon* *season* n

сейф ⓜ seyf *safe* n

секс ⓜ seks *sex (intercourse)*

семейство ⓝ se·*meyst*·vo *family*

сенна хрема ⓕ *sen*·na *hre*·ma *hay fever*

сервитьор/сервитьорка ⓜ/ⓕ
ser·veet·*yor*/ser·veet·*yor*·ka *waiter*

сестра ⓕ ses·*tra* *sister*

сив seev *grey*

сиди ⓝ see·*dee* *CD*

сим-карта ⓕ seem·*kar*·ta *SIM card*

син ⓜ seen *son*

син seen *blue*

сироп за кашлица ⓜ
see·*rop* za *kash*·lee·tsa *cough medicine*

с климатик s klee·ma·*teek* *air-conditioned*

скоро *sko*·ro *soon*

скоростна кутия ⓕ
sko·rost·na koo·*tee*·ya *gearbox*

скулптура ⓕ skoolp·*too*·ra *sculpture*

скъп skuhp *expensive*

скъпоценен skuh·po·*tse*·nen *valuable*

сладкарница ⓕ slad·*kar*·nee·tsa
cake shop

сладък *sla*-duhk *sweet*
след *sled after*
следващ *sled*-vasht *next (following)*
следобед ⑩ *sle*-*do*-*bed afternoon*
слушам *sloo*-sham *listen*
слънце ⑩ *sluhn*-tse *sun*
слънцезащитен крем ⑩
  sluhn-tse-zash-*tee*-ten krem *sunblock*
слънчеви очила ⑪ pl
  sluhn-che-vee o-chee-*la sunglasses*
слънчево изгаряне ⑩
  sluhn-che-vo eez-*gar*-ya-ne *sunburn*
сляза/слизам *slya*-zuh/*slee*-zam
  get off (train, etc)
смазочно масло ⑩ *sma*-zoch-no *mas*-lo
  lubricant
сменям *smen*-yam *change (money)* v
сметка ⑪ *smet*-ka *account · bill · check* n
смешен *sme*-shen *funny*
снимам *snee*-mam *take a photo*
снимка ⑪ *sneem*-ka *photo*
сняг ⑩ snyag *snow* n
собствено име ⑩ *sobst*-ve-no *ee*-me
  first name
София ⑪ so-*fee*-ya *Sofia*
соча *so*-chuh *point* v
спален вагон ⑩ *spa*-len va-*gon*
  sleeping car
спален чувал ⑩ *spa*-len choo-*val*
  sleeping bag
спално бельо ⑩ *spal*-no bel-*yo*
  linen (sheets)
спално място ⑩ *spal*-no *myas*-to *berth*
спалня ⑪ *spal*-nya *bedroom*
спасителна жилетка ⑪ spa-*see*-tel-na
  zhee-*let*-ka *life jacket*
спешен *spe*-shen *urgent*
спешен случай ⑩ *spe*-shen *sloo*-chai
  emergency
спирачки ⑪ pl spee-*rach*-kee *brakes*
споделя/споделям spo-*del*-yuh/
  spo-*del*-yam *share (a room, etc)* v
спортен магазин ⑩
  spor-ten ma-ga-*zeen sports store*
сребро ⑩ *sreb*-ro *silver* n
стар *star old*
стачка ⑪ *stach*-ka *strike* n
стая ⑪ *sta*-ya *room*
стая с две легла ⑪ *sta*-ya s dve *leg*-la
  double room

стол ⑩ stol *chair* n
стомах ⑩ sto-*mah stomach*
струвам *stroo*-vam *cost* v
студен stoo-*den cold* a
студент/студентка ⑩/⑪
  stoo-*dent*/stoo-*dent*-ka *student*
стълбище ⑩ *stuhl*-beesh-te *stairway*
субтитри ⑪ pl soob-*teet*-ree *subtitles*
сувенир ⑩ soo-ve-*neer souvenir*
супермаркет ⑩ soo-per-*mar*-ket
  supermarket
сутиен ⑩ soo-*tee*-en *bra*
сух sooh *dry* a
събрание ⑩ suh-*bra*-nee-e
  small conference
събудя/събуждам suh-*bood*-yuh/
  suh-*boozh*-dam *wake (someone) up*
съвременен suh-*vre*-me-nen *modern*
сън ⑩ suhn *sleep* n
съобщение ⑩ suh-ob-*shte*-nee-e
  message
сърбеж ⑩ suhr-*bezh itch* n
Сърбия suhr-*bee*-ya *Serbia*
сърдечно заболяване ⑩ suhr-*dech*-no
  za-bo-*lya*-va-ne *heart condition*
сърце ⑩ suhr-*tse heart*
сянка ⑪ *syan*-ka *shade · shadow*

Т

таблетка ⑪ tab-*let*-ka *pill*
такси ⑩ tak-*see taxi*
таксиметрова стоянка ⑪
  tak-see-*me*-tro-va sto-*yan*-ka *taxi stand*
там tam *there*
тампон ⑩ tam-*pon tampon*
танц ⑩ tants *dance* n
танцувам tan-*tsoo*-vam *dance* v
танцуване ⑩ tan-*tsoo*-va-ne *dancing*
твой tvoy *your* inf sg
твърд tvuhrd *hard (not soft)*
театър ⑩ te-*a*-tuhr *theatre*
тежък te-*zhuk heavy*
телевизия ⑪ te-le-*vee*-zee-ya *television*
телевизор ⑩ te-le-*vee*-zor *TV (set)*
телеграма ⑪ te-le-*gra*-ma *telegram*
телефон ⑩ te-le-*fon telephone* n
телефонен сигнал ⑩
  te-le-*fo*-nen seeg-*nal dial tone*

телефонен указател ⓜ
te·le·fo·nen oo·ka·za·tel *phone book*

телефонна кабина ⓕ
te·le·fon·na ka·bee·na *phone box*

температура ⓕ tem·pe·ra·too·ra
temperature

тенджера ⓕ tend·zhe·ra *pot (cooking)*

тенис ⓜ te·nees *tennis*

тениска ⓕ te·nees·ka *T-shirt*

тенискорт ⓜ te·nees·kort *tennis court*

тетрадка ⓕ tet·rad·ka *notebook*

ти tee *you* inf sg

тиган ⓜ tee·gan *frying pan*

тирбушон ⓜ teer·boo·shon *corkscrew*

тих teeh *quiet*

тлъст tluhst *fat* a

тоалетна ⓕ to·a·let·na *toilet*

тоалетна хартия ⓕ to·a·let·na har·tee·ya
toilet paper

той toy *he*

ток ⓜ tok *current (electricity)*

топъл to·puhl *warm* a

тостер ⓜ tos·ter *toaster*

точно toch·no *exactly*

трибуна ⓕ tree·boo·na *platform*

тролейбус ⓜ tro·ley·boos *trolley*

тука too·ka *here*

туристическа класа ⓕ
too·rees·tee·ches·ka kla·sa
economy class

туристическа спалня ⓕ
too·rees·tee·ches·ka spal·nya
youth hostel

туристическо бюро ⓝ
too·rees·tee·ches·ko byoo·ro
tourist office

Турция ⓕ toor·tsee·ya *Turkey*

тъмен tuh·men *dark*

търговия ⓕ tuhr·go·vee·ya *business*

търговски център ⓜ
tuhr·gov·skee tsen·tuhr *shopping centre*

тъст ⓜ tuhst *father-in-law (wife's father)*

тъща ⓕ tuhsh·ta
mother-in-law (wife's mother)

У

уговорена среща ⓕ
oo·go·vo·re·na sresh·ta *appointment*

удобен oo·do·ben *comfortable*

ужасен oo·zha·sen *awful*

уикенд ⓜ oo·ee·kend *weekend*

улица ⓕ oo·lee·tsa *street*

уличен пазар ⓜ oo·lee·chen pa·zar
street market

уличен телефон ⓜ oo·lee·chen te·le·fon
public phone

уморен oo·mo·ren *tired*

универсален магазин ⓜ
oo·nee·ver·sa·len ma·ga·zeen
department store

университет ⓜ oo·nee·ver·see·tet
university

уста ⓕ oos·ta *mouth*

утре oo·tre *tomorrow*

утро ⓝ oo·tro *morning*

ухо ⓝ oo·ho *ear*

учен oo·chen *scientist*

учител/учителка ⓜ/ⓕ
oo·chee·tel/oo·chee·tel·ka *teacher*

Ф

факс ⓜ faks *fax*

фамилно име ⓝ fa·meel·no ee·me
surname

фар ⓜ far *headlight*

фенерче ⓝ fe·ner·che *flashlight • torch*

ферибот ⓜ fe·ree·bot *ferry* n

филия ⓕ fee·lee·ya *slice* n

филм ⓜ feelm *film (cinema/for camera)*

фонокарта ⓕ fo·no·kar·ta *phonecard*

фотоапарат ⓜ fo·to·a·pa·rat *camera*

фотограф ⓜ fo·to·graf *photographer*

фотография ⓕ fo·to·gra·fee·ya
photography

фризьор/фризьорка ⓜ/ⓕ
freez·yor/freez·yor·ka *hairdresser*

футбол ⓜ foot·bol *football (soccer)*

Х

харесам/харесвам
ha·re·sam/ha·res·vam *like* v

хартиени кърпички ⓕ pl
har·tee·e·nee kuhr·peech·kee *tissues*

хартия ⓕ har·tee·ya *paper* n

хладилник ⓜ hla·deel·neek *refrigerator*

хлебарница ⓕ hle·bar·nee·tsa *bakery*

хотел ⓜ ho·tel *hotel*

храна ① hra·na *food*
хранителни стоки ① pl
hra·nee·tel·nee *sto·kee groceries*

Ц

цветарски магазин ⑩
tsve·tar·skee ma·ga·zeen *florist (shop)*
цвят ⑩ tsvyat *colour* n
цена ① tse·na *price* n
цена на билет ① tse·na na bee·let *fare*
центьр ⑩ tsen·tuhr *centre* n
центърът на града ⑩
tsen·tuh·ruht na gra·duh *city centre*
цигара ① tsee·ga·ra *cigarette*
цип ⑩ tseep *zip/zipper*
цирк ⑩ tseerk *circus*
църква ① tsuhr·kva *church*

Ч

чадър ⑩ cha·duhr *umbrella*
чаена лъжичка ①
cha·e·na luh·zheech·ka *teaspoon*
чакалня ① cha·kal·nya *waiting room*
чакам cha·kam *wait*
чанта ① chan·ta *bag · handbag*
чаршаф ⑩ char·shaf *bed sheet*
час ⑩ chas *hour*
часова разлика ① cha·so·va raz·lee·ka
time difference
частен chas·ten *private* a
чаша ① cha·sha *cup · glass*
чек ⑩ chek *cheque (banking)*
червен cher·ven *red*
черен che·ren *black*
черно-бял cher·no·byal *B&W (film)*
Черно море ⑩ cher·no mo·re *Black Sea*
четка ① chet·ka *brush* n
четка за зъби ① chet·ka za zuh·bee
toothbrush
чиния ① chee·nee·ya *plate*
число ⑩ chees·lo *number* n
чист cheest *clean* a

чистене ⑩ chees·te·ne *cleaning*
чист памук ⑩ cheest pa·mook
cotton balls
чистя cheest·yuh *clean* v
човек ⑩ cho·vek *man*
чорапи ⑩ pl cho·ra·pee *socks · stockings*
чорапогащник ⑩ cho·ra·po·gasht·neek
pantyhose
чувствам choovst·vam *feel (emotions)*
чувство ⑩ choovst·vo *feeling (physical)*
чудесен choo·de·sen *fantastic · great*
чуждестранен choozh·de·stra·nen
foreign
чуплив choop·leev *fragile*

Ш

шал ⑩ shal *scarf*
шапка ① shap·ka *hat*
шивач/шивачка ⑩/①
shee·vach/shee·vach·ka *tailor* n
шия ① shee·ya *neck*
шорти ⑩ pl shor·tee *shorts*
шофьорска книжка ①
sho·fyor·ska kneesh·ka *drivers licence*
шумен shoo·men *loud · noisy*

Щ

щастлив shtast·leev *happy*
щепсел ⑩ shtep·sel *plug (electricity)*

Ю

юг ⑩ yoog *south* n
ютия ① yoo·tee·ya *iron (for clothes)* n

Я

ядене ⑩ ya·de·ne *dish · meal*
яке ⑩ ya·ke *jacket*
ям yam *eat*

The topics covered in this book are listed below in Bulgarian. If you're having trouble understanding Bulgarian, show this page to whoever you're talking to so they can look up the relevant section.

KEY PATTERNS

When's (the next bus)?	Кога тръгва (следващият автобус)?	*ko·ga truhg·va (sled·vash·tee·yuht av·to·boos)*
Where's (the station)?	Къде се намира (гара)?	*kuh·de se na·mee·ra (ga·ra)*
Where can I (buy a ticket)?	Къде мога да (си купя билет)?	*kuh·de mo·guh da (see koop·yuh bee·let)*
How much is (a room)?	Колко струва (стая)?	*kol·ko stroo·va (sta·ya)*
I'm looking for (a hotel).	Търся (хотел).	*tuhr·sya (ho·tel)*
Do you have (a map)?	Имате ли (карта)?	*ee·ma·te lee (kar·ta)*
Is there (a toilet)?	Има ли (тоалетна)?	*ee·ma lee (to·a·let·na)*
I'd like (the menu).	Дайте ми (менюто), моля	*dai·te mee (me·nyoo·to) mol·yuh*
I'd like (to hire a car).	Искам да (взема под наем кола).	*ees·kam da (vze·muh pod na·em ko·la)*
Can I (park here)?	Мога ли да (паркирам тук)?	*mo·guh lee da (par·kee·ram took)*
Could you please (help me)?	Моля ви/те (за помощ). **pol/inf**	*mo·lyuh vee/te (za po·mosht)*
Do I have to (pay)?	Трябва ли да (платя)?	*tryab·va lee da (plat·yuh)*